MAURICE CLARETT
WITH BOB ECKHART

ONE AND DONE

HOW MY LIFE STARTED WHEN MY FOOTBALL CAREER ENDED

MAURICE CLARETT
WITH BOB ECKHART

ONE
AND
DONE

HOW MY LIFE STARTED WHEN MY FOOTBALL CAREER ENDED

Copyright © 2019 by Maurice Clarett and Bob Eckhart
All rights reserved.

All trademarks are the property of their respective companies.

Cover Design by Jessica Angerstein

Cover Photo by Shanikka Flinn

Cataloging-in-Publication Data is on file with the Library of Congress.
ISBN: 978-1-64687-000-4

Proudly Printed in the USA

Dedicated to:

Shane Curry (1968-'92, Georgia Tech/Miami Hurricanes '87-90)
Sean Taylor (1983-2007, Miami Hurricanes '01-03)
Darrent Williams (1982-2007, Oklahoma State Cowboys '02-04)
Jovan Belcher (1987-2012, Maine Black Bears '05-08)
Adrian Robinson (1989-2015, Temple Owls '08-11)
Greg Bryant (1995-2016, Notre Dame/UAB '14-16)
Aaron Hernandez (1989-2017, Florida Gators '07-09)
James Hardy (1985-2017, Indiana Hoosiers '04-07)
CJ Fuller (1995-2018, Clemson Tigers '14-17)
Jordan McNair (1999-2018, Maryland Terrapins '17-18)
Marquis Brown (1998-2018, Duquesne, '16-18)
Kevin Ellison (1987-2018, USC, '05-08)
Korey Stringer (1974-2001, Ohio State Buckeyes '92-94)
Kosta Karageorge (1992-2014, Ohio State Buckeyes '14)
Will Smith (1981-2016, Ohio State Buckeyes '00-03)
Terry Glenn (1974-2017, Ohio State Buckeyes, '92-95)
Mike Kudla (1984-2018, Ohio State Buckeyes, '02-05)
Zachery Slagle (1988-2019, Ohio State Buckeyes, '06-09)

. . . and many, many others just like them—none of whom had to die from violence, suicide, or neglect.

TABLE OF CONTENTS

Introduction i
Author's Note v
Prologue vii

ACT I

1. Reese 1
2. Little Hustler 11
3. Falcon 27
4. Raider 37
5. All-American 51
6. Army All-Star 59
7. Buckeye 65
8. Starter 83
9. Champion 127

ACT II

10. Outcast 149
11. Hustler 163
12. Plaintiff 171
13. Angeleno 179
14. Bronco 185
15. Cut 191
16. Ashley 195
17. Big Hustler 201
18. Defendant 209
19. #529-720 213
20. Machine 229
21. Out 241

ACT III

Epilogue 251
Acknowledgments 259

INTRODUCTION

min'is-ter: any person thought of as serving as the agent of some power or force

IN 2008, I published a book called The Winner's Manual. In this book, there were 12 chapters about many different aspects of life. The last of these chapters was Hope, in which I wrote about my relationship with Maurice Clarett. I expressed my sincere good wishes for his rehabilitation and redemption:

WHEN HOPE IS TESTED

If you follow Ohio State football, you may recall that Maurice Clarett was an outstanding football player and an integral part of our national-championship team in 2002. He had a fantastic season, and his future looked bright.

Maurice's story is complicated and it would probably take an entire book to detail all the hardships he's been through, but the bottom line is that he made some poor decisions along the way and is now paying the consequences. He is currently serving a prison sentence in Ohio.

Maurice was a great kid with a wonderful sense of humor. He came to Ohio State after graduating from Warren G. Harding High School in Warren, Ohio. I remember that when he first filled out

his goal sheet, he said that he liked football a lot but what he really wanted to do was become a minister. As I did with other players, I told him to put that on his goal sheet and we'd talk about how we might help him reach that goal.

After he distinguished himself in the first couple of games, I called him into my office and showed him a list of about fifteen things that I knew would happen to him as a result of his visibility on the team. I said, "Just so you know and can be prepared, these are some things that are going to happen."

I told him that women would be knocking on his apartment door. Gamblers would try to get next to him. The media were going to focus on him. The students in every class were going to watch his every move and tell everyone they knew everything he did, good or bad. I listed all the things I'd seen happen to other players in his situation and warned him that he needed to be prepared to handle himself properly.

He looked over the list and then looked back at me. I could see the wheels turning in his head.

After one season at Ohio State, Maurice left the team and tried to gain early entry into the NFL draft—an endeavor that didn't work out for him. Eventually, he got into some real trouble and wound up in prison. So why am I including his story in this book, and specifically in this chapter about hope? I'm still hoping that Maurice's story will have a happy ending and that what has happened to him will serve a good purpose in his life and result in a greater good for him and for others. I believe he still may become the person we talked about when he wrote his first set of goals as a college freshman.

It turns out that Maurice accomplished his goal—he is a minister now. Not from a pulpit, but on so many other stages. He tours the country talking to athletes, prisoners, church groups, court systems, and schoolkids.

INTRODUCTION

Maurice has also founded two social service agencies called The Red Zone—that crucial area inside the 20 yard-line where positive yardage gets even harder to gain—and this is his ministry. Maurice is serving a higher power: social justice. He is seeking to create a just world for athletes, prisoners, schoolkids, and all of us.

> *I think it's healthy to talk about Maurice to Ohio State fans, as well. Many of our fans have a great deal of bitterness about what Maurice put the school through. They'll never forgive him for the way he mistreated the university and abused the privilege of being a player here. My perspective is that Maurice was a young man when he came to us. He was a kid. He made some bad decisions because he was acting like a kid. It doesn't excuse what he did, but it does put things in perspective. And I'm still hopeful Maurice will be able to turn things around in his life.*

Maurice has turned things around and I am as proud of him as I am of any of the thousands of players I've coached in the last 40+ years. Everyone knew that Maurice was a talented and gifted football player—that much was obvious from his outstanding freshman season in 2002—but what we should be finding out now is that he is simply a talented and gifted human being. Since getting out of prison, Maurice has been sharing his gifts and talents with people all over the country. When you are rooting for your favorite football players every weekend in the fall, it is hard sometimes to see that they are so much more than just an athlete. Maurice is showing everyone now what he has to offer and our world is a better place for it.

– Jim Tressel, 2019
President
Youngstown State University

AUTHOR'S NOTE

I'M NOT trying to capitalize on any aspect of my story or sensationalize violence. I apologize to everyone for all the negative things that I did. Everything in this book happened and I'm not proud but I'm not hiding from it, either. It's truth.

All proceeds from this book will go to support the mental health of people who need it. Opportunities for drug and alcohol counseling, and the kind of psycho-social-emotional development programs I participated in while in prison, are sorely needed and I am trying to provide them wherever I can. This is God's plan for me—not carrying a football and scoring touchdowns. My life didn't end when my football career did…that's when it started.

– Maurice Clarett, August, 2019

PROLOGUE

IN THE summer of 2006, I made the decision I was going to try and kill two people who were supposed to testify that I robbed them.

It was only a few years after I scored the game-winning touchdown for the Ohio State Buckeyes in the national championship game, but my life had spiraled completely out of control since then. Alcohol, drugs, mental illness, criminality.

I had been hustling for a while and after my baby was born in July, I panicked completely. I decided that if these people refused to be paid off, then I was going to kill them. I had learned their address weeks before and decided to make my move.

I woke up in Youngstown on August 8th and drove down to Columbus. I was just bouncing around visiting people all day—just going to see whoever I could, because I knew what I was going to do that night. There was no question about what I was trying to accomplish. I was going to kill those witnesses.

The last person I was with was a buddy who I was trying to get to drive for me. It was 1 or 2 am, I was drinking from a bottle of Grey Goose, and I told him what I was going to do. He tried to talk me out of it.

He was saying, I've been down this road before, I've been to prison—in fact I've been to prison for homicides and it's not like what you think.

He was a good friend from Youngstown, living by himself in Columbus. The fact that he had killed before made me think driving for me would be no problem for him. But he had been super-responsible after he got out of prison, doing his job, handling his business, and had nothing to do with the streets anymore. He was straight and clean and not in the life.

I told him the situation—how these people were going to testify about me robbing them and put me in prison for a year at least, maybe more, and he kept saying it wasn't worth it. He was shooting down the whole idea but I wasn't hearing it. Honestly, I think I was just wasting time, stalling. I wanted to hang out somewhere for a few more hours so I stayed at his place until I set out on my mission.

I could have chosen a guy's house who was still in the life, but I wanted to be careful about who to get involved in what I was doing. I could have also taken a fraction of what I had offered them not to testify, given a young guy $1500, and he would have killed them for me.

You can probably even get someone killed for $1000 dollars in the street. It's sad to say that someone's life is that cheap or someone would do that for so little. But in my head, as twisted as it was at the time, I knew not to ask anyone else to commit murder and put them in a situation where they might spend their life in prison.

I don't know if that was a good thing or not, but I didn't want to ask anybody else to clean up my mess. If you get into a mess and something bad happens, at least you should shoulder it yourself—that's what I was thinking. I didn't want to screw up someone else's life.

But those two witnesses—they had to go. I knew more or less where they lived, in a house off of Brice Road. My plan was to kick in the front door and storm the house. When someone kicks in a door, it's a massive intrusion and people are too stunned to react.

A home invasion is super-dangerous because you have this aggressive human being with a gun coming through your front door. Nobody is prepared for a home invasion. I didn't even know if they had kids, or had guns in the house. I had robbed people before and I don't care if you have a gun or not. You could have fifty guns but if someone kicks in your door while you're sleeping and gets right up on you, it doesn't matter.

I say this with certainty, in fact. The person who has the element of surprise will almost always prevail. You could have a gun right next to your

PROLOGUE

bed but you're going to be so shocked that you can't think. It's not what people are conditioned for.

Most guys carry guns either for show or to defend themselves in an extreme situation. But most times shootings are not like this combat, U.S. Ranger, Navy Seal-type of back-and-forth gun battle. By kicking in someone's door, you catch people with the element of surprise and they freeze. It's 3 in the morning and they are asleep and out of it. So my thought was to bum-rush their house, run up the stairs, shoot them in their bed with my AK-47, and take off.

I knew exactly what I needed to do. I was medicated with the alcohol but I was still thinking clearly. I knew good and goddamn well what I was doing and what my intentions were. Was it the right thing to do? Absolutely not. Was it the responsible thing to do? Of course not. I shouldn't have been in the situation where I was trying to kill these people.

It's hard to talk about it now. In fact I'm ashamed. But I need to talk about this and everything else in my life in the mind-frame of what actually took place 10 or 20 years ago. Looking back on everything, of course I wonder, What the hell was I doing? To be there in my mind where I was ready to kill these people—I was ready to kill these people because I had actually tried to rob them and they insisted I get punished for it.

But what had me panicking the most, more than just the thought of going to prison for a year or two, was that my baby had been born a few weeks before, in mid-July. That got me thinking, what am I going to do about this robbery charge? Now I got this baby in the world.

This is when I decided I needed to make these people go away. I knew so many people in my neighborhood growing up who had been killed or killed other people and nobody ever gets punished for that shit so the thought of going to prison for murder never crossed my mind. This shows how I was thinking then.

First I had a guy I know who knew the witnesses reach out and offer them $15,000 to not testify against me, but that didn't work. So I decided I would kill them, 100%. Because I thought killing them was going to stop them from coming to the trial to testify and then there wouldn't be a case against me. In my street way of thinking, this made sense to me.

Even though I hadn't killed anybody before, at this time I was thinking my life would always be in the streets, selling drugs forever or doing something criminal in some capacity because that's all I knew. I never thought, Oh I'll live a straight life someday.

When I was driving over to their house, I didn't realize that Brice Road had two different exits—one to go north and the other to go south. When I had scouted their house earlier, I had come from a different direction, so the next thing I knew I got off the exit and I realized I was going in the wrong direction, away from their subdivision. I made a U-turn in the middle of Brice and I don't know if the officer was in the Home Depot parking lot or just in the vicinity and saw me but the next thing I knew he was pulling me over.

I pulled to the side of the road and I'm thinking to myself—because I had seen this on an episode of Cops—that as soon as the guy got out, walked up to my car, and knocked on the window, I would race away.

This is exactly what I did and he ran back to his car and started chasing me. I got on the ramp to I-70 East that was only about 100 yards ahead of me and I saw him behind me as I headed in the direction of Pickerington.

This chase was going on for a few minutes and then there were a few more police cars behind me and I was like, Damn, these cops must have been in the area. This seemed such an immediate response to me. I was flying down the road and the further I got out of town, I started to get scared because as I went further east, I started to see woods. There was nothing but woods on both sides of the highway. And I'm thinking to myself, like, My black ass ain't about to run in the woods.

In fact, I was trying to figure out how to bring my black ass back to Youngstown, because brothers don't do the woods. We have seen too many horror movies and the black kid in the group always gets killed first in the woods. That's a fact.

So I made a U-turn in the median of I-70 and when I made the U-turn and was headed back towards Columbus I saw there were no cars on this side of the highway.

PROLOGUE

Also, as I was heading back west on I-70, I noticed that the police officers stopped chasing me. The further I got, I thought they were calling to officers downtown so I just thought I'd get off on Livingston, before getting to downtown, and get out of the car and run and get away somehow. But before I could get anywhere close to downtown, there was a cop standing right in the middle of the highway and he threw down the spike trips and BOOM they busted my wheels.

So at this point, as I kept driving, my car was making loud grinding noises and smoke started coming from everywhere as I kept flying down the road on flattened tires.

I managed to call my mother though and I told her I was about to get out and have a shootout with the police. That came more from like I was going to kill myself, because I was just tired of living. It wasn't like I wanted to kill any police. I was just tired. I had been screwing up for so long and I was ready to give up. Life was just too hard and I couldn't go on. I was done.

I forget all the other things my mom said, but I remember her screaming, NO, MAURICE! She said I should just give myself up and live to see another day.

I was still headed back downtown and there were the loudest banging metallic sounds coming from the car, so I decided, Okay, I'll get off at the next exit and give myself up and face the consequences. I pulled off the freeway and into the parking lot of Tee-Jaye's Country Place, an all-night diner.

As soon as I got stopped, a police cruiser crashed into me from behind, BOOM. The cop sprinted to the car with his gun drawn and immediately recognized me. I heard him yelling to the other guys, Hey, we got Maurice Clarett here and he's got guns.

He was screaming—telling me to get out of the car and put my hands up. So I put my hands up and this is where some unnecessary bullshit happened.

I got out of the car and was 100% giving myself up. But as soon as the cops realized I had a bullet-proof vest on, and there were weapons in the car, they started slamming me around. One cop came in and kicked me really hard in my leg, and then punched me in the face. Another cop hit me on the top of my head. And then it was just like over-aggressive roughing me up.

I was like, I get it. This is the part where I'm down on the ground with my hands behind my back and the guy is giving me instructions like, Stop Moving!, and I was done moving but he started tasing me anyway.

So as he's tasing me and I'm trying to get the barb off me, I was thinking, like, Dude, I'm not going anywhere. I'm done. I'm not running.

I wasn't handcuffed at this point, but I was on the ground, and they were still tasing me. One cop was tasing me and I was trying to knock the barb off and he tased me again and I was actually able to get up and I was thinking to myself, like, Man, you all are some bitches. I had been drinking but I knew everything that was going on. I wasn't incapacitated at all. I knew it was just a handful of Columbus Police Officers roughing me up. That was clear to me.

If nothing else, it was the same thing from when I played football. I can remember pictures in my mind. I have visual memory and I can remember every aspect of this, from going onto the ground, getting up, and walking to the police car with my hands behind my back after they cuffed me.

But I had blood in my mouth from getting punched in the face and I was spitting blood on the ground and this guy goes, Oh, you're spitting on an officer? I wasn't spitting on any officer. They were all behind me anyway. I was spitting on the ground because I had blood in my mouth.

So that dude ran up on me, sprayed me in the face with mace and stuck a damn bag over my head. So next thing I know, I'm in the back of the paddywagon and I was screaming, I can't breathe.

I was on the floor, with my hands behind my back, and I couldn't breathe so I started scraping at the floor with my face just to try and get the mask off.

When I finally got the mask off my face, I looked up and saw there were two officers sitting in there already—a white dude and a black dude.

PROLOGUE

I looked right at the black police officer in the back of the paddywagon with me and I said to him, Man you're a bitch—you're really going to let these racist cops do this to me? I said, Man, I done gave up a long time ago, and they kicked my ass for no reason.

I said, Dude, I didn't hit them—they kicked my ass and then got me sitting here like a dunce and I could barely breathe and you're sitting there doing nothing? But the guy just stared at me for a second and then looked away.

The next thing I knew, we were downtown and for whatever reason, legit, I started asking them, Yo, can I wash this mace off my face because this shit is burning. But they didn't let me. To this day, I have a brown stain on my forehead from the mace. This scar is not from a football helmet rubbing my forehead like everyone thinks. They left the mace on my skin the entire night.

So when I went to court the next morning, it had irritated my skin. If you look at the photos, my whole face had swollen up by the time I appeared in front of the judge. My face had swollen up and my eyes had swollen up. The mace eventually burned my skin. I looked like a beast.

After court that day, I said to my lawyer, I understand what I did by fleeing a traffic stop, but these dudes kicked my ass for no reason. I was giving up. He must have filed a complaint because next the cops told me they were going to do an internal affairs investigation.

I actually went to an IA hearing a few days later and I took my mother but as soon as I sat down, after about 3 seconds, I said, Y'all aren't going to do shit for me so just take me back to my cell because this is a waste of time. They said they needed to get the information about what happened to me but I said, Dude, y'all, this is a formality—you aren't trying to serve justice, I get it, just take me back to my cell. And after that, I was locked-up for the next four years.

ACT 1

"How tough is it to buy an inner-city kid? Buy him some shoes, take him to dinner, get him some nice clothes, maybe a car. You become his best friend, and he gets hooked. Like a junkie. Then you control the product. The secret is controlling the product early. It's just like slavery. Modern-day slavery is what it is."

— Rudy Washington, Black Coaches Association
From Forty Million Dollar Slaves,
By William C. Rhoden (p.178)

CHAPTER 1

REESE

On Black Monday, September 19, 1977, Youngstown Sheet and Tube shut down and 5,000 people lost their jobs. Before the wave of steel factory closings was over, around 40,000 jobs had been lost at the steel mills in and around Youngstown.

This reverberated throughout the economy of Northeastern Ohio, but completely devastated the south side of Youngstown, where my mother was living with my two older brothers, Michael and Marcus, when I came into the world on October 29, 1983.

The first thing I can remember is growing up at my Grandmother Mary's house when I was younger. My mom always dropped us off at her mom's house on her way to work in the morning. I can start remembering when I was 3 or 4 years old, getting dropped off at Grandma's house before preschool. She lived on the bottom half of the south side, down the hill and we lived on the upper part of the south side, about 5 minutes away.

Grandma looked after all eleven of my cousins and me and I was the youngest so before I really started growing, I was the smallest and had to compete with my older cousins.

My Aunt Gwendolyn had three kids: Antjuan, Andre (who we called Butter), and Andrew. My Uncle George had five: George Jr. (Junebug), Vivian, Kim, Chad, and Troy. Then there were the three of us—Michael was three years older than me and Marcus was two years older.

All my earliest memories are of everybody being over there along with our aunts and everybody growing up. Most of my memories are pretty hazy, but one part I remember in detail is her garden. Whenever Grandma wanted anything done in the garden, I would do it because I loved working in the garden and eating homegrown tomatoes and peppers.

My dad wasn't around when I was a kid but I didn't even have a context for that like I do now that I'm raising my daughter and realize the millions of things a dad does for his kid.

On the south side of Youngstown in the 1980s, nobody's dad was around. I can only think of one guy who had a father so it didn't even register with me that my father was missing.

It's embarrassing to say it now, but I just don't know that much about him. He went to Cardinal Mooney High School and went to Bowling Green State University. He died in 2012.

All I know is that he was an entrepreneur. He ran a courier business, Myke's Same Day Delivery, and lived about 10 minutes away, but on the same side of town as us. He played football at Mooney and I know bits and pieces from what people told me, but I have no clue what he was like.

My mom and dad had dated in high school and he started at Bowling Green State University in 1977. Mom started at Youngstown State University after graduating from Youngstown South in 1978. She went there for 2 years until she had my oldest brother Mike in 1980 and dropped out.

Marcus was born a year later and I came two years after that. My brothers and I have the same father and our parents were married until 1984. They stayed together long enough to have three kids and my mom raised all of us.

My grandma's house was the flophouse for our whole family. At this point, my mom was working at Northeast Ohio University College of Medicine (NEOCOM), in Rootstown, Ohio, an hour away. She started her job as an educational coordinator in 1982.

My mom lives in the same house now on Ravenwood that I grew up in. She would drop us off at Grandma's house every morning and pick us up in the evening. I couldn't wait to get dropped off there because that's where all the fun was.

CHAPTER ONE: REECE

My cousins just loved being around each other so every day was exciting, especially for me as the youngest because I could pick up on all the things my older cousins were doing. We played red light/green light, hide-and-seek, and football in the front yard. There were 9 boys so the 2 girls pretty much had to adapt and play whatever games the boys wanted.

This is where I first got infatuated with football. Chad played for the South High Warriors and I can remember him bringing his equipment to Grandma's house after practice. He was #3 and played tailback and I remember thinking how cool it would be just to have a uniform. I would put his equipment on and run around the house carrying a football and look at myself in the mirror, thinking I was going to be a football player too someday.

Even after my mom picked us up on her way home from work, I still had 2 brothers to hang out with when we got home. My brothers and I used to fight. I fought Marcus more than Mike and I never won a fight against them but getting beat up got me tougher. That's part of growing up.

The first time I really remember getting out and exploring Youngstown was when I went to preschool at the ABC Corral. They would pick us up at grandma's in the morning and take us there. I remember having activities and making friends and getting back on the little school bus and coming back to my grandma's house.

At this point, in the late-1980s, I don't remember a whole lot of the criminality and madness that Youngstown is known for because I was always at home or at Grandma's house, playing around in the yard or in the neighborhood. I wasn't really doing too much or seeing any hustling going on.

A lot of my earliest memories revolve around the game of football. The first time I played football was in the summer of 1988 when I still only 4. My mom signed-up my brothers for the South Side Little Braves and I can remember I wanted to play so bad because they had these bright orange helmets and orange and blue uniforms. The Braves played down at Volney Rogers football field and I thought it was the coolest thing in the world. So,

I went and tried out and they just put me on the team because back in that day they didn't care how old you were and I was already big for my age.

I probably shouldn't have been playing tackle football when I was only 4 years old but I was tough from playing with my older brothers and I really enjoyed going to practice and running into people. People couldn't believe I was only 4 years old because I was so big. I was playing on the team for kids under 90 pounds. When you're that young, tackling doesn't hurt anybody. There's not enough speed generated or power between the kids to have anything actually hurt.

This is where I really caught the football bug. I just thought this is fun, this is competitive, I was wearing my own pads, going to practice, running through the drills, catching the ball, learning the plays, and getting coached. It was fun because it was a challenge to learn everything and try to figure out the game of football. Even as kids, there are blocking assignments and things you're supposed to do on each play.

In Northeast Ohio, pro football is a big deal. The Cleveland Browns and Pittsburgh Steelers were very big obviously because Youngstown was halfway between both those cities.

I remember watching Browns games growing up. Bernie Kosar, from Boardman, right outside Youngstown, came back to Cleveland from the University of Miami, where he was a star, and led the Browns to three AFC championship games. Those teams played their hearts out even though they never made it to the Super Bowl. I decided then that being a football player was going to be my ticket out. Think about it, the only men I saw succeeding in life, and I mean really succeeding and not just surviving the streets, were athletes on TV.

So, I was always going outside and playing with my friends: Dale, Andre, Aariss, Kevin, JR, Deshaun, Keon, and Frankie. We had a neighborhood in the south side of about 30 boys who were all within three years of each other and if it wasn't football, it was basketball, and if it wasn't basketball, it was something competitive that everyone did together. All the way through elementary school, everything revolved around sports. Every day after

CHAPTER ONE: REECE

school, that's all we did was play sports and I was so big for my age so I was a star no matter what the sport.

My brothers and I and some of my cousins were going to St. Patrick's Elementary at the time. My Great-Grandma Harvey was an entrepreneur who owned her own motel and she agreed to pay for our schooling. So I was at a Catholic school first and second grade, taking communion and everything. It was a cool experience—it was all black kids and we had to wear green and white uniforms that looked fine. Obviously, the day was very structured. It was helpful and I had a lot of fun with some of my friends who went through that school with me. I got paddled but I don't even remember what for, just being bad in class and being a knucklehead, I guess.

Toward the end of second grade, I remember going to my great-grandmother's house and that was the first time that I remember seeing my father. Even though my parents weren't together, we still maintained the relationship with his grandmother because she was paying for us to go to school. But, that day at my great-grandmother's house, what I remember is that my father was beating my mother up.

What started the fight was that my mother had gone to court and put my father on child support and he got furious and beat her up. I don't know the details of the story—I just remember being in the other room while my mom and dad were in the hallway. We heard a loud BOOM and when we went out to see what was going on, my father was on top of my mom hitting her. Then my father's brother got him off her. She was crying and she grabbed her stuff and we got in the car and left.

After this, my great-grandmother quit paying for us to go to St. Patrick's, so when third grade started, we were put into Sheridan Elementary. My mother was working but just couldn't afford to keep us all at St. Patrick's. We were still going to my grandmother's house after school though, and having a blast. But around that same time, I remember the house, where my whole family had always gathered, burned down.

I was in the 3rd grade and my mother showed-up one day to get us before we could walk over to Grandma's. I guess my cousin's son, who was just a toddler, must have knocked something over, maybe a candle, and something caught fire and the whole house burned down. This had been the meeting place, the gathering place for all the holidays—everything took place in this house and now it was gone.

Actually, both of my grandmothers died within 7 months of each other around the end of 1990 and the beginning of 1991. Both of them were gone and grandma's house had burned down, so everything that had kept the family together from a tangible standpoint of seeing each other regularly was disrupted. From this point on, we basically dispersed and stopped having all the family get-togethers at my grandmother's house.

Mom needed to make new arrangements for us after school, so now we started going up the hill, and our older cousins started babysitting us. This was the first time I was seeing drugs. It was 1991 and I was 8 years old. My older cousin Vivian was supposed to be watching us but she was using drugs and would pass out and then me and the young boy cousins would sneak some beer or get high.

Not long after that was happening, my brothers and I were staying full-time at my mother's house, which was considered up the hill on the south side and we just started living from there. It was basketball every day, football every day, and just having a lot of fun being kids.

I don't even remember wanting to be mischievous or thinking I had to be bad or terrible towards anyone at that age, but after I started at Sheridan, I was known as the class clown and troublemaker. It wasn't even anything with girls yet. I was just starting to get into trouble and if I saw a girl and liked her, I would just do something crazy to get her attention because I didn't know how to talk to her.

I think things definitely started changing when I went to Sheridan. I wasn't used to all the freedom of the public school setting. I can remember the difference. At the Catholic school, if you were bad your name went into the red book and they paddled you. There was accountability.

In the public school setting, the first teacher I knew was Ms. Johnson. I remember just how different public school was—it felt cooler than the Catholic school. I can remember being defiant for no reason…just getting

CHAPTER ONE: REECE

into trouble for attention. I would just be bad and go to the office and now, I guess looking at it with my adult mind, I just wanted some sort of attention for some reason. I don't know what it was. We were just being mischievous. Part of it was the guys who were around me. I had Juwan Phfifer, Brian McGauley, and other friends like Otis Simmons.

Our neighborhood on the south side of Youngstown had a ton of boys, dozens of them. It didn't seem weird then but now, to have that many boys running around in one neighborhood would be unusual. Back then, Youngstown was still pretty heavily populated and not deserted like parts of it are now.

I did start going to football camps at YSU during this time and I first learned who Jim Tressel was. He had been the head coach of Youngstown State University since 1986 and won his first national championship with them in 1991, when I was 8 years old. That was a huge deal to me as a kid. Everybody in Youngstown worshipped him it seemed, especially after they won it all again in 1993, 1994, and 1997.

When my friends and I weren't playing sports, we were trying to get girls. In third and fourth grade, it was about being a clown, but in fifth grade, we really tried to have sex. It was an adventure—would a girl let you grab her bottom or show you her breasts. I was successful with some girls but other girls slapped me. In thinking about my daughter right now, in the 6th grade, she has no concept of some of the things we had a concept of then.

I had one teacher in 5th grade who was always on me about being smart. Her name was Mrs. Freeman and this was my best year academically. My head was totally in the space of chasing girls, but she was constantly on me about doing well in school and arranging activities for us. We had a DARE program to tell kids not to do drugs and she also talked to us about respecting women.

In 6th grade, we had 4 different teachers, which didn't help. It was like chaos. The first teacher quit, then there was a substitute. Eventually, they brought out a new permanent teacher but she didn't last so we were going back and forth with too many teachers and there was no stability.

We were just spending all day in class passing notes to girls, asking them to let us walk them home. There were lots of girls who lived within a few blocks of me and I was always trying to go to their houses after school and just hang out on the porch with them. Most of the fooling around happened at people's homes when their mom was still at work. There was this one girl whose grandmother used to be at work all of the time. Sometimes when grandparents are raising little kids, they aren't as vigilant. It's a relaxed space and we always figured out how to manipulate those grandparents.

Putting this in context, the pressure for inner-city kids to have sex is huge. It's almost a competitive thing. We are all trying to establish ourselves. There are only a few things that get you noticed or make you popular in the 'hood. One of those is violence and another is if you have cool clothes and know how to dress, or know how to dance. And another thing is sex. The pressure to have sex was huge.

The first time I had ever known about sex or saw sex was when I was 5 or 6 years old, at my grandmother's house. My cousin Vivian was having sex with this older dude when she was supposed to be babysitting me. I also remember all my older cousins would have copies of Playboy around, and having access to those magazines was a big deal before the internet.

The first time I kissed a girl was in 6th grade on my buddy's porch. She was a girl who lived up the street from us so we grew up together in the same neighborhood. The older dudes were always saying to us, you're nobody—you haven't got any girls, you haven't had sex, you haven't even kissed a girl.

And the same thing went for the girls. Now I'm speaking from the responsible adult perspective. You had some older girls in the neighborhood who were pressuring the younger girls to do the same things they were doing with guys and the younger girls weren't ready for that. Neither were the older girls, but that didn't stop them.

The first girl I had sex with was in a group of friends my buddies and I hung out with. We had three little groups of girls me and my buddies would float between and we were all just trying to have sex with any of them. My next door neighbor Dale, he probably started having sex in 3rd grade. He didn't mess with sports—his whole focus was girls, girls, girls.

CHAPTER ONE: REECE

His house would be the flophouse and we would try to get girls to go over there with us.

His house was usually the house where we would have sex, but the first time I had sex was around the corner from my house and this girl's grandmother was gone. Basically my friends and I went over to her house on a Saturday and there were four of us and four of them and each of us little boys and the little girls went into a room and was doing their own thing. Even saying it now sounds crazy but that's what was happening back then.

This became the cool thing to do all the time. We had condoms which was the only thing we knew about birth control at that point. Everybody carried condoms because that was cool, even if you didn't use them, you carried them in your wallet. It made us feel like we were grown and bad.

Once I had sex the first time, it became like a mission to have sex with as many girls as I could in 7th grade. It was probably three at the most but it consumed all my energy even though it was just casual sex.

So I can see how young kids have kids. I can see how it starts out and it's fun and free and innocent because kids don't have anything else to do and having a connection with someone feels good, because in the inner-city you're constantly chasing that feeling of connection with anyone.

Also, you have to remember, that I was 5'10" 185 lbs in 7th grade. So I looked like a man. It's not surprising to me now to realize that I think a lot of this, for me, was trying to get my oldest brother Mike to see that I was cool because I got girls and was trying to have sex with them.

That came directly from him because I can remember as far back as third or fourth grade thinking how cool he was. He always had cool clothes and women around him in some capacity from hustling and selling drugs. So for me, I wanted to be like that, too. I wanted to get me some girlfriends and have sex and prove to myself and him that I had taken a step into manhood. I wanted to be somebody.

CHAPTER TWO
LITTLE HUSTLER

THINGS HAD already been rolling in the wrong direction for a while when I started at Hillman Junior High. You gotta realize, I was 5'10", 185 lbs when I started 7th grade, so I was becoming a man. I looked like a man and I thought I was doing what men did.

I was still playing sports but I remember the inner-city culture of America in the mid-90s and, in Youngstown especially, crime was at an all-time high. There were lots of murders and robberies. The gangs in Youngstown at the time were real heavy. There was the whole Bloods and Crips thing, and the Folks. At that time, crime was just a big thing going through America.

Gangsta rap had really hit the scene, Menace II Society, and it was cool to be tough and hard. I can remember that whole feeling and that whole era. I can remember Michael basically being involved in gangs and all that stuff was around and at my front door. So I just wanted to mimic it because I saw what my brother was doing and saw how the girls responded to it positively and so I wanted to emulate it unconsciously. I just wanted to roll with it.

The first time I saw someone getting killed with my own two eyes was when I was 10 years old, in the 4th grade. I was playing basketball in the park down the street from my house and saw a young man get murdered. I don't even think he was 20 years old–he was probably in his late-teens, and I watched him get shot once through the heart and die right there.

None of us even knew what it was about but we had seen both the shooter and the victim many times around the neighborhood. The shooter walked right up to him, shot him under the basket on the court next to ours, and then took off.

We all ran up to the young man who was shot and I guess we would have helped if we could but it was too late. He was gone. The police came but there wasn't anything they could do either and I don't think the shooter ever got caught.

Even when I sit here now thinking about it, I am pretty numb about it. Menace II Society was out, gangsta rap was big, we saw this stuff everywhere, and the whole neighborhood felt like that movie. That was the first time I'd seen anything like that first-hand, but I can remember this was sort of a normal thing.

There was also another guy I saw getting pistol-whipped right in front of me. This was just two houses up from mine. Cornelius, a guy from our neighborhood, ran up on Marcellus and whupped his ass with a pistol right while we were playing in the street.

I can also remember playing in the street and on the hottest summer days there was a dude who used to open up the fire hydrant so us kids could cool off. Then the firefighters would come and close it back up. Well they did this twice and the third time, the dude grabbed the fireman's wrench out of his hand and busted him upside the head. This little white firefighter got his head cracked by this huge wrench, BOOM, and the other firefighters had to carry him outta there and they didn't come back. This was the south side of Youngstown.

There was even a hit put out on the prosecutor, Paul Gaines. I can remember hearing about this as a kid and this was like normal stuff to me then. Being around people getting high all the time, doing gangsta things, this was very normal. From 3rd to 8th grade, the violence I witnessed just blurs together in my head because there were so many random shootings and killings. Mass amounts of murder.

So, hell yeah, I was scared growing up on the streets. I always had a sense of fear, as long as I can remember. I want to pinpoint it sometime around the 5th grade—11 years old—when I started to be like on edge, and kind of uncomfortable on a daily basis. I was worried and I could feel the

CHAPTER TWO: LITTLE HUSTLER

tension all throughout the city. My brothers and I actually wouldn't go too many places outside the neighborhood but when we did, I felt the tension.

I can feel that same sort of tension down here in Columbus now on Parsons Avenue. It feels like you are somewhere in a dire situation, but when you go out to a suburb like Upper Arlington, you certainly don't feel that. It feels like those people are actually living in a country club. People underestimate the toll going through daily life in a constant state of tension takes on kids. That constant stress of being on edge breaks down a kid's mental health for sure, every day.

All that violence around me in Youngstown is where my tough guy attitude came from. I had to be tough at a very young age to survive. If you come from the suburbs, that's not anything you can understand in terms of how it dictates the behavior of a kid. You've got no framework for it. But violence just permeated the entire south side, which was basically my whole world at the time. There wasn't any escaping to the suburbs for me. This violence running through my neighborhood became the pervasive reality of my life and everyone's life in Youngstown. For heaven's sake, our city was known as Murdertown, USA in the mid-90s. Murdertown.

The history of Youngstown is that organized crime ran the city. First it was the Italians who brought drugs in and sold them to black people and it just escalated from there. But when you see it in person, that's how people like me picked it up. And you combine that with the TV, news, movies, and gangsta rap and you just think it's cool and it becomes part of you.

The next thing I know from there, I was wanting to get into trouble just to make a name for myself and be somebody. So I would corral my friends up and we started with stealing bikes and it went from bikes to stealing out of stores and then stealing different stuff. Kohl's was a new store over in Boardman. We would go to Boardman and hit up Kohl's and I would take my shoes off and put some new shoes on and walk out. You know, just little silly, petty stuff, but to kids it was a big deal and you could brag about it like you were a big dude.

Of course the older dudes were stealing cars. At that time my little friends and I weren't stealing cars yet. At first, we were the guys just being the lookout and things of that nature. So from that standpoint, we were just being knuckleheads and helping to steal cars, then going on joyrides. But things kind of progressed from there.

Eventually, what I would do was walk across Southern Boulevard, to the white part of town, and steal cars and go for joyrides. This was actually around 6th grade, I guess. I would say I probably stole 10 cars back then.

I remember one time even being a kid around that time period, I was going over to my older cousin's house and we were sneaking and drinking beer or smoking joints. I was 11 or 12 years old. I can't remember the exact age but I remember drinking 40s of St. Ides malt liquor was real big then.

Back then, you could go to the store if you were 10 or 11 years old and if they knew your cousins you could grab a beer. That was the fun part about it. It was just the time period. It wasn't even like you were looking for trouble or it was a bad thing to do.

Like if you saw a kid walking down the street carrying a beer now it would look crazy, but at that time, a kid could carry a beer home and it was no big deal. You could go to the store with a note back in the day and get yourself a beer. And people were selling $5 bags of weed. So sneaking and smoking weed and cigarettes, that was the cool thing to do. All that stuff was going on in 5th and 6th grade, in fact.

My brothers and I would never get caught because my mother worked an hour away at NEOCOM so by the time she would come home at the end of the day, the mischievous behavior would have already taken place. We would just be in the house eating dinner and going to sleep by then, getting ready to start the next day.

So by around 7th grade, things went to the next level for me at least. I was really living pretty independently by the time I was in 7th grade. My mother was working all the time and I was on my own.

I never carried a gun myself, but the first gun I got my hands on I stole from a friend of my mother's. There was a gentleman she was dating and he must have hid it in our attic because one day I was messing around up there and I found it and stole it.

CHAPTER TWO: LITTLE HUSTLER

This guy dated my mom for 7 years, from 1993-2000. It was weird because sometimes he was there and sometimes he wasn't. He had a few kids before dating my mother. He would go to work, then come back to our house, stay for a minute and then go do whatever he did. Like, literally he was almost never there but when he was there, he would just stay in the bedroom.

He and my mom used to go to the Baptist church all the time but I didn't have much of a relationship with him. One of his sons went to Wilson High School and was really smart. Another one of his sons was a mechanic and a third son had special needs. So he had his hands full and didn't need me to be another son to him and I wasn't looking for him to be like a father either. I was following in the footsteps of my oldest brother Michael.

For some reason, my mom's friend must have brought a gun into the house and once when I was in the attic, I opened a drawer and I thought, Oh Damn, that's a gun right there. I left it alone for a few months but then later I went back up there and it was still there so I just took it. It was only a little .22 but I could still take it over to my friend's house and be cool because I had a gun. This went on for a while but eventually my friend's dad was like, I'll give you fifty bucks for that gun so I sold it to him and neither my mother nor anyone else ever said anything to me about missing it. My friend's dad was smart to get that gun away from me—not that I had plans to use it, but guns are nothing but trouble.

The thing is that to this day, I don't even like guns around me. The reason I say that is maybe it's me and I'm different but I don't keep guns around me because I believe that when people have guns around them, they become an option. I think if you just take that shit away, you don't even have to think about whether you're going to shoot somebody.

The summer before seventh grade was the first time I got caught stealing a car. I had stolen a car from a nursing home. I stole the car and we went joyriding in it for a day. We wanted to steal a car because the 4th of July was the next day and we wanted to have a car to ride around in and show off for the girls. You know, everything was showing off for the girls.

The day after we stole the car, I went to pick my buddy up in the north side of town. And as we're leaving the north side, I was making a left turn at a stoplight and the car window was broken out and a police car was sitting next to us. We must have looked suspicious as hell because he put his lights and siren on. I floored it and started flying through downtown Youngstown. Crazy as it sounds, Bill Clinton was in town that day campaigning for re-election in 1996 and I was flying up Market Street from one side of the town to another and going through traffic and barely missing people and probably endangering everybody.

I finally got to the south side of town, slammed on the brakes, jumped out of the car, and ran through a church parking lot, until I got to my buddy's house. I hid in his house but the police started going door-to-door through the area. They found me and arrested me, and took me to juvenile.

I stayed for a few days and at this time I thought it was a real big joke. I mean you're handcuffed but you just ride up an elevator and then go to the intake room. Then you take off all your clothes, they spray you with this anti-lice spray, you take a shower, you get your little jumpsuit, socks, and you go upstairs to the floor with guys your same age.

Guys 12-14 are separated and the 15-18 year-olds are separated. It was juvenile so you're locked down all day and don't interact with anybody. It was like solitary so I didn't have a roommate. At our local facility, we got a bed, a toilet, and a sink. We could go get a book out of the library whenever we wanted but we could only go out of our room to take a shower one at a time. We could listen to the radio through the speaker in the hallway but lights are out at 9 o'clock and we didn't even get to go to the gym every day.

After I got out, I was actually more popular amongst my friends because I had been to juvenile and experienced the intake process and actually slept there. Being in the jail system in urban areas, even at that point, was like you've earned some credibility or developed some level of toughness just because you went to this place that was supposed to be so hard and punishing and intimidating and you survived it and came home to talk about.

It's not surprising to a 12 year-old that I actually thought that I had done something cool and amongst my friends it was cool. But at that time, my mother said I needed to get into AAU basketball, football, and anything to channel my energy. She kind of hoped sports would straighten me out.

Mr. Butch, the math teacher at Hillman, was our football and basketball coach. I had known him since he came to my elementary school and was recruiting kids. He was saying this is what we have to offer and letting us know what to expect and informing us about the tryout dates. When he came, I raised my hand and said Excuse me, but I don't listen to coaches, I just do my own thing. I was just joking and it's funny to think about it now in the context of how I grew to love instruction in the intricacies of running and blocking and breaking down film.

Mr. Butch said Well, if you come to my school, you are going to listen to me. So we just went back and forth and as it turned out when I got to Hillman, he was one of the 7th grade football coaches. I always listened to him then and started to learn the basics about football and 20 years later I still get great advice from him.

I had fun just playing and he was one of those coaches that if he had room in his car and players didn't have a ride home, he'd drop them off. Or if we were hungry, he would take a group of kids to eat and spend $30-40 feeding us.

In 7th grade, we barely had enough people for a team. Mr. White was the head coach and Mr. Butch was the assistant coach. Mr. Butch was always supportive and fatherly to me when I played for him in 7th and 8th grade. He was full of wisdom and always expected me to make the right decisions.

We only played 6 games but by then I was 5'11" and probably about 190. I was playing tailback and having fun because I was usually the biggest kid on the field. I had so much fun running over the kids on defense. We won all 6 games and I just dominated on raw size and strength. I was gaining hundreds of yards each game and scoring as many TDs as I wanted.

In fact, the only time I ever lost at anything in junior high was track. We were undefeated in football and undefeated in basketball two years in a row. Because of this, I started getting a reputation around Youngstown for being an athlete. I was even getting good grades because in Youngstown City Schools there wasn't homework and it was easy, even math. I just understand and enjoy numbers. Numbers make sense to me and I love crunching numbers in my head now when I'm thinking about doing or not doing certain deals.

I was playing sports like my mom wanted and doing everything I was supposed to do from a teenager standpoint, but what I wanted was the respect from my friends. That was a little more important than the respect from my mother. I didn't want to get in trouble from my mother but the respect from my friends and how I was impressing girls was a lot more important to me. Of course now I can look back on it and understand some of the foolishness I was involved in.

Even though I had guys like Mr. Butch trying to look out for me, I only saw him during school and sports. All of my criminal behavior was after school when I didn't have anything else to do. That was the difference. When I didn't have anything constructive to keep me occupied, like sports, the criminality was all I was focused on. The easiest way of feeling like I was doing something, accomplishing something, was getting money or getting girls.

About a month after my first arrest for stealing the car, 7th grade started and I was still involved in this foolishness. There was a back-to-school Teen Night at a club in Austintown, a richer, whiter town next to Youngstown and I got into a fight that resulted in my second arrest.

My buddies were the ones who got into the fight first and I had to jump in to help them out. I don't even remember what it was about. With guys from the inner city, it could be as trivial as I'm from the south side and you're from some other part of town. It wasn't a huge brawl, just little pockets of kids fighting around the parking lot, and then the Austintown police came and arrested everybody and actually took us to the Youngstown police station for some reason.

If you were around the fight, you got arrested. And because it was within 30-days of my last arrest, I had to stay in juvenile for ten days. They basically put me in the system, made me do a bunch of community service, put me on house arrest and this time the warden said Man, if you don't stop what you're doing, you're going to get sent to Indian River Juvenile

CHAPTER TWO: LITTLE HUSTLER

Correction Facility in Massillon or the Training Institute of Central Ohio (TICO) outside Columbus. These were sort of like the prisons for juveniles. So, after that happened, I calmed down and I thought, you know what, I don't want to go to TICO. Going away for like a year would have felt like a life sentence to a 12- or 13-year old. Man, I was thinking I'm not about to go away for a year. That seemed like an eternity.

But I was still doing little miscellaneous stuff like stealing things, breaking into cars, and breaking into pawn shops. For some reason, I didn't think this was bad enough to jeopardize my freedom. So in the middle of 7th grade, this was the time when drugs were huge, especially to my older brother. Michael was hustling on the streets. He had moved out of the house a year or two earlier, when he was around 15. I was 13 now and knew he was hustling, not really in a gang but in a group of guys in our neighborhood.

You have to remember the feeling in the mid-90s. There was the Bloods and Crips and that hardcore feeling of that shit you see on television and in the movies was real. Gangs in California or Chicago were more organized, but in Youngstown, you had different small neighborhood groups and drugs were everywhere, weed was everywhere, and alcohol was everywhere.

I can remember that era so vividly and I can still feel how it felt, even now. I can just flat-out feel that whole era. It was wild and raw—not just with drugs and alcohol but with guns and crime too.

Michael was just putting my mother through hell. He just left the house and my mother couldn't control him. It was terrible for my mother. Michael didn't care about jail. He just kind of like flew the coop so to speak. He was getting into fights at school, ripping and running around the streets. He was always going back and forth to juvie. It was constant mayhem for my mother. When he didn't come home, she would leave the house, trying to track him down and find out where he was. But I would see the money he would have, when he did come home, and I would think man you know, this dude is making money, he's selling drugs, and I could also watch the process of him selling the drugs and I thought man I want to do that.

Marcus had his own little group of friends. When I said we grew up around probably 30-40 boys in our same age range, that's true, but you can still have 5-6 friends doing their own little deal and that's what Michael had. They were in the streets hard.

Luckily, my middle brother Marcus wasn't hustling; Marcus was just like a regular guy growing up. He might have been doing some little neighborhood bad stuff but he wasn't following in Michael's footsteps. He did end up in juvenile detention one time for getting into a big south side/east side fight, but that's about it.

So one day, when I was in 7th grade, basically there was a woman who helped get me into selling drugs. She was a teacher's aide at my school. She came and found me during lunch, because she was actually looking to score some drugs from my brother. She came up to me in the cafeteria and asked for Michael's number. She said, I've seen you out and about with him and know he's your brother. I said I don't know his number but I told her that I was looking to buy some dope too. I'd seen the money my brother was making and I thought I wanted to make money like him.

So I lied to her but she said, Well if you're looking to buy some, I know somebody else we can get it from. I basically played my brother and took his place and his money. I don't even know how I came up with $250—from cutting grass or shoveling snow I guess—but a few days later I gave her $250 and she told me I could buy a quarter ounce of cocaine. Now that I know all the details, she ripped me off. She said come over to my house after school and I'll show you what to do to cook it up.

She lived about three blocks from the school so I walked over there after basketball practice and she had already cooked up the dope and laid it out. All I had to do was go to the corner store and get the little plastic crack bags. She said I could make five hundred dollars off this stuff. She even said she'd bring her friends over during the next week so I could sell to them.

And so, over like a four- or five-month period, she was teaching me, as a 13 year-old kid, how to hustle drugs and cook them up and learn the whole process. I thought it was the greatest thing in life. I know how this sounds now, totally crazy. I mean I imagine someone coming up to my daughter at her school and then teaching her how to sell dope. But to me, this was very normal for what was going on around Youngstown and I just thought it was like the coolest thing in the world.

The way it worked was that I would go to practice and I would have prepared everything in the morning so after practice all I had to do was go over to her house and hustle, sell drugs, and make myself some money. This went on throughout the rest of 7th grade.

I thought it was super-cool to buy myself Air Jordan shoes at the time or new clothes and stuff. I had to hide it all from my mother though because she couldn't know. I didn't keep my shoes or anything else out in the open. Mom would go into work about 7:15 each morning and I had to be at school at 8 or 8:15 and I would put them on and put them back in the closet before she came home. There was also an easy excuse if I ever got caught to say Michael bought this stuff for me.

It seems ridiculous now that a 7th-grader would do this but it was just a different time and place. I still enjoyed going to school, not to learn but to be around my homeboys and chase girls and play sports. That's basically what school became for me until summer came and I could sell drugs full-time.

Not surprisingly, when 8th grade came of course I was still doing most of the same stuff, being a knucklehead. I was still playing sports and doing petty crimes and stuff of that nature. I was breaking into homes and it was all about how do I make money? I would say that 8th grade was 100% about how do I make money, how do I get my first car because turning 16 was right around the corner, and how do I get the clothes I need to look cool.

I only broke into a few homes but the bigger thing was stealing cars because I needed those to sell drugs. I still had the teacher's aide who was letting me sell from her house but a car let me sell to a wider clientele all over Youngstown.

It got to the point though where I didn't even steal cars anymore, because there were drug addicts who would let me rent their cars for around $30/day. This way, I could move around and sell weed anywhere. Guys my age wanted to smoke weed all the time. It sounds crazy, but in 8th grade, those guys wanted to smoke weed every day.

It was also in 8th grade that my house got shot up. Our house, where my mom still lives, got blasted when I was 14 years old. It was about 2 o'clock in the morning and my brother Marcus and I were still awake, playing video games and laying around on the living room floor. The next thing I knew, there were probably twenty or thirty shots throughout the entire house.

I heard glass breaking and bullets going through the drywall, but it probably only lasted a couple minutes, at the most. This happened because Marcus had gotten into it with these guys earlier. To this day, I don't know what it was about but it could have been a basketball game or any little thing. He came home and didn't tell anybody anything and that night whoever it was came back and shot up our house. This was how they did things on the south side of Murdertown.

Soon after that came the turning point of my childhood, which in a roundabout way really put my high school football career into motion. A guy who was my brother Michael's age, just 3 years older than me, came to my house one morning that I stayed home from school and he was like Yo, you know, there's some people down the street. He said you know, Reese, these guys are not home today—let's break into their house and take their PlayStation and some other little goods that they had. They lived at Ravenwood and Firnley, just a block away from me.

The truth is, I figured out later that this guy was probably coming to rob my house, but then I heard him on my back porch when I happened to be walking to the kitchen so I went to the window and asked what he was doing. I said, What's going on?, and he pretended like he was going to knock on our back door. Then at that point he said, Let's go rob this house right down the street. The sad thing about it is that we were friends with the people living in that house then and they are still friends with my mom now.

I didn't have anything else to do, so we went over there and broke into the house. We were rummaging all around. I had a pillowcase and was stuffing CDs into the pillowcase and PlayStation games into another bag. Eventually, I went upstairs and into a bedroom and as I was stuffing stuff into my bag, I heard somebody come walking down the hallway. Of course it was one of the people who lived there. So my buddy sees him and I heard

CHAPTER TWO: LITTLE HUSTLER

him saying, Oh Shit, because they recognized each other. Then my guy runs down the steps and so I take off and I'm running, too, trying to get out of the house. The guy who lived there just ducked into a bedroom and shut the door and tried to hide. He didn't confront us in the least.

The next thing I knew, my buddy climbed up on the table in front of the kitchen window that we had come in through. Then I come sprinting into the kitchen cause I'm scared and I thought I would just skip climbing onto the table and try to dive right through the open window. The problem was that I hit my head on the windowsill and busted my head wide open. After busting my head, I fell onto the concrete patio, hit my head again, then got up and started running and tried to jump over the wooden fence. I didn't make that either because I was dizzy and woozy already so by then I had busted my head a third time on the sidewalk and I ran home with blood gushing out everywhere.

I was jogging up the street to my house and my head was straight leaking. To make a long story short, I sat in my house all day, thinking I was going to die because I was seeing more blood than I've ever seen in my life coming from the top of my head and it wouldn't stop. I'm putting all these cold towels on my head and that's not working. So I called my mom after my buddy was like My man, you gotta go to emergency. I didn't even know what the emergency room was as a matter of fact. I'd never been there or anything.

I called my mom about 3 o'clock and told her I got hurt playing basketball and my head wouldn't stop bleeding. She came home and by about 5 o'clock we were at the emergency room in Boardman. They put 13 staples in my head, which is why I wore #13 on my jersey at Ohio State. But by the time we're driving home from emergency, my mom gets a call from my brother Marcus that the police stopped by the house looking for me. When we got home, mom called them and they asked her to bring me to the station the next morning.

The next morning, I went to the police station and the officer was like, Hey tell me what happened yesterday. I said, Look, I don't know what happened at that house—I was playing basketball and hurt my head. I had a hat on to cover up my staples and he said go ahead and take your hat off. So I took my hat off and he asked me again. He said, Look I'm not going to lie to you: look at this statement. They had caught my buddy and since he had two prior drug cases, he tried to act like I put him up to everything.

The next thing I knew, the officer said, Either you're going to lie to me or you're going to tell the truth. I told him again I didn't know what he was talking about. I was denying everything and he said, I'm going to tell you the truth, if we run the sample of your blood and the blood on the window, it's going to come back to say that you did it. So I was like, Alright man, I did it, whatever the consequences are go ahead and lock me up.

Basically, I get sent back to the juvenile facility. I took the elevator up there, went through intake, got my cell, and settled in. I was thinking at this point, Oh shit, I don't want to go away for a year. This was my third strike and the punishment was going to be real this time.

But just then, on my first night there, the corrections officer at the place, a guy by the name of Rollen Smith, came into my room around 2am, and took me to his office.

Rollen had seen me play football in 7th and 8th grade. He was an assistant coach at Youngstown Ursuline High School and a corrections officer at the juvenile facility. Basically, he was a very serious guy—straightforward, stern, and tough. He was about 6'2" and muscular as hell. He wasn't intimidating, but he was real serious. In fact, he had been a defensive back at University of Arkansas back in his day. He might have been 50 years old but he got respect and everybody on the south side knew him from going to juvie.

Rollen said to me, Maurice, man, what are you doing? You went down the wrong path. He knew this was my third time down here and he wanted to help me out. He knew my parents—they grew up together—and he knew both my brothers because they had been locked up before at this place. He said what I did was something stupid but it was not the end of my life.

He said, I've seen you play football—let me try to help you out and get you on the right path. In addition to being an officer there, he was also supposed to be recruiting junior high football players to go to Youngstown Ursuline, a Catholic high school in town. So he said, let me go to the judge and ask if I can mentor you and we'll keep you out of the system. And that's exactly what happened.

Rollen went to the judge and he convinced the judge to put me on house arrest and let Rollen mentor me. The judge allowed me to go back and forth to Ursuline that summer to lift weights and basically go into a structured program before my first high school football season.

And so the next thing I know, I'm at home every day that summer unless I was training. My guys were coming over and we were playing Madden all the time. I couldn't go anywhere, I couldn't even leave the porch unless I was with Rollen. I couldn't do any moving around the neighborhood and couldn't sell any drugs. I put all that behind me. I was just going back and forth to Ursuline, lifting weights, and trying to get back on the right path. But the message I was getting into my head was as long as I was good at football, everything would be okay.

I think from the time I was identified as an outstanding football player, all the adults who were supposed to be correcting my behavior stopped saying No to me, stopped telling me I couldn't do certain things. This was the message I got anyway.

In fact, when I look back at my life, I ask myself how was it so easy for me after I got kicked out of Ohio State to tap into the criminal part of my upbringing? I realize now that whenever I got arrested as a kid, nothing changed in terms of my behavior.

The only thing that changed for me, fundamentally, was I kept getting better at football. There was never any intervention. There was never any psycho-social-emotional development happening, until I got to prison. There was no re-direction of my behavior or my thought.

Teenagers who are standouts at football get to call their own shots. Of course it needs to be up to our parents to teach us but you can dig a little further into that. A lot of these guys, the really highest-level college football and basketball players come from single-parent homes. So the dynamic of a lot of inner-city mothers is that the success of their son is the greatest thing that has happened in their lives, too. This is the greatest level of attention they've received and they are going along for the ride because they've always wanted to be noticed and be somebody as well. When you're as good as I was coming out of high school, your mother is also getting recruited by the coaches, and she's never enjoyed that level of hospitality either.

The message that comes across loud and clear is if you're good at sports, you can have anything. In a lot of cases, like mine, sports were getting me out of all the trouble I get into. Football was my get-out-of-jail-free card. There was never anything enforced behavior-wise when I was screwing up and never anything enforced academically either. It was just that I got to be so good at football that football excused or minimized everything else and made everything else secondary to the success I could bring to my high school or college.

Once big-time college football coaches started begging me to come to their school, when I was 16 years old, I got the wrong message that football would let me do anything as long as I was good enough.

CHAPTER THREE

FALCON

I PUT IN about a month of training at Ursuline but it was late-June when we found out I couldn't go there because I lived south of the dividing line for the two Catholic schools in Youngstown.

When we figured this out, my mom and I went back to Rollen and he said, I don't necessarily want you to go to Cardinal Mooney but when we started naming possibilities in the area, he said I'd rather have you go there or Fitch. Youngstown City Schools were off the table as part of the deal with the judge. He thought there was just too much temptation to keep going down the wrong road there.

My first visit was at Mooney. I knew one of the other assistant coaches from basketball, Donald Deliscio. He basically gave me a visit to Mooney and my father was actually there.

I knew my dad was going to be there at the school because he went to Mooney and he wanted me to go to Mooney. I think the relationship between my dad and my other two brothers was so messed up—my first brother was going to juvenile, and my second brother wasn't around, and I imagine my dad was thinking I was the last chance to try and get it right with one of his sons. I don't know if there was communication with my mother about whether my dad could step in at this point though. I was 14 years old, and just a kid.

Meeting with Don was real cordial. He showed me the gymnasium, the weight room, the locker room and once we got downstairs to the football offices in the basement, I got to meet Coach Bucci. He's legendary. He had won a bunch of football games and he has a presence in Northeastern Ohio. He was even my dad's coach 20 years earlier. He was your traditional, straight-up, old-school football coach.

To put it in context, in the area, people feel like it's a privilege to go and play for Mooney. It's not surprising that Coach Bucci had no interest in me. Mooney had solid players but in that time period, it wasn't a big thing to have a great player. Now, every high school in America wants the great tailback. In the 90s, they weren't recruiting that much.

When I met with Coach Bucci, I asked him a direct question: could I play varsity football as a freshman? He said No, we've never had a freshman play varsity football. And that's why I didn't go to Mooney.

So then I had to go back to Rollen. He wanted to steer me away from trouble. Rollen was a mentor for a lot of men. It didn't matter where you were in life and whether you had my talent or no talent at all. He was all about helping young kids. He actually cared about us.

Remember, I couldn't go to any Youngstown high schools. My judge just thought I needed something different and he was probably right. I had been in front of him before, my brothers had been in front of him, and he knew I needed a change of environment.

Somehow, the option of going to Austintown Fitch came up, probably because Mr. Butch lived in Austintown. He had been my junior high football and basketball coach and I think I must have asked him.

My first thought was just to get on the field. I wasn't even thinking it would be possible to start at tailback. I was thinking about Liberty or Austintown because I had traveled to play there in junior high football and basketball. I wasn't even hoping to dominate at the varsity level but I wanted to see the field.

Mr. Butch connected me to Coach Brian Fedesci at Austintown very soon after the meeting at Mooney. By early-July, it was decided that I could go to Austintown and I immediately started training with them to get ready for two-a-days. Coach Green was picking me up and taking me to conditioning. I didn't know anybody on that team when I started conditioning with them.

CHAPTER THREE: FALCON

I was just so happy to be outside the house and lifting weights and being cool. I was having fun at football practice and it started showing that I had a lot of natural talent. I wasn't coached up or anything specifically for the running back position but I just had a desire to play football and had natural talent from what I'd learned in little league and junior high football.

It was a big switch for me going to Austintown Fitch. Youngstown was an all-black or predominately black school system, even in the Catholic schools. My school was all-black in first and second grade, then the public schools were all-black as well. Austintown City School district was completely different. I wouldn't call them rich, maybe upper-middle class, but they were rich to me. My mom would drive me to Austintown, which only took 15 minutes, but once we got across Glenwood Avenue, that was like the dividing line between the haves and the have-nots.

Austintown was a completely different world. There was an all-white school, with an all-white administration, teachers, and everything. It was totally different for me—not shocking but just different how they did things, with different classrooms and a whole different setting. From a social standpoint, I didn't fit in, just because I had nothing in common with my teammates.

When I came into this high school and started playing varsity football, I didn't identify it at the time, but I was breaking up the system of a lot of these kids playing junior high football together, freshman football, junior varsity, and then varsity. And then you had me, this kid who a lot of people knew was basically placed out there by the court.

In fact, the first time I went there during the summer for conditioning, I still had 13 staples in my head. When they saw those staples, the guys were asking me, What the hell happened to you? I told them I was in the juvenile system and that I came out here to play football and get away from the inner-city. And now I go out there and I'm dominating the varsity guys in practice and then after practice Coach Green, the strength coach, would drop me off after practice, taking me across Glenwood Avenue and back into my world in Youngstown.

Actually, there were 4 other black kids on the team: JT, Chance, Mike, and Josh. Everybody was cool during practice, because we were just doing drills, running, catching balls. When I came in, it was already established that these were the seniors, these are the guys on the the JV team and I was a freshman so nobody was thinking about where was I going to fit in. I was 5'11" and weighed 220 lbs. so I was big but not the biggest guy out there.

Just like at Mooney, the first question I had asked the head coach at Fitch was whether I could play varsity football and he said if you're good enough, you can play. And no one had ever seen me play so I was just another guy coming into the team. The separation between me and the other guys didn't start until we put on the pads.

During the two-a-days in August, I started to distinguish myself practicing with special teams—kick return and kick coverage. When you don't have a starting position on offense or defense, they just throw you on the special teams.

On coverage, I was flying down the field, making tackles, and blowing up the punt protector, all that stuff. They also had me returning kicks which I loved—getting a full head of steam and looking for holes, making cuts, and running dudes over. But I really started making an impression on the coaches as the scout team running back. I was hitting all the holes, breaking tons of tackles, and hitting tacklers as hard as they hit me.

Frank Giordano, a senior, was the starting tailback and also a captain. He probably never thought for a second I could ever replace him but I started to make my case in the first game.

It was against the Chaney Cowboys, and I started on kickoff coverage, punt coverage, and returns. This is where I broke out—I had a 78-yard kickoff return in our opening game.

We were losing at the time, but I returned one of their kickoffs for a touchdown, and that was a spark for everybody so the coach put me in for a few plays at tailback. But still, Frank wouldn't have been worried. We were getting our ass kicked and I was moving the ball but it was the end of the game. I played most of the 4th quarter and I had 6 carries for 33 yards. It was the only time we moved the ball that day.

CHAPTER THREE: FALCON

In practice after the first week, I was still on practice squad because Frank was a senior captain and there was another upperclassman who was second-string. I still wasn't believing they were going to start me because I was the third-string tailback at this point. Frank was a senior and I thought he would continue to play. He had been playing together with all these guys since peewee football and now they were seniors so everybody expected it to be their time to shine.

But in the second game, against Youngstown Rayen, I had even more carries and gained 127 yards. Frank went out for the first two series and we weren't moving the ball and I went out for the third series in the beginning of the second quarter. I had 2 touchdowns and we won. That's when things started rolling. Here I was, still 14 years old, just running dudes over.

In the third game of the season against Berea, they started me. I went out and ran for 248 yards. Coach Tressel was actually at that game because his nephew was playing for Berea. He was so famous and I had gone to his camps in the summer as a kid and I really wanted to impress him. At the time, if you had told me I could play for Youngstown State, that would have been like telling me I could play for the Steelers.

After the third game of the season, it was clear I just had natural talent to be able to play at the highest level. Even at 14, I was dominating 18-year olds.

But in the second quarter of the fourth game, I broke my fibia and tibia. It was a pitch to the left. It had been raining and I slipped and the tackler's helmet crashed into my lower leg. I just laid there before they carried me off, knowing it was broken.

At the emergency room, they gave me an air-cast and I started going to rehab after that but I had broken my leg, so my season was over. Even after only four weeks though it was pretty apparent that I was playing at a very high level.

At this time, just based upon the fact that I was going to school fifteen minutes away from my neighborhood, I wasn't around the same people. I was around a whole different crowd of people. My free time was spent a lot differently. This whole notion of wanting to be someone cool on the streets wasn't happening anymore because by then, I was like, Man, I could play football and get away from the streets. I was just like, Man, this shit with the street life is over. I didn't want to get in trouble anymore or go back to juvie. I just wanted to play football and basically become this football hero.

You know, this attention that I was starting to get from the streets, I was getting it also from fans and in class from the students and even the teachers. This is why I can understand why kids just want attention from somebody to make them feel special and feel like somebody. That's how I was starting to feel from football.

So from that standpoint, I ended up going to school and I was enjoying it. The school was visibly nicer, kids were driving cars to school. It felt like a completely different place. It wasn't impoverished. I wasn't shocked or intimidated by anything other than the schoolwork and the expectations on me academically because I was so far behind.

Even though there were no girls for me in 9th grade, I didn't mind. When football became a fascination of mine, I didn't care about messing with girls. I remember this is when I first thought I could go to college because of football. That's when the spark really went off.

After I started at Fitch, I didn't even mess with those girls in my own neighborhood. I just made friends with the black dudes on the team, but the white students at Fitch weren't bad to me at all. I'll say this, even though all those guys came up together, even though I took Frank's position for a minute, even his close buddies were never like, Screw you—you took Frank's spot.

The schoolwork was real tough though. As far as being at grade level for 9th grade, I was behind on technology, didn't know how to type, didn't know how to write, didn't know how to put a paper together. The only thing I was decent at was math. But science, computer, and language arts, and all that other stuff, it was just real tough for me. Every class I was in, outside of math, I didn't have a clue what to do. I didn't know how to study, didn't know how to take notes, or how to do homework. I didn't even know homework existed and now I was supposed to do it in multiple classes. I just wasn't prepared. I was constantly asking teachers questions all the time. It was evident and I was thinking, Man, I don't know how I'm going to do all this work. But I survived and got by, barely. I don't remember my grades but I can't imagine they were good.

Because of my immediate success, all the way through football season, I was already plotting and planning on leaving. There was a school called Warren Harding that was 30 minutes away from my house and they were sending guys to Michigan, Ohio State, Penn State, and all the Big Ten and other prominent MAC schools. They were #2 in the country and they were so close to Youngstown. So I was thinking, I was playing against Joe-Blow for Austintown and these dudes are ranked #2 in the country. We were cooking on the grill in the backyard and these guys were going to Smith & Wollensky.

All in one year, all these seniors at Harding signed letters of intent: Carl Diggs went to Michigan, Derek Tolls went to Penn State, Anthony Simpson went to Toledo, another guy named Anthony went to Temple. Somebody went to Akron. And I remember thinking, man, I'm getting out of Austintown and going there. We actually played Warren Harding in our last game. I was on their sideline on crutches as a ballboy and I remember asking coaches how was it that I could go there? Warren kicked our ass that night. They had like 9 guys going to Division I. They were a powerhouse in the Steel Valley Conference. So at the end of the season, I was talking to these guys asking how could I be a football player there. I got their contact information and I started recruiting them as a school and a place that I wanted to go.

When the winter came around, I was still going to Austintown and I went out for the basketball team. In my head, I was hoping the same thing that happened in football was going to happen in basketball—I was going to get to prove I could start on varsity. My leg had healed and I went out every practice and did my best but Coach Conley was a little more adamant about me not playing. In his head, he thought everything was given to me in football and he didn't want the same thing to happen with his basketball team. So many of these guys came up through freshman, JV, and varsity together, just like with the football team, but he wasn't going to let me crash their party.

It was clear that I was better than some of the guys on the varsity team and it frustrated me. I had no interest in playing JV but I did. In each game, I would score and I would do well but coach would not let me play for varsity. The fact that he was so bitter toward me made it very easy for me to leave Austintown. I didn't need him making an example out of me. I was like, I don't want to be here—you know, I'm just going to go to Warren Harding.

I actually left Austintown in the middle of the school year. Coach Conley didn't bother me at first until we were playing the JV games and I was performing and I was like, Yo, can I play? The JV games were always right before the Varsity games and for selective games, I would dress for Varsity. It was a decent team and I could have contributed.

All of the resistance came because the varsity guys had gone to summer camps together and been playing together since junior high. Nobody wanted to say it to my face, but the attitude with the coaches was these are my guys and I'm sticking with them.

Of course the team was bunch of white guys except Jared Ellis. He was a junior when I was a freshman. He was real good. I had known him because he also started out at Youngstown City Schools. He had family who lived in Youngstown so I would see him periodically and whenever we played pickup basketball, Jared would be there. He understood the system that was going to stay in place with Coach Conley and he was already good in that system so he wasn't going to rock the boat to get me any minutes.

There were two things that made me decide I couldn't stay at Austintown. The first explicit problem the coach had was with my shoes. All the varsity guys had bought a team shoe—some Adidas. But I had some Gary Payton shoes that were white and blue and Coach Conley wasn't cool with my shoes. I didn't have the $90 to buy another pair of shoes like the varsity team bought. The freshman and JV just wore any shoes they wanted. So I bought my shoes planning on playing for JV but then they told me if you want to play varsity you have to get the team shoes. But, damn, I didn't have the $90.

CHAPTER THREE: FALCON

Coach Conley was just looking for a reason not to play me and that was it, I guess.

And then the first time things with Coach Conley actually blew up was coming home from Liberty. We went up there and I had a great JV game, scoring probably about 15-20 points, with lots of rebounds, and played great defense. So, I was thinking I'm about to get in for the varsity game. I was playing the 2 or the 3 at that time and I dressed for varsity that day.

But what Coach Conley did was put in another JV guy into the varsity game before me—a guy who didn't play as well as I had in the JV game. And then Coach put me in with less than a minute left and us getting our ass kicked at that time. I could have had more pride sitting on the bench instead of getting in with 40-seconds left. So a sort of argument started on the bus on the way back to Austintown. I was mad about this and I was sitting about four rows back from the coaches, talking to the guy sitting next to me saying, Man, that was some bullshit—he put me in with 40-seconds left. I wasn't trying to have the coach hear me, but he was listening. I wasn't ranting and raving in front of everybody but I wasn't trying to be discreet either. I didn't care that he could hear me.

After the coach heard me, he said something to me on the bus. He wasn't that harsh and didn't yell at me but he was defending why he put me in when he did but I wasn't hearing it. When we got off the bus, he came up to me and we had a little discussion outside the bus while the rest of the team went into the school and got their stuff. It was just a few minutes but I was like Look, man, 40 seconds—I deserve to be playing more. He was just telling me I needed to be a better teammate. He wanted me to suck it up and pay my dues and not expect to come to this new program in my first year and expect to play. The coach was basically saying, this is the way it is and I don't care if you don't like it.

The next game was at Canton Hoover. I had another good game for the JV and played well enough that I thought I should be getting some minutes for the varsity. But Coach Conley put me in again for garbage time when the team was getting blown out. This was a much longer ride back home than Liberty and I was like, I don't want to put up with this. This time on the bus the coach and I were actually arguing. In the middle of the argument, I quit. I was cussing and we were going back and forth with each other while everybody else was just being quiet. I was big, 220 pounds, from Youngstown and I thought I was the man because I was playing football and I was feeling the same way as when I went to the Mooney coach and said, I just need an opportunity. It didn't make any sense to me why he wouldn't give me an opportunity, especially when we were getting blown out.

When we got off the bus, I went to the locker room, got dressed in my street clothes, grabbed all my basketball gear, and gave it to the coach and told him he could have it because I was done. My mom had been following the bus so she was waiting in the car to take me home.

At this point, I started making plans to go to Harding for real. Before, it has just been a thought but it wasn't serious. Around this time though I told my mom I wanted to transfer schools. She was mad too because she had seen me not getting to play but she still tried to talk to Coach Conley and get me to stay at Austintown even though she knew I was interested in going to Harding. I went for a few more days to Austintown but I was making plans to get out. I called the football coach at Harding and asked him what the process was to transfer there immediately. By the end of the week I was at Harding.

CHAPTER FOUR

RAIDER

I DIDN'T KNOW a soul when I started at Warren G. Harding either but it was a refreshing change because the school was very diverse. It wasn't odd for black and white people to be talking to each other. So there wasn't like any racial dynamic and it was the total opposite of the one I had experienced at Fitch, which maybe had 50 people who were black in the entire school.

Marcus was going to school in Youngstown, but he had done really well against Harding when they played them. He was a defensive lineman, who made a lot of tackles. When I approached the coaches at Harding about whether I could play for them, they asked whether Marcus would come too at the start of the next school year. They were thinking they could have me as a sophomore and him as a senior. He was 6'2" and 275 lbs and was being recruited already by Tressel to go to YSU.

Starting in February of my freshman year, my mom drove me back and forth to Warren, which was 30 minutes away. And then by the beginning of my sophomore year, Marcus was driving me. He was happy to transfer there for his senior season because more college scouts would see him play.

At Warren it was just about a 50-50 racial split. Black and white people socialized—they talked to each other in class and in the halls and they hung out with each other after school. When I got there, this was refreshing. They took football serious—there was some real pride about sports. The school day was shorter, and that was the first time I ever heard of trimesters in my life. They didn't have lunch—that was the biggest thing. You went to school at 930 and got out at 130 and you were responsible for feeding yourself. I was like, cool, five periods and you skip lunch. I could get my own lunch. I was programmed to take care of myself anyway.

Everything about Warren was different. The guys' approach towards football was different, the camaraderie was different, the pride of the town—everything was more intense. Warren is like one of those old-school towns where all high school sports mean something…soccer, swimming, and they had a bunch of support for every sport. It was like a big deal. So when I came over there, guys were receptive and I was able to help their team. Weightlifting was a class in my schedule, so I was working out and getting to know the guys on the team. We didn't have gym class; I just had to lift.

I was also conditioning after school and playing 7-on-7. I hadn't heard of that before. My new teammates knew who I was because of my three games at Austintown and they knew about the injury which ended my season. The tailback for WGH was Omar Strader, who was going to be a junior. He was the backup to Deryck Toles and was expecting to be the starter the next year. He wasn't that cool with me actually because I was his competition. He was 5'7" but was super-fast, so he was a different sort of back than me.

I wasn't doing anything from a criminal standpoint, I was obviously living in Youngstown and I would come home so late at night and see my guys getting into things. At this point, Michael was out of school and in the streets. My guy Juwan Phifer, who I was with as a kid, had basically got a sentence of 18 years for robbery and felonious assault when we were 16. He's been incarcerated my whole adult life and just got out.

I can remember all that criminality taking place and as silly as it sounds, that life seemed so distant to me even though I'd only been out of it a year or so. I was only 15 years old, but I was still going to high school, training my body seriously, and playing football.

But rewind one year and Juwan and I were running around trying to sell drugs together and stealing cars together. But only a year later, that life felt distant to me even then. I was even thinking about college—all because I excelled at football and someone who became a real mentor to me snatched me off the pipeline to juvenile detention. Football was my ticket out and probably saved my life—it was all I was thinking about then.

Well, if I wasn't thinking about football, I was thinking about girls. Since sports were so central to Warren, it was easier to get girls. It was a huge football town and some of the older guys on the team were famous for throwing parties. I would go up there sometimes and hang out and the girls were always around.

So I conditioned the rest of the school year at WGH and played 7-on-7 all that summer. I was getting more serious about football. The difference was that compared to everyone else in the area, WGH was like the Ohio State Buckeyes and everyone else was like a small college.

In June, I went to a camp at Indiana University with some of my new teammates. The coaches drove us and dropped us off. About 15 of us went. This was a big deal. We stayed in a dorm, which was a really big deal to me. Kam Kameron was the coach then and he offered me a scholarship while I was there based on how well I did in the drills. I wasn't even a sophomore but I was getting paired against seniors and doing well.

This camp was 4 days and before I left, one of the coaches, Anthony Thomas, sat down with me and said I can see where your talent will take you and we want to offer you a scholarship. He had spent about half the day with me getting to know me and then he invited me to his office. I didn't accept the scholarship on the spot—I said Thanks, that's cool, that's a nice offer and I told my coach they offered me a scholarship on the way back to Youngstown.

This is when it first felt like, Damn, I'm getting out of Youngstown and off the streets. I was thinking I could do something with myself and my future. Getting out of Youngstown was like a major deal at that time. I wasn't thinking about being a major college star and dominating—I was just trying to keep improving my situation.

That was the only camp that summer but all through the rest of the summer Coach Reardon, the wide receivers coach, was picking me up and taking me to WGH. He was going to work and I was riding with him. He would drop me off and then go up into his office. It started to become obvious during 7-on-7 in the spring actually that I could be the starter if I got a fair chance.

Two-a-days started in the beginning of August and I was loving it. Omar had left school so that cleared the way for me. There were a couple other guys, Josh Cayson and Artemis Edington, who were also going out for tailback. Josh was about 165 and Artemis was about 205 but I wasn't going to let them beat me out. In my mind, I was going to do everything I needed to do to be the first-team back.

When we got our uniforms, I was #5 and I was named the starter. There were huge expectations on me since I had been the starter at Fitch as a freshman and then transferred to Harding.

The season opened with a big victory over Cleveland Benedictine, 36-13. I had a huge game with around 150 yards and two or three touchdowns and was looking forward to a breakout season on a powerhouse team

The next game was at Cincinnati Moeller, though, which was always one of the best teams in the state. We just couldn't move the ball against them and they shut us out 19-0. It was a horrible rainy night which made getting crushed somehow even worse.

Late in the 4th quarter, I hurt my ankle which made the 5-hour bus ride back to Youngstown last forever. It was throbbing with pain and we were soaking wet from sweat and rain. Those bus rides from Cincy all the way to Northeastern Ohio after getting your ass kicked just seemed to take forever.

We bounced back with a 37-14 victory against Dayton Meadowdale the following week. This was a big game for me and next up on the schedule was Mooney.

I didn't have many yards because our offense just couldn't move the ball against them. They beat us 29-6 and by this time, it was clear that my ankle was really hurt.

I played the rest of my sophomore season on a bad ankle. I just kept doing a little more damage to it because I didn't want to get the surgery. I wasn't taking painkillers—I was getting double- or triple-taped and just running on it. I had a bone chip on the inside of my ankle from my injury freshman year that never healed and a separated tibia and fibia and the more I ran on it, the more I separated it.

CHAPTER FOUR: RAIDER

I had 1100 yards as a sophomore and we finished 7-3. We lost to Cincinnati Moeller, Mooney, and Ursuline. We got our ass kicked in those losses. We were beating the teams we were supposed to beat but getting whooped by the better teams.

But in the last game of the season, on my 16th birthday, we beat Fitch 32-14. This felt particularly sweet since I had played for them the previous year and they were gunning for me for sure. We ended the season with four straight wins so things were looking up but I realized soon that my ankle was really messed up and I needed to get it looked at.

I already had my learner's permit because I turned fifteen-and-a-half that summer, and I got my driver's license after the season was over. I bought my first car with money I made doing dishes at DiLucia's banquet and catering facility in Warren. I was working holidays and on the weekend. This guy Bobby Dellimuti, who owned the restaurant, would hire the football and basketball players on the holidays or whenever he needed help—Easter, Mother's Day, etc.

We could go in for the weekend and make some money. He would pay us cash as spot labor. Basically, he was the booster for high school sports. I was actually going and working—making $8-10/hour doing dishes and there were other guys on the team who were doing it too. If we wanted to make money and he had work that needed to be done, we would call him up and ask him if he needed us. There were always dishes to be done and floors to mop. There were some nights when we didn't get out of there until 1 or 2am but we weren't getting checks—we were getting cash at the end of the night so we didn't mind.

My first car was a 1988 Oldsmobile Ninety-Eight, so it was about ten years old when I bought it from my neighbor for $1200. I was driving back and forth to Warren and wasn't getting tickets or getting in accidents. I was just staying out of trouble.

In basketball as a sophomore, I was on the varsity and started at the 4, power forward. We were a run-and-gun team and our center was only 6'3". We were a fast team and played good defense. Once we started playing games, my ankle was just killing me so I played the whole season on a bad ankle and had surgery on it as soon as the season was over. I couldn't run track that year or play 7-on-7 in the summer and I knew I was probably going to miss the first half of my junior season.

The boosters in Warren started helping me out during basketball. They would just give me some money, stuffing it in my pocket. When the NCAA came after me in college, these guys caught a lot of flak, but it was actually pretty honest. I don't think they got anything out of it and were just being generous and kind because they saw a kid who could use a little help.

I spent the entire spring lifting every weight that I could. This is when I became stupid strong. I would lift after school and stay as long as I wanted because I had my own car and was driving myself home. I wasn't drinking or smoking weed—I was committed to staying in shape and I was like the ideal kid. I was around people who were running in the streets but I wasn't involved with that at all. I wasn't associated with criminality—I was hanging out in the neighborhood with my brothers and cousins who were doing it but I wasn't involved in it directly. I just had no interest in the streets at this time.

When I was coming up, I just wanted to be somebody to my friends. So when I was younger, I was being a knucklehead to become somebody amongst my friends. So, football helped me make that name for myself and I became identified as cool playing football and started thinking I could take this shit to college and do something with myself. Just think about it, I was in high school and I wasn't even thinking about the NFL: going to college was like the bigtime to me at this point.

At the beginning of my junior year, I was about 230 pounds but a compact, strong 230. I had been lifting weights for about 6 months straight. I couldn't participate in two-a-days though and had to sit out at the beginning of the season. I couldn't even run on my ankle until the beginning of August but I wasn't getting hit. I wasn't cutting, exploding, or running until now.

CHAPTER FOUR: RAIDER

Right before my junior season started, I moved into an apartment in Warren. Some of the boosters had gotten it for me but it wasn't any big deal. They weren't trying to bribe me or give me any additional incentives—I was already enrolled at Harding and wasn't about to go back to high school in Youngstown—they just saw that I was driving a half-hour each way back-and-forth to my mom's house and thought it made more sense for me to live in Warren. All I had was a bed, a couch, a TV, and one table. I kept a few clothes there, but that's it. I stayed there most of the time but would go back to Youngstown on the weekends if I could.

You have to think about this given the statistics at the time. When you talk about Youngstown in the 1990s, there was heavy crime. Murders, killings, and intense danger. There were more than 500 murders in Youngstown in the 1990s and I think the boosters just thought if we could get him up here, get him out of there, we could get him in a better situation where he would be safe.

During the NCAA investigation a few years later, I had to go through a lot of this. When I thought about it then and even when I think about it now, do I think it was wrong? Hell no—I don't think it was wrong. I grew up living in a war zone, watching people get murdered in front of me. Having my house get shot up in a drive-by. And the NCAA wants to say I have to suffer my fate in that neighborhood even though people want to help me out? That doesn't make any damn sense.

It was just a situation that's no different than if a kid is good at hockey and he goes and lives with a family for a couple years to play on a better team. Say what you want about it, but these guys were just trying to help me out. They weren't getting anything out of it, believe me. It wasn't helping them at all. They were getting me off streets where I could have been murdered.

I must admit the apartment was a little bit of an added benefit with the girls though. I could mess around with girls at night, go back and crash at my apartment, sleep in, and still make it on time to school, which was only a few minutes away. But mainly it just helped keep me out of the street life.

In Warren, there wasn't any pressure to sell weed and I didn't have the stress of surviving the streets every day like I had in Youngstown. So from that standpoint, it accomplished exactly what those boosters wanted it too. It gave me a place to feel safe and relax as a normal teenager. And that comes up three years later as an NCAA violation?

I came back in the 6th game of my junior season and the team was 3-2 at that point, losing again to Ursuline and Moeller. We got killed by Moeller again, 42-0, but Ursuline barely beat us, 15-12. I was on the sidelines for all these games and it was killing me not to be out there. Josh was the tailback for those five games and he was running hard and doing a good job.

I had been going to physical therapy in Warren at this place down from the school and then in the 6th week of the season, I got cleared for full contact practice. I was the strongest I'd ever been and I knew I needed to put up some film for the college scouts. I was stronger and more confident and could do everything they asked of me at the clinic. The day I finally got cleared, we had finished our rehab session and the lady said if you can do these 10 sprints, I'll clear you to play. I did them and she said alright, cool, you're done with therapy.

I had been practicing—doing the non-contact drills—so I knew I would be ready when I got cleared. I was also watching film every week with the team. During that 6th week, I practiced hard and my first game back was against my old team, Austintown Fitch. The coach was going to let Josh stay as the first-team tailback, but I knew I would get a lot of carries. This was a home game for us and there was still some animosity between me and Coach Fedesci because I had left.

Josh went out for the first three series and the coach put me in for the fourth series. I knew our little competition for tailback was over already. I was healthy and stronger than I'd ever been. It didn't matter that we were down by 10 points when I went in, because the first play, I ran for 75 yards and a TD. It was a counter to the left and I followed the guard through the line, stepped over a guy, and broke one tackle and went for 75 yards. Then I went back out for the next offensive series and did the same thing. It wasn't on the first play but I took it down and scored another touchdown. I finished the game with about 180 or 190 yards. At that point, it was just like I

CHAPTER FOUR: RAIDER

took off and we beat them decisively. A lot of guys on their team were jawing at me but I didn't get into that.

At that point, we were 4-2. We lost to Boardman the next week but we won the rest of our games to finish 7-3 again. I had 1200 yards in just five games. I was just rolling for the rest of the season and was getting contacted by a lot of college coaches.

I had already taken a visit in fact to Notre Dame. Urban Meyer invited me and my mom to South Bend for their night game against Nebraska on September 9th. He was the receivers coach at Notre Dame and the scout in charge of Ohio. Even though my ankle was still healing, I was on the sidelines when Harding played Friday night and then mom and I drove to Notre Dame the next morning.

It was a close game but Eric Crouch beat them in double-overtime on an option keeper. They did everything for my mom and I, including taking us down on the field and meeting all the other recruits. After the game, my mom and I went out with Coach Meyer and his wife, who was pregnant at the time. At the end of the night, he offered me a scholarship and I could see that it was really happening—I was going to have the chance to go to Notre Dame if I wanted.

I also went to Penn State games. Jay Paterno was an assistant and he was in charge of my visits. These weren't official recruiting visits but they were allowed to invite us to the game and give us some money for food.

In terms of academics, Warren wasn't challenging. I was doing fine and there wasn't any homework. I was getting As and Bs and maybe a few Cs. I was getting As in weightlifting but my big problem was with German, which was the only foreign language they offered.

During my junior year, I started again at the 4 on the basketball team. We were a little better team but we were young. In the tournament, we only made it to the second round where we lost to Cleveland South.

I didn't run track my junior year so I could concentrate on conditioning. I was serious about football at the time. I was running short sprints and doing drills on the football field and this is when I started breaking down film. I got into a routine of watching film with Coach McDaniels. He really knew the game and taught it to me as well as his own son, Josh McDaniels, the offensive coordinator for the Patriots.

Coach McDaniels was the one who taught me how to break down film. I would see him doing it and he would explain the game to us Saturday mornings after the game. He would call the entire team in the next day after the game at 9 or 10 in the morning. We were in the auditorium and he used a projector to show all of us the film of the game the night before. He would tell us what we were supposed to be doing and what we were supposed to be looking at.

Everybody learns at a different level based on what they are interested in and already know. So you could say that in 9th and 10th grade, I was just playing on instinct and talent. But then Coach McDaniels started to explain to me why teams were in an in/over defense, why they were in cover-two, what are your leverage points, why do we audible. So, during my junior year, I learned football.

That spring, I was watching VHS tapes over and over again, in the coach's office during the day and then at my apartment at night or in Youngstown if I decided to drive home. My brother Marcus was away at Buffalo and it was just me and mom at home. Around this time, my mom started working at the court in downtown Youngstown. This meant she didn't have to drive an hour each way and was around a lot more.

After my successful junior year, I was like, Oh shit, I can do this. Notre Dame had made me an offer and I committed to them. When Urban Meyer was driving me around in his Explorer, I was in the back seat with Rex Hogan, the recruiting coordinator.

Nobody will believe this, but my thinking wasn't that I was going to the NFL but that I was going to go to Notre Dame and get an education. I wanted to be smart and graduate from Notre Dame. I wasn't thinking about making money in the NFL. In fact, going to the NFL seemed so mysterious to me—like I had no idea whatsoever how a player made it there. You have to think about visibility and what I'd been exposed to at that point.

I hadn't ever seen guys go beyond college so going to college was like the highest possible level of attainment for me. In my mind, going to the

CHAPTER FOUR: RAIDER

NFL was so far-fetched that it seemed like an impossibility. I hadn't seen it happen, and didn't have a roadmap for it so I don't care how good I was, I couldn't conceive of the thought of going to the NFL. I just accepted the offer to Notre Dame and really started thinking about my future.

In fact, after gaining 1200 yards in 5 games as a junior, I decided that I had already proven myself as a high school player and I didn't need to play at that level anymore. I also saw how punishing football was and knew my body only had a certain amount of hits it could absorb. The way I ran, breaking into the secondary where safeties had open season on me, every play could have been my last in terms of knee, neck, or spinal cord injuries.

So, I wanted to skip my senior year of high school football and enroll at Notre Dame in the fall of 2001. Unfortunately, I didn't have the English credits I needed and couldn't get them in time to do that. Coach Meyer told me to take summer school at Harding and graduate in December so I could enroll in January and participate in winter conditioning and spring practice at ND. So I took senior English before my senior year. He also told me I needed to get a 17 on the ACT.

At this point, I had already taken the ACT once, in the spring of my junior year. I didn't take any practice tests and I actually thought I was going to do well but I had no idea what the test was going to be like and I bombed it.

Based on the classes I was taking, I was getting good grades and I thought I'd be alright. So I just showed up at my high school one Saturday morning with a #2 pencil and my driver's license and a week later I got my score—a 13. It wasn't high enough to qualify with the NCAA clearinghouse to be eligible but I figured I would be alright because there were more chances to take that test or the SAT.

The next time I tried to get my qualifying score, I took the SAT. It was in the summer before my senior year and I got a 1220, which was way more than I needed. I'm ashamed to admit that I cheated off the girl next to me. She was a white girl from Struthers who probably didn't even know who I was. She was sitting catty-corner in front of me and she happened to have the same color test I had so it was easy to tell I should look at her answer sheet instead of the guys on either side of me.

Once I had the score I needed, I was ready to go to ND, but there was a pivotal moment right after I got the test result. Bob Davie was fired as the head coach of Notre Dame and Urban Meyer left ND to be the head coach at Bowling Green. He wanted me to go there, but I wasn't about to go to Bowling Green after I already had offers from most of the Big Ten and Notre Dame. When he called me, I said, No offense, but that isn't what I have in mind for my future.

Another completely unpredictable thing that happened was that our hometown hero from Division I-AA Youngstown State University, Jim Tressel, had been hired as the head coach at perennial college football powerhouse Ohio State.

So, all of a sudden, my future became very clear—I was going to go to Ohio State. The thing was though, they hadn't been recruiting me yet. But I knew Tressel from camps, he had been in my house recruiting Marcus to go to YSU, so I figured all I had to do was reach out to him.

After spring conditioning one day, I walked into Coach McDaniels' office and we called Coach Tressel. They knew each other already so Coach dialed up Tressel and handed me the phone. I said, Hey I'm coming to Ohio State. He laughed and said we didn't offer you a scholarship and I said you will after you watch my games this season.

When I had Coach Tressel on the phone, I also told him I was going to take summer school so I could graduate one semester early and come to OSU in January of 2002. Staying close to home was cool because I didn't want to have to fly that much. I was also infatuated with Tressel because of his national championships at YSU.

To tell the truth, it wasn't that surprising that the Buckeyes hadn't offered me a scholarship. At that point, I didn't have an Ohio State stat line. I only played 3 games my freshman year before I broke my leg, I played my whole sophomore season with a bad ankle, and I only played 5 games in my junior year. I had only gained something like 2000 yards total at that point and some high school all-stars were getting more than that in one season.

CHAPTER FOUR: RAIDER

But I was serious going into my senior year. I was focused on school, focused on practice, and focused on football. I was locked-in and focused. I was doing everything I could to excel in school and in football. I was as focused then as I am in my life right now. I was going to succeed. I was going to have incredible success—I could visualize it and nothing was going to stop me.

CHAPTER FIVE

ALL-AMERICAN

Summer school was Monday-Thursday from mid-June to July. There were two classes each morning with just a handful of students from different districts and after that was over, I would grab lunch somewhere, and then lift weights and then go to practice. Summer school was so relaxed and informal and I wish that I had taken classes each summer.

Summer workouts were pretty packed with people—we were good my junior year and had a lot of players coming back so everybody wanted to come and build for the future. I hadn't been named a captain yet but it was pretty much known that I was going to be a captain.

Marcus was already at Buffalo so I wasn't talking to him that much. I was proud of him but I wasn't that connected to what he was doing there because my high school also played on Saturdays. I didn't get to make any visits to Buffalo or watch Marcus because I was always playing myself. Warren Harding football was such a big deal that we would sell-out 25,000-seat stadiums on Saturday nights. We were the biggest draw in the area.

So unlike most high school football players, we had Friday nights to ourselves. After school on Friday, we had our walk-through, then most of my teammates would go see some local game in the area but I would usually go back to Youngstown. I didn't hang out with my teammates outside of school. I still had a group of friends in Youngstown that I would hang out with.

Sports were a big deal in Warren and everyone there knew I was part of the team but they all knew I wasn't from there. I would go to Perkins or some local restaurant with my teammates after the games sometimes but I hadn't grown up with them so we never got close like a family or anything.

Since we played on Saturdays, I had to drive back to Warren in the afternoon. For a home game, we would meet around 3:30 and have a pre-game dinner in the cafeteria then went back to the practice facility where we had offensive, defensive, and special team meetings to talk about what we were going to do. If the game was at 7:30, we'd go back to the stadium about 6:30, get dressed, listen to the national anthem, and then it was game time.

For away games, we might have to meet a lot earlier if we played in Cincinnati or Cleveland. We would eat our meals earlier, have our meetings, and then get on the bus to whatever stadium we played in.

The first game of my senior year was against Cleveland South at home. It was August 24th and we beat them 76-0 which wasn't saying much because they weren't good. In fact, we had beaten them 82-12 the previous year. I had over a hundred yards and a few touchdowns. This was all in the first half and I didn't play the second half. They didn't need to protect me but they would tell me before the game that if we were winning pretty big I would sit the second half.

Our second game was also at home against Cincinnati Moeller, a perennial powerhouse in big-school football in Ohio. It was fun to beat them 55-0 because they had beaten us so many times before including 42-0 last year so it was great this year because we physically beat them up. We kicked their ass and I was just ripping it up on punt returns, kick returns, runs, receiving. I was the starting tailback but I wanted to get the ball in my hands as much as possible. I was super dialed-in, super focused, and wasn't worried about getting injured. I was strong, healthy, and ready to go.

Our third game was against M. M. Robinson, a team from Canada. They came down from Canada for a whooping, 71-0, which was worse than the year before when we beat them 55-6. I had more yards, more touchdowns, and was really rolling.

The big game was our fourth game, against Youngstown Ursuline. They had beaten us both my previous years 15-12 and 23-14.

CHAPTER FIVE: ALL-AMERICAN

Everyone in the region thought Warren had stolen me from Youngstown. Everybody knew I was from Youngstown and if you're from Youngstown, you're supposed to stay in Youngstown. When we played against Ursuline, that coach was bitter that he had let me go. That didn't matter though, because we whooped them 56-16.

The next game was against Toledo Witmer and I got hurt. I got hurt in the first quarter on a slippery field. I literally pulled my groin. I wasn't hit. I planted, slipped, and strained my groin. We were already beating them and I played a little bit after that and we won 30-0 but I only played sporadically and the offense sputtered after I came out. Our offense was mainly a rushing attack so I was responsible for a large portion of the offense.

The game the following week was at Austintown Fitch. I wasn't 100% but I played. That game was special to the Fitch guys because it was their senior year and we had beaten them the two years after I left. They felt like I started there and they really wanted to beat me after we left. We beat them 26-14 in my sophomore year and 32-14 when I was a junior.

This was a good game and closer than it would have been if I were at full capacity. In fact, I didn't play the first half even though I was dressed and on the sideline. It was a real struggle and there wasn't any offense in the first half but we led 7-6. The coach came to me at halftime and asked if I could play. I said, Hell yes, and I went out on the first series and we were moving the ball and then I ripped off a 50-yard run. We scored to go ahead 14-6 and in the fourth quarter they scored a touchdown to make it 14-13 and they tried an onside kick but it came straight to me, standing there up close on the hands team. I caught it off the bounce on the dead run and scored a touchdown so we won 21-13.

At the end of the game, the coaches from Fitch didn't even talk to me. I had beaten them 3 times after I left. Even to this day, there's still a small level of bitterness between me and the coaches on those other teams. They all knew I could have helped make a difference on their team. They weren't wrong but I had to do what was best for me.

After the Fitch game, we were 6-0 and had to play Boardman. I was doing physical therapy for my groin but all they could do was tape it up and stabilize it. The trainer was a guy named Jeff, who worked with YSU. He would tape me up and make sure I wasn't going full speed or getting hit in practice.

Boardman had beaten us the year before 20-6 so we really wanted to beat them. This was a back-and-forth game and they sent me in on defense which hadn't ever happened in a game before. I went in at nose guard in the second quarter even though I'd only practiced there a little bit. But I was the strongest guy on the team, squatting 750 pounds, and benching 375. I was so unbelievably aggressive. I was serious about it and couldn't get out there and hit people enough. I used to do this in our own practices sometimes against our offensive line, exploding into the center, blowing these dudes up, disrupting everything.

So, Boardman was beating us up in the running game and I went to the coach and told him to put me in. They were kicking our ass so I just said show me where to line up and I'd just go off the snap and blow up the gap. I was making tackles, sacks, and even though their lineman were 260-275, I was just blowing them off the line. I was so explosive, blowing the center up, blowing the guard up, even sacking the quarterback. I was disrupting the whole flow of everything for them. We ended up beating them 43-28 but it was back-and-forth until I went in there and then we pulled away.

Canton McKinley was our next opponent and this game was really personal for Coach McDaniels because he had come from there. He had retired from there, sat out a couple years, and then started back up coaching at Warren Harding. So with the added incentive, we laid a total ass-whooping on them. Coach had a noticeable focus on whooping them all week and the weeks prior in fact. We won that game 57-9 and he was still allowing me to play in the fourth quarter. I just wanted to play so I didn't mind. Now we were 8-0.

We went on the road the following week to play Cincinnati Elder. We had escaped with a victory against them the previous year, 24-19 at home. That was a tough-ass game and they had everybody back this year and were also undefeated. They were ready and we got physically beaten by them. They had this outstanding running back and I don't think they passed the ball against us at all. They just lined up with 9 men on the line and physically beat us up on both sides of the ball. Our offense depended on the run so when they stuffed our line, we didn't have any answer for them. When you are getting your ass kicked, the game seems to last forever. We just weren't moving the ball. Every adjustment we made, they were already there. Coach tried to pass it to me, tried splitting me out, and they just had our number.

This was a Cincinnati Catholic school so they had the biggest and best people in the area. They were a lot bigger than us. These guys were the biggest of the big and the best of the best. They were all big and white, with a huge-ass line. Their only black guy was their tailback.

I just remember from the moment we pulled-up to the stadium to the moment we left that everything was purple. The stadium was called the Purple Pit and they had purple everywhere. From the moment we got off the bus, they had a different level of intensity. I had been averaging almost 150 yards per game but only had 42 yards on 16 carries against Elder. It wasn't close. They beat us 24-14 and Michael Philips had both our TDs. Needless to say, it was a long 5-hour ride home.

So, we were 8-1 and had one last game of the regular season against Youngstown Mooney. We whooped their ass 33-0, taking out our frustrations on them. If you want to talk about running guys over, and breaking long runs, we just beat them and we made the playoffs for the first time in my high school career, which was a really big deal.

In the first round of the playoffs, we had to play Boardman again at home and it was a really tough game. Man, that was a great high school football game. I think we had a safety at some point and most of the game we were ahead 9-7. I didn't play defense in this game, out of respect to the defensive line coach and the nose guard himself. I mean, of course that's disrespectful when you send your starting running back in to play nose guard. We ended up scoring on our last drive to make it 16-7. It was an intense final drive of all running plays to me. The touchdown was a sweep to the left and that sealed the game.

But I broke my left thumb in this game.

I don't remember what quarter, but I gave a guy a stiff arm and my thumb got caught in his facemask and he went down. My thumb got stuck, and when he went down, it felt like my thumb got ripped off. I didn't want to see a doctor though so I just got it wrapped up for the playoffs. The trainers taped it and stabilized it but they couldn't do anything to fix it at the time without me sitting out and there was no way I was going to miss the playoffs.

If I were going to think of legendary games, I would say both of the Boardman games my senior year. Those were hard fought games, just two teams with great form tackling, who were blocking really well, and taking care of the football. That was really good high school football. At the end of our first playoff game, I followed my usual routine and got in the cold tub in the locker room to start getting ready for the next game.

Our second playoff game was against Cleveland St. Edward, which was #1 in the state and ranked in the country. We played them at Kent State University, which was less than an hour from us. It was closer to us than it was to Cleveland in fact. We won this game 42-26 and I had 404 yards that game and 6 TDs. My first run was 75 yards. Then I had a run of 85 yards. I had over 300 yards in the first half when the game was relatively close. The interesting thing was that we couldn't stop them on defense. They were having these long time-consuming drives and would score a touchdown, then we would get the ball and I would score really quickly in the first few plays. This was a big upset and our fans rushed the field and we were heading to the state semi-finals against Cleveland Ignatius, who was also ranked.

We felt like we had already beaten the #1 team so we thought we were going to kick their ass too.

This game was at the University of Akron and we filled that stadium as well. We lost 40-33. At first, we were beating them by two touchdowns. I had 176 yards in the first half and we were really controlling the game. But right before halftime, we were still up by 14 and on their 6-yard line about to score again. Coach McDaniels called a slant pass but Anthony Gonzalez, who ended up playing for OSU, jumped the route and intercepted the ball and took it for a 100-yard return.

CHAPTER FIVE: ALL-AMERICAN

So, we go into the locker room at halftime only up by one touchdown but thinking that's not a problem. On the kickoff to start the second half, our returner fumbled the ball. Ignatius got the ball on about the 30 and went in to score and all of a sudden it was a tie game. They held us on our next drive and we punted and they scored again on a bomb so within a few minutes, we went from up 2 TDs, about to go up 3 TDs, to being behind. I started to get pissed off and only got the ball twice in the second half. To this day, I have no idea why. This is a mystery still for football fans in Warren. Everything was happening so fast and we were just throwing the ball and before we knew it the game was over and we lost 40-33.

This was the first game in my life where I ever cried. I used to see people crying after football or basketball games and I would ask myself, what the hell are they crying for? But I went into the locker room after this game and I was really hurt. I was like, Oh shit, now I get it—this shit really hurts. Coach McDaniels was broken-up too after the game. He had a look like he really let us down.

I never confronted Coach McDaniels about it, and even now, I don't know why I wasn't getting the ball in the second half. It was harder for me to catch because of my broken thumb but I had 16 carries in the first half and didn't fumble at all. In fact, my only three fumbles of the year were in the St. Ed's game when I had 404 yards.

But Coach McDaniels and I are cool. He taught me the game of football. He knows everything about it and almost everything I know, I learned from him. In my three years playing for him, we only had one confrontation, before the Ursuline game my junior year. It was in Youngstown, I was hurt so I wasn't playing, and I called him on Saturday morning to ask if I could just meet the team at the YSU stadium, where Ursuline played. I only lived 5 minutes from there but I lived 30 minutes from Warren. The thing is, Coach said No. He wanted me to drive all the way to Warren and leave my car there and ride back to Youngstown with the team and then ride back to Warren after the game to get my car. I honestly thought he was bullshitting me.

So, at the end of the phone conversation I just told him I was going to meet him at YSU's stadium but when I got there, he banned me from the locker room. He had one of the assistant coaches tell me I couldn't go into the locker room. He didn't want me on the sidelines either. It was like I wasn't part of the team. He basically just blew me off. Coach DiGiacomo was sent out to reconcile with me but I ended up staying on the opposite corner of the sidelines during the game, which we lost 15-12. I didn't go out to the school the next day to watch film with the team but I had to go in on Monday to apologize, which I did out of formality. I regret to say this, but it's been almost 20 years and the two of us never actually cleared the air about this.

Even though he taught me so much, I can't say I was very close to Coach McDaniels. He was just like the teacher to everyone. He was never a father figure to me. He was just a total football guy. He taught everyone a lot about football and it wasn't like he took me aside especially, but I was dialed-in and I learned. We were respectful and close but I wasn't going to his house and eating dinner and he wasn't giving me advice about life. Once he saw everything I was doing to help the team, he didn't hesitate to let me do what I wanted most of the time as long as it benefited the team. If it was 3rd-and-1 and I said I wanted the ball, he would give it to me, 100% of the time. He also let me tell Michael Philips, our QB, whatever I saw and what I thought we should do based on what I was seeing. So he let me be a leader and got me ready for my time at Ohio State.

CHAPTER SIX
ARMY ALL-STAR

For the season, I had 2400 yards and 42 TDs. My high school career was over and everybody knew I was going to Ohio State. Losing in the state semifinals was still a disappointment though. In the past, Warren had been very good for a lot of years and we were hoping to get back to that pinnacle. We had been working since spring to win the state championship so it just hurt that we didn't.

After I committed to Ohio State, Penn State and Michigan were the only ones who were still trying to recruit me. They were calling and saying they would love to have me. I was also still getting handwritten letters in the mail, which was a big deal, and coaches telling me to call them if I needed anything. I hadn't ever signed a letter of intent to Ohio State so they thought maybe I would switch schools. I could have gone anywhere at this point but I wasn't thinking about that—I was determined to go to Ohio State.

I was a Jim Tressel fan. That was the biggest reason why I wanted to go to OSU. When I was a kid, Youngstown State was good. Whenever my mom and I would go out to eat in local restaurants, I would see all these posters of the team and their championships. YSU won the national championship in 1991, 1993-4, and 1997.

Another big thing was how black people treated Tressel. Black people in Youngstown loved him. He was the most popular guy in town and a hero to everyone. Everybody loved him whether they were black or white.

I had already passed the Ohio Proficiency Test in 9th grade so I didn't even have any exams to take before I was going to graduate. After we lost in the state semifinal, I just went back to Warren for a few weeks of classes and then to the fall sports banquet at St. Anthony's. I also came to Columbus in early-December for the Touchdown Club luncheon.

At this point, I didn't know any boosters at OSU and didn't even really know Tim Spencer, the running backs coach. He had been a star running back at OSU himself and had a great career in the NFL. I had met him at a top-50 seniors camp before my senior year but didn't have any relationship with him. Spencer wasn't one of Tressel's own hires—John Cooper had hired him.

Coach Spencer had brought in three running backs the previous year: Maurice (Mo) Hall from Columbus, Jaja Riley from California, and Lydell Ross from Florida. These three guys had all been back-ups for Jonathan Wells the previous season, while I was playing as a senior at Harding. So it seemed like he had a full complement of backs—a pair and a spare, as they say.

I was named Parade High School Player of the Year and USA Today Offensive Player of the year in December. I also got invited to the Army All-Star game at the end of the regular season. I got a letter in the mail from the organizers and all I had to do was call and reserve a spot. My plan was to go to this game and then fly straight to Columbus to start at Ohio State.

So, after Christmas, the 26th, I got on a plane for the first time in my life and flew to San Antonio. A lot of my fear of flying comes from this trip. I went from Cleveland to Memphis first and after switching planes, when we were backing away from the gate to go to San Antonio, the plane just shut off. The lights went off, the fans went off, and there was no power at all. In my mind I was thinking, What the hell? You have to put it in the context of an 18 year-old on the plane by himself, flying for the first time, and this happens. Anybody would be scared.

As for the Army All-Star game, I didn't know any of the guys on my team. I had heard of some of them, but I flew down there by myself. In fact, I didn't play in the game because of some bullshit that happened and I was standing up for one of my teammates. I chose to sit out that game. I was practicing under the high school coaches and enjoyed the festivities including New Year's Eve at a BBQ with all 100 guys but I didn't even dress for the game.

Three days before the game, we had an issue with the person I thought was the best quarterback on my team who got caught smoking a Black & Mild outside the hotel. This shouldn't have even been an issue because he was 18 and it's not illegal to smoke a cigar.

On the other side, the West, were the guys from Texas. Vince Young was their quarterback. At all the social functions, in a friendly competitive way, these guys were talking shit. Not in a bad way—they were just saying, man, we're going to kick you all's ass. Our squad, the East, had two of the national players of the year—me and Ahmad Brooks, who went to Virginia and then played for like 13 years for the 49ers.

So, after all the talking from the West all week, we wanted to win really bad. We wanted to be in the best position to win. So our guy Tremaine Banks from Indianapolis, who was going to Tennessee, he was just killing it at practice. This guy was Michael Vick in the making. Running everywhere, passing, he was that good in high school.

But then this other guy, Tyler Palko, a white guy from Pittsburgh who ended up going to Pitt, his father was our head coach. And his son was competing against Tremaine to be the starting quarterback for the East. It was so obvious that Tremaine was better. Everybody kept saying this on our team.

But then Tremaine got caught smoking a cigar and Tyler's dad said, Well, you're not going to start—Tyler is going to start. So they bench him and everybody on our squad was pissed off. When we were at practice, everybody knew that Tremaine gave us a better shot at winning. Not that Tyler was bad, but we wanted to win. So, a lot of us were dogging it at practice and the coaches said there was going to be a meeting after practice because they knew guys were disgruntled. After practice, we went upstairs to a meeting room on top of the stadium and the coaches asked if anybody had anything to say. It was dead silent…nobody was saying a word.

So I stood up and said Look, the bottom line is that we want Tremaine to be the quarterback because we want to win. Everybody seemed to understand what was going on—Coach Palko wanted his son to start. We just felt like he didn't like Tremaine, period. I mean, Tremaine was 18, he was allowed to smoke, and he wasn't even trying to hide he was doing it, because it was legal. He was doing it out in the open.

In the meeting, we went through this whole song and dance but there was no response other than, it is what it is—Tyler is going to be the quarterback, we don't care what you're saying. They pulled me to the back of the room after the meeting and I told them I'm not practicing anymore because my hamstring hurts. I told everyone that. I was like, I'm not playing because this is some bullshit, and I don't even want to play for you. This was my way of saying, I'm more than just an athlete. When my mind is straight, I fight for justice on many levels. Above everything else, justice is what I believe in. Even when I got sentenced to prison, I wasn't bitter—I knew that was justice.

Well, Coach Ted Ginn, Sr. was down there as an assistant coach and they tried to have him talk to me about going out to play. I told him, No, this is some bullshit. Me and him had a bunch of discussions and it was cordial but I couldn't figure out why he didn't see the injustice being done here. He was being a father figure to me at the time, just like he was a father figure for all those guys at Glenville. I didn't even know him before that but now I was close to him and I would sit next to him on the bus for the rest of the week going back and forth to practice but I couldn't figure out why he didn't see the same injustice I saw.

He was still trying to get me to play but I kept saying, No. it wasn't that I cared that much about Tremaine but I just knew it was bullshit. They even threatened to call Coach Tressel but I just said, I don't care, go ahead and call him. It's not like he could have made a difference about me playing either. I just wanted them to know I knew it was bullshit.

This is the same feeling I had with Troy Smith a few years later, sitting in my car at the Woody Hayes Practice Facility when I was about to get suspended by OSU. He was begging me to stay and saying why don't you just go in there and be cool with those people and I said, Hell no, I'm not doing that. I don't give a damn. I don't care if I lose everything. I was not

CHAPTER SIX: ARMY ALL-STAR

about to shuck and jive to no psychological treatment and basically make an admission that I was lying to these people when I wasn't. I wasn't about to do that so they could label me. I said to Troy that change only happens when people stand up to power and I wasn't about to get psychological treatment when I knew I wasn't wrong.

At the Army All-Star game, I couldn't articulate it but I knew Tremaine was getting victimized by the system. I wasn't aware of all the moving pieces of the system I was in, but innately, there was something in my spirit that I just knew this was some bullshit.

I just knew with Tremaine that this was just an 18 year-old kid and this was a part of growing up so for Coach Palko to act like the reason he was starting his son over Tremaine was the cigar smoking was bullshit. This was serious to me and I could feel amongst my peers that I was in a different mental state than them. But this was very clearly a black and white issue for me even though I didn't have any formal education about the civil rights struggle. I just knew what was right and what was wrong and this was wrong.

Ultimately, Ted Ginn Sr. said that it was my decision to play or not. But I wasn't about to play even though Tremaine himself tried to come to me and say it wasn't that serious. To be honest, I don't think he understood what a big deal this was when someone is abusing their power over you. Maybe if I talk to him now he might get it but then he didn't think it was that serious.

But I stood my ground and I didn't practice after that meeting or play. I was in jeans and a jersey on the sidelines and the coaches were mad as hell. Gerald Riggs was the backup running back who played instead of me. And I didn't pay close attention but I know we got our ass kicked. I was just counting the minutes until I left. My mind was on Ohio State at that time and trying to be the starting running back when the season started next fall.

After the game, I went back to my room at the hotel and watched TV. The next morning, I checked out and flew to Columbus where Coach Spencer picked me up at the airport and got me started as a Buckeye.

I didn't mind missing the all-star game because still to this day I'm not that interested in football. As silly as it sounds, I just enjoy working hard. If I find something I'm interested in, I can work on it endlessly and find a joy in doing it. Later in my career when people threatened to take football away from me, I didn't even care about it. My identity wasn't being a football player—football was just a tool to get respect, be somebody, and survive. But I didn't love it per se. It wasn't my life or my identity. Even back then, I considered myself to be more than just an athlete.

CHAPTER SEVEN
BUCKEYE

I REMEMBER EVERY single detail from landing in Columbus as a recently-graduated high school senior to winning the national championship, less than a year later.

Tim Spencer picked me up at the airport. I didn't have any relationship with that guy or understanding of who he was. He didn't recruit me. I recruited myself and he had recruited 3 other tailbacks the previous year. I don't think he was interested in a kid from the streets because that wasn't his background and he didn't know how to deal with all that. There's a way to deal with kids from the streets and a lot of coaches who don't understand the streets don't have any idea how to reach those kids. When everything is going okay, it's no different working with them, but when there's any difficulty at all, it's a whole other ballgame.

I arrived Sunday January 6th, the day after the all-star game, and stayed at the Cross Country Inn right near campus. They didn't have my dorm room ready so Spencer took me there. All Spencer did when he picked me up was take me to the hotel and tell me where I had to be the next day to meet my adviser. I had a suitcase and a map and he just showed me where I needed to be.

I stayed at that hotel about a week and a half and then I moved over to Steeb Hall, near where the Black Cultural Center used to be. I didn't last long at Steeb though because my roommate and I got into it over me talking on the phone all night, just being super-loud I guess. So, next I moved over to

Morrill Tower. Chris Gamble was living there so we would walk or take the bus to the practice facility during winter conditioning and spring practice.

My aunt had a condo in Columbus, near Gahanna, and I moved to her place as soon as I could. I literally left the Towers as soon as spring ball was over. I packed up my stuff and left because after spring ball it was just basic lifting and conditioning. You have to remember, for the last two years of high school I had been living by myself, so living in the dorms was a big difference and just wasn't going to work.

From an athletic standpoint and a confidence and independence standpoint, I was ready for Ohio State. The thing was, I was always so much of an isolated person; I'm just really comfortable being by myself. I could strike up a conversation with anyone and feel comfortable, but I prefer just to be solo.

In my high school, it was always known that I was cordial and respectful with people and cool but I never did the hanging-out thing. I never even had a letter jacket in high school. I never thought I needed to broadcast that I played football to everybody.

I came by myself to Ohio State that January. I didn't have a recruiting class. I started the whole graduating early from high school thing and I was just cool with it. I didn't feel awkward or scared on the first day. I felt like I was part of Ohio State. I didn't feel like this isolated person.

I got here in January, lifted weights for a month, and actually had surgery on my thumb in early-February. I had injured it toward the end of my senior season and I kept taping it up but it was hurting and getting worse. I didn't want to say anything to jeopardize my whole entire plan to come early and participate in spring practices, but eventually the trainers got an X-ray and they got me the surgery. But I still played all of spring ball. There was no way I was going to miss that.

When spring practice started, I knew where I stood. In practice, you are naturally grouped with your unit. I had made it known previously that I was a threat to them. When I showed-up, there was history to my relationship with Lydell, Mo Hall, Jaja, and Brandon Joe.

CHAPTER SEVEN: BUCKEYE

My history with them started during my junior year of high school. It wasn't an official visit but I had come down to Columbus and watched a home game with them and some other recruits. After the game we all got into a van to go to dinner. I'm just setting the stage and I need to say this was my personality at the time—I was a little Mike Tyson-ish. I was raw and in your face when it came to football.

One of the backs, but I forget who it was, said, You know we're deep in running backs. So I was like, I don't know what you're talking about—I'm coming here to be the starter.

I just casually said it. People say there's truth in subtle moments and those guys helped me out when they didn't say nothing in return. This actually helped me believe I could do it even more because when I said it, I was like, Oh shit, they are not even going to contest it.

So I was like if you're not even going to contest it, in my mind, I could do it. I loved Mike Tyson and I had heard Mike Tyson say one time, Dudes like to compete on teams but are scared to compete face-to-face. So he would just tell them, I'm going to knock you out and it's up to you to do something about it.

He was basically saying, sure, people like to compete and we're all here saying team Team TEAM but somebody's always scared to say, I'm going to whoop all your asses. Nobody wants to take that stance and make that claim. But I did.

And what I found was that he was basically saying people are scared to openly compete against each other. Like when you put it out on the table, now it comes down to are you going to work harder than me every day to beat me out?

For me, when I don't have any drinking, drugging, or partying distractions in my life, it's like I'm going to flat outwork you. I'm coming to take the starting position. After I said that in the van, it was out in the open and we didn't have to hide it from each other.

Coming in, it was already on the table that this dude is coming to play and he's going to take the position. So like every day at spring practice it was something that I was doing, you know, every damn day I was doing stuff to aggravate the other backs. I would get to practice early and I would stay longer than them. Just trying to aggravate them and let them know I was serious as hell.

The aggravating part is that if you've got somebody who is going to show up before you, leave after you, watch more film than you, and he's not the starter? Well, then he's banging on the door and that person becomes aggravating because it becomes a stamina thing, like, can I outwork this person?

Meanwhile, it just makes me better. And lo and behold, when the time came, I was prepared for it and it was fate—it was supposed to happen. Even though I was still 4th on the depth chart after spring ball and through most of two-a-days in August, it was fate that I would become the starter by the home opener in the fall.

In spring ball, I was just playing special teams but I got some reps at running back on the scout team. Spencer's belief was that at some point later in my career, I might be somebody but he was 100% riding with Lydell Ross as the starter in the fall with Mo Hall right behind him getting a lot of carries as well. One was strong and one was fast and they were a great pair.

But I was still frustrated during spring practice because I thought I would get more reps at running back. I thought that I would be in a better position than I was. I was just doing special teams, like grunt work. I was frustrated because I knew I was grinding and outworking them. I understood how to do that since high school, when Matt Richardson was my running back coach and Tom McDaniels was the head coach and just from a work ethic standpoint, that was preached to me in high school—always outwork the other guy.

Where I was making my mark during spring ball was special teams, because I have always been strong and aggressive. I was just messing people up on special teams: coverage, punt block, and every chance I got to hit people. I was running down on kicks full-speed and blowing people up on the wedge. I was just being hyper-aggressive towards everyone on the field.

Academically, I didn't have any expectations about college. I honestly thought that there would be some classes that I would take and be able to

CHAPTER SEVEN: BUCKEYE

do with no problem, just like high school. I thought there would be some classes that would keep me eligible. I wasn't intimidated but I wasn't fooling myself that I had any level of academic prowess. I don't think I was scared—I just thought I would be able to pick some classes to stay eligible.

When my older brother Marcus had gone to Buffalo, I knew he kept the party going. He didn't take school seriously, either. He stayed eligible the entire time but ever since we were kids, he was always smart and willing to do his work. He tripped up a little bit when he had a baby in high school but he never had a problem in school. He played well, and went to college, but we hadn't ever communicated about what to expect academically. He never would have had any reason to talk to me because when I was at Warren Harding, I had good grades. When you're dealing with inner-city school districts, the work isn't that tough. There's not a tremendous amount of homework or responsibility.

But I remember in the first few weeks of January getting called by the coaches asking why did I miss study tables. I remember I thought 730 a.m. was way too early and I didn't wake up that early in the morning. All incoming freshman were supposed to go to study tables so I was supposed to be there with Lydell, Mo, and Jaja. They were all still freshmen and technically I was, too. You have to remember that I was one of the first to graduate early from high school and start college in time to participate in spring ball. I didn't have any sort of orientation or even a peer group to relate to.

So classes were grueling at first because I wasn't used to homework and responsibility. I wasn't used to studying. I also got a late start because when I showed-up, I didn't even have a schedule. My adviser had to make that for me during the first week. The only thing that was left was a math class and a geography class about globalization if you can believe that. A kid whose whole entire life had revolved around the south side of Youngstown taking a class about globalization. I would probably love that now but not back then. I didn't have any level of preparation or any strategy for how to attack schoolwork or school life because I hadn't developed that in high school.

My whole focus was staying eligible. My adviser connected me with a tutor but I didn't even have any expectation when I met with him. I was just told I needed some help and my adviser would get me a tutor. Everybody knew I needed some assistance.

I had learned in high school that if I took care of things on the field, everything else fell into place. And it's what nobody wants to talk about. Anybody in any industry who generates a bunch of money, they will be taken care of in some capacity. You're going to figure out how to keep doing business with them or in this case how to keep them eligible.

It was simple math even in high school: I was bringing in 25,000 fans and tickets were $8 and there were 7 home games. Warren G Harding was making a lot of money if you do the math. The high school football coach and AD were making 90-grand. So there's a level of importance to sports because the coach is making three times as much as the teachers.

I didn't personally care too much about this but it let me know what was important and just being blunt, this is what is important, this is what is going on, and if you walked around the school the main thing at Warren Harding was football and walking around Ohio State, the main thing is football. It becomes easy to say to yourself, I don't need school—I just need to play football because this is my profession. But there's other requirements in the way based upon the rules and regulations that govern it.

Between me and Tim Spencer there was always a butting of heads from day one because I wasn't a guy he recruited. He recruited all three of the other tailbacks and in his defense, he was trying to get me to display a level of humility I didn't have. I had an ego, which fueled me, and I had a relationship with Tressel. I don't think that he necessarily cared for that because he felt like I was undermining him by talking to Tressel all the time.

In my defense, the ego was what basically allowed me to play with so much confidence. Look at Floyd Mayweather, if he didn't walk around like that he wouldn't be able to beat all those people. You have to make up your mind that you're a superhero and then play like one. Guys who are truly humble, and not just pretending to be humble in interviews, don't win too many championships. Why would a position coach try to break you down anyway? It doesn't make any sense.

CHAPTER SEVEN: BUCKEYE

So I stayed as the 4th tailback all throughout spring ball. But even during this time, I felt like I was completely better than the people in front of me. They kept putting me on the scout team though. So I was running, breaking tackles, running tough, getting my ass beat up. I was making some sort of impact and the other tailbacks and everybody was noticing what I was doing.

One day at practice though, I ran a play and got crushed and I slammed the ball down and yelled out, Man you guys need to block. I was saying this to the scout team offensive line because I was getting crushed. I said it with a lot of conviction and I meant it, but what I really meant was that I didn't really deserve to be running behind the scout team offensive line. I was getting killed.

The offensive coordinator, Coach Bollman, came running up to me and grabbed me and said don't you ever slam the ball again. Coach Spencer was talking to someone else but he came over too and I told them, Man you guys don't get it, I don't belong on the scout team.

After practice, Spencer called me into his office and his conversation was the same old thing—you can't do this, you can't do that, you have to wait your turn, and all that bullshit. My mind still to this day works different. I don't believe in waiting your turn. I don't believe in that.

I just believe if you're good enough to do something, you just need to do it. I don't think there needs to be a gatekeeper to anything. Whoever is better should play but most fans don't realize that doesn't always happen. Sports aren't always a pure meritocracy when authority, control, and power are involved. Nothing is, I guess.

At this time, Tressel was talking to me but not getting into this issue of who should be the starter. Looking back on it, I think everybody saw my willingness and passion to play but they wanted to make me prove myself and it got to the point, like, Damn, what more do you want me to do? It got to that point with me internally.

So of course nothing changed after I slammed the ball in practice that day. I was on the scout team and stayed that way through all of spring practice. Nothing much happened in the spring game either. I didn't get a lot of touches. I was 2nd string on one of the squads and played special teams but there wasn't a space for me to make anything happen in the environment of that scrimmage.

I was frustrated because I thought I would move up the ladder faster in the spring but it wasn't happening. It frustrated me but it also motivated me. I was like, I have to figure out some way to get on the field—any way. I was killing it in the weight room. I squatted 870 so they were noticing me in the weight room but it wasn't transferring into me having the ability to move up the depth chart.

Will Smith was my first friend on the team because I had stayed with him when I came down on my visit. I was already committed to OSU but wanted to meet some guys and have some fun. Chris, Will, and Darrion Scott were my friends but I wasn't hanging out with them. I wasn't partying. I was just dialed-in to football, 100%.

Spring practice ended and I hadn't done what I set out to do, moving up towards being the starter. I moved to my aunt's condo as soon as spring ball ended and after spring quarter ended all I did over the summer was train. The entire time. I was down at OSU training at Larkins in the pool because I felt my body getting beat up and this would take the pressure off my joints. I was also doing speed training in the pool with Chris.

I didn't take any classes that summer. All I did that summer was train and the one fun thing I did was going to Red, White, and Boom on July 4th. I just watched the fireworks downtown and I was anonymous at the time. Nobody had any clue who I was. I could have walked past 50,000 people and unless you were a huge OSU football fan you wouldn't know who I was.

We moved into the Fawcett Center hotel for camp in August. I don't remember who my roommate was but I know that I did nothing, zero, with the recruiting class that entered that fall. I didn't go to any of the orientation sessions or meetings. All I knew was that I kept working with my academic counselor to schedule classes. I thought I was rockin' and rollin', with no academic issues. It hadn't dawned on me that I should have a good major or take classes where I could get some skills.

CHAPTER SEVEN: BUCKEYE

All I wanted to do was get to the NFL and my whole goal, serious as can be man, was to get on the show MTV Cribs. To me, that would have been my goal: buying a house and having fancy cars. I remember this one episode with Snoop Dog, LIT, and Silkk the Shocker and that's what I wanted my life to be like. My mind hadn't expanded very far up to that point.

At the start of camp, my only thing was—and I told you I'm a huge Mike Tyson fan—my only thing was to continually aggravate the running backs. This was my strategy. I just wanted to aggravate them by being the first guy in the running backs room, the last one to leave, and just outworking them.

I don't care what field you're in, people in general are traditionally quick to find more reasons why not to do something and why not to work. I think people in general have a hard time focusing on a mission and I just thought to myself I'm just going to outwork these guys and these guys aren't going to be able to keep up. Just from a capacity to work, I knew they couldn't work endlessly with weights, film, and drills like I could. I was going to become the starter by any means necessary.

I also sensed from watching the other backs in spring practice that they didn't love running into people and running people over like I did. That's what I lived for as a back—straight running dudes over, giving them a stiff arm, putting them on the ground. So I decided I was going to do everything these guys wouldn't do.

Most guys in football—the public perceives them as tough but the actual tough guys are the ones who aren't scared to run directly at people. It's easy to get tackled from the side. I can tackle you from the side and it isn't going to hurt. But when you're running up against dudes who are 250 and you're 230 and you're banging over and over again, that takes a lot of fortitude. Put it like this, before the game starts—or even before practice—I'm consciously deciding I'm going to have a massive headache the next day because every play can be like being in a train wreck. It's all one big violent collision after another and I knew these guys didn't want to do that. But I did.

I can remember putting my helmet on and banging my head against the wall at the practice facility just to condition myself to take a hit. I can remember doing massive amounts of neck curls just to strengthen my neck so I had a level of stability and just consciously doing crazy things like this so I could get used to banging into people. Those were just things that I knew I had to do to get through practices.

Every day I knew we had to go to the facility during camp and I would beat the entire team over to the facility. I would be the first one there, before everybody. Brother, I beat everybody, every day, during the entire camp. I wanted to let it be known to the coaches that I'm here to play, period. I didn't come to be just another guy on the team, wearing a jersey, on the sidelines. I came to ball. That was it. With anything you do in life, if you just go above and beyond, when you start to outwork everyone in the space you're in, you naturally ascend to a different level. You're not going to stay in the same space.

I actually saw ways that the other backs could have become better. If you take the time to figure out how to leverage your skill set, I think you can always improve. I wasn't the fastest, Mo Hall was the fastest one. Jaja Riley was the most elusive. He was a little taller and limber and had a different running style. And Lydell Ross was just a tough, solid runner. These guys were good backs for sure.

The only thing that separated me was that I was tougher and stronger than them. So I had to figure out how do I leverage this in the offense that we played. These guys never explored that because they didn't watch as much film as I did. At the end of the day, this comes down to playing to your strengths in the system you're playing in. There's a lot of people almost as good as Kobe and LeBron, there's a lot of guys 6'8", but they have to ask what's my skill set and how does that fit in this system if they want to dominate.

I was trying to follow in the footsteps of Jonathan Wells, the starting tailback from the previous year, who was a big strong downhill runner. So his style was something to guide me.

I was outworking everyone, and watching more film, to find every advantage, but the biggest advantage I had before I ever ran my first play at Ohio State is that the offense we ran in at Harding was the same offense we ran here, 100%. We used the same language and everything. I already had all the language and analytical framework in my head. My coach at Harding used to feed players to YSU when Tressel was there and when Tressel came to OSU, everyone who played for Coach McDaniels was prepared to succeed here.

It was just all the same language—46-dave, 47-dave, 36 and 37-counter, 38 and 39-boss. McDaniels used the same plays and the same overall system. So for me coming down to Columbus, I knew probably 85% of what we did already. So I knew the defensive fronts and how to identify linebackers and what defenses were trying to accomplish based on down-and-distance and I had a sense for this stuff already from watching so much film in high school with McDaniels.

When we would be in the RB meeting room during camp and we would be watching film, I'd see how challenging it was to the other guys but this stuff was like hardwired in me. These guys weren't brought up like that. They came out of different systems. I was fortunate to come up under McDaniels because that's what put me in a position to become the first true freshman to start at running back for Ohio State.

Two-a-days were obviously awesome and a lot of fun. The coaches were seeing me practicing and busting my butt on scout team still. So two-a-days was where I started to emerge but it was still slow-going. The interesting thing is that I was the only back doing the scout team. Jaja didn't want to do it and he was just like this is grunt work and he didn't want to take the hits. So at the start of August, Lydell was first string, Mo Hall was second, and Jaja was third, but I knew I was better than them. I just knew it and nobody could tell me different.

I decided I was willing to get crushed on every play and I got my ass kicked probably 80% of the time but I was out there. Listen to me, I wasn't backing down, I wasn't missing practice, I wasn't faking hurt, I took all my lumps and bumps running behind a bullshit scout team offensive line. Those guys did their best but they were just bodies in there trying to block guys who were way stronger and faster than them.

Nobody wants to be getting hit by Mike Doss or Matt Wilhelm but I did. Our defense that year was stacked with guys who played on Sunday so who would want to get crushed by them over and over. But I did.

I remember getting tackled all the way off the practice field and driven into a fence by Cie Grant. On this particular play, the defense just blew through the scout team line and I had to bounce the run outside and try to get the edge. This was full speed, full equipment, full everything and the next thing I knew I went to turn up the field and I didn't even see Cie Grant coming and he smacked the shit out of me. I rolled all the way up under the fence and he rolled under the fence and I laughed and I said to him, Damn, that shit hurt. This is how Cie and I got cool. The rest of the scout team offense wasn't balling like I was so the first team defense loved me for what I brought to practice. Those guys want to be tested by the best competition possible.

Cie used to totally mess me up. He probably got like 5 clean legendary hits on me where I can say he totally destroyed me and that's how I can say we got cool. It was like a respect thing. If you're an older guy then you're trying to get the younger guys to beg for mercy. But when you got a dude like me who kept getting up—I just wouldn't let these guys get me. I kept coming back and they kept kicking my ass but all that developed me and made me better and put me in a position to prevail. I thank them for it.

There was one day where it finally happened—when I went from 4th-string to 1st. A few weeks into camp, toward the end of camp really, we were doing a drill that was all inside runs on the goal line drill at the end of practice. This late into camp, people were believing that the depth chart was set the way it was. Lydell was sitting out because he was dinged up and figured he was the starter with nothing to prove. So Mo Hall got his chance with the first team to do these inside runs—between the tackles.

But this wasn't Mo's strength—he was our speed back and going outside and getting the edge was his thing. So, when the goal line drill started, he was getting the carries but plowing into and through the line wasn't his forte. Not every good running back is a power back.

CHAPTER SEVEN: BUCKEYE

I noticed the coaches were getting mad because the defense wasn't getting the good looks they needed to improve. I mean, they need their starters to practice stopping power backs crashing through the line so when they needed to make a goal-line stand against Wisconsin or Michigan or any other team with a power back, they'd be ready for it.

After Mo ran a few plays, they put Jaja in and he's running straight into the line and nothing was happening either. At this point, I was just sitting on the side with the other scout team guys because I don't traditionally get in during this period.

But eventually, Coach Tressel himself finally grabbed me and he put me in. I had waited for him to do this for eight long months—since winter conditioning and spring practice. I had waited for this chance to run people over. So I said to myself, just run right at these dudes. This is first team D and first team O and it's the first time I was finally in the mix.

Everyone on defense knew I was going to get the ball and just run straight through the line. Cie was waiting, Matt was waiting, everyone was just waiting to try and stuff me. The whole design was that I was supposed to take the handoff and find whatever hole I could and score. This is like inside the 5-yard line. Not just inside the red zone but on the goal line. This is strap-up-your-shit-time, because it's time to hit. You know what I'm saying? This is what I was built for.

This could have been the reason Lydell didn't want to participate. Listen to me, you can look in people's faces and see if they're scared or not and for most people, running full speed into dudes, even if they're on your own team, is pretty damn scary. But the biggest difference is that I wasn't scared out there. Being scared is a luxury I didn't have. I had to be fearless if I wanted to be successful.

You know, inside running in the middle of the field is different. Linemen and linebackers will hit you and stand you up but on the goal line the defense takes this shit personal like, Man, you're not scoring. So they put me in and I took the handoff the first time and I scored, no problem. I got hit, but I wanted to get hit. Got it? We lined up again and I took the handoff and BOOM I collided with Donnie Nickey but for sure I scored. I

77

had trained for this for my whole life. They gave me the ball the third time and I scored again. There was no way I wasn't scoring. I was hardwired for this shit, mentally and physically. It was a great feeling and a great way to end practice that day, showing everybody on the whole team, who were standing around watching every play, that I was the man.

The next day, I showed up at the facility before everyone else, like always, and I saw that the coaches took me off the scout team and put me with the first team. Practice that day started with individual inside running plays, group plays, team plays, and then special teams. So now they put me in at first string on the team part and I'm running all the plays with the first team offensive line now. And not just the running plays, but pass blocking, pass receiving, and everything.

So we go out there and I'm performing very well. It's more than just crashing through the line for a few yards. It's like, Oh shit, this dude is doing everything well so let's try this dude tomorrow as well. At this time, I don't know who was making the decisions but I had another good practice and Coach Dantonio, the defensive coordinator, who I had never talked to before, he pulls me aside and tells me I'm giving his D some good looks. He said I was giving his defense the best looks they've seen in camp.

All during camp, these other running backs were doing great taking plays outside, but now you had a back who was 235 pounds running right at them. Straight up the gut. To be honest, I'm sure our linebackers and safeties—Donnie, Cie, Matt, Mike Doss—they would have rather tackled the other guys than try and tackle me. They were probably relieved I was on scout team all during the spring and most of camp.

In my heart, I believe Dantonio is the one who helped me break out from the scout team and get a chance. He must have been the one who spoke up the most in coaches meetings saying this is the guy who is prepared to take this team to the next level because I was going nowhere until he pulled me aside and said, Man I was impressed and I feel we should give you more looks. This guy had never spoken to me before but if it wasn't for him it would have never happened.

CHAPTER SEVEN: BUCKEYE

It's not like our quarterback was taking sides or had a preference either. Craig didn't really get involved with the running backs. Craig is a cool guy, and tough as nails, but he stayed out of who the starting running back should be. It was always just Craig and Ben Hartsock sticking together on offense—that was his closest friend and he was a reliable target to throw to. They made each other better.

Craig didn't have a special relationship with any running back—it was like he was there to lead the team and try to make good things happen with the offense but as far as I was aware, he didn't have any special feeling about who the starting running back should be. Nobody was thinking about a championship then.

So, the next few days in practice I was still first team. After being stuck as the scout team running back for what seemed like an eternity, I went from 4th to 1st overnight. The reaction from the other backs was a lot of animosity and jealousy and it was like this dude doesn't deserve it. It was like blatant.

It was weird with the entire team dynamic on the offensive side as well because everybody knew like, Oh shit, this thing has changed—it is no more Lydell and Mo as the pair and Jaja as the spare. But everyone probably understood why I was up in front and the other guys were behind me. I was the real deal. I had come in with so much hype and I started to deliver once I got the chance.

Everybody wanted to win and the entire team could see that's why I was there too. All I wanted to do was run through a wall if I had to in order to win. It wasn't even like a subtle difference between me and the other backs. There was a distinct difference the way I ran the ball and the other guys and everyone on the offense finally saw that when I ran behind the first team line: Ivan Douglas, Adrien Clarke, Alex Stepanovich, Bryce Bishop, and Shane Olivea.

Those were the guys who started on the offensive line, and we had Nick Mangold who came in from time to time. He was the backup center as a true freshman and we knew he was going to be great then. Then you had Rob Sims and Mike Stafford who rotated in as well. Those guys either all played in the NFL or should have. It was an outstanding line and to tell the truth, any of the other backs would have run for a thousand yards behind them as well.

I actually liked Lydell, Mo, and Jaja and trying to beat them out made me better. They were my competition but also my teammates.

Mo Hall was a very good teammate and is a great guy. I congratulate him because he's in LA acting now. Me and him never had any problem. I could see he wanted to play for sure but for college football you have to be hard and raw and willing to get hurt. Maybe he was too smart to want that.

Listen to me, in order to play this shit, you gotta be tough. I don't care who you are, you have to have some extreme level of toughness to compete at a high level. There has to be something in your brain that just isn't right. And that's the way it was with me. You can't be a nice guy—you've got to be a machine built to destroy people or get destroyed.

That's college football at the highest level—young kids out there trying to destroy each other or being destroyed. Don't ever let anyone tell you anything different. Football is a beautiful game but it's a violent game by nature. There's no other way to play it except violently. And most of the time, to be the best, you have to have 2 things—supreme skill and supreme toughness—to survive that violence.

Chris Gamble didn't have that level of supreme toughness but his skill level was so high that it just transcended everything else. And at cornerback, you can succeed on supreme skills. Craig didn't have supreme skills but he was smart as hell and he was a tough dude. He was tough and smart. He wasn't afraid to get the hell knocked out of him. He wasn't afraid to run into people. Craig was a tough dude. He was 6'4" on a bigass frame and had a confidence about himself like most guys who succeed in college football. It's not arrogance—it's confidence. It's believing in yourself, and he had it. Confidence and toughness.

Dudes who play at the highest level are usually just plain tough. When you watch the best guys on the best teams, you have guys who are just flat-out tough dudes. Like Will Smith, god rest his soul. Will didn't have supreme skill—he was just one tough dude. He was flat-out tougher than everyone else. He was probably the toughest guy I ever played with.

Actually, the majority of players in the NFL are tough dudes. Look at John Lynch, he wasn't supremely skilled at what he did but he was smart—he knew what he was supposed to do on every play—and he was just a tough dude, man. James Harrison, tough dude. The majority of people who play on Sundays are just incredibly tough guys. It's very rare that you get somebody who is just doing it on skill. Like, Randy Moss was another level of skill so he didn't have to be tough. He was fearless and could play as long as he did based on his supreme skill. The same with Tom Brady—the greatest QB of all time—he's a tough dude, man. The measurables on most people are all about the same, so it's the intangibles like toughness that set people apart.

CHAPTER EIGHT

STARTER

TUESDAY BEFORE the first game, they make the announcement I'm going to be the starting tailback for the opener. I found out from the news because Tuesday was media day and you had to name a starting roster. Back at the Fawcett Center I was watching TV and it wasn't a big deal to me because I already knew I was practicing with the first string. I didn't get what a big deal it was—a freshman starting at tailback in his first game. I didn't understand it. It didn't dawn on me.

When it hit though, later that night, I was nervous as hell. Super nervous. I was like Damn, this is almost gameday. I had success against our own team in practice but at that point, I didn't actually know how good our defense was. By the end of the year, we were going to have the #1 defense in the country. But when I was running against them in practice in August and having some success, I didn't know they were that good. So there was a level of nervousness from that.

But I was confident in the O-line, and confident in Craig. I was just nervous as to whether I could perform and whether I could get this done. I also knew it was a big leap to Division 1 football physically. Mentally, I understood the plays and offense. There was only doubt about the physical aspect of the game. I just questioned myself, like damn, can I get this done?

There wasn't anything memorable the rest of the week, we just practiced the rest of the week, looking at film, looking at their defense. The only player who stood out on their team was their senior quarterback Kliff Kingsbury who was setting all sorts of NCAA passing records. He led a great offense so I figured we'd have to score a lot of points to win.

I never had a ritual to prepare for games and I didn't expect anybody other than my mother to come to the game—that was about it. But she came and a bunch of guys from the neighborhood came but I didn't invite them and I don't even know how they got tickets. My mother was the the only person I put on the list.

The night before the game, we stayed at the Blackwell and we went to individual meetings and the big team meeting. Spencer still hadn't warmed up to me. I can never remember a time when we had a decent relationship. There was a distance. There was a real, like distance—like you play running back and I'm your coach but you're not my choice.

I wouldn't say he didn't like me, I would just say I didn't come across to him the way these other guys did. You dig further into it, look at Mo, Jaja, and Lydell—all of these guys had visible and present fathers in their lives. Mo Hall was from Columbus, and his father came to almost every practice in fact—he was around and he cared.

So, when those other guys saw Coach Spencer they may have naturally had a level of respect for him. Me on the other hand, I had no respect for this guy. Like zero. I just knew he didn't buy into me and I wasn't his favorite and as an 18 year-old kid, I didn't know how to manage this relationship. I saw a guy who didn't want me so I wasn't about to invest anything in that relationship outside of being professional about it and going about the business of reaching my potential, and achieving as much as I could to help the team win.

I just went to practice and watched film with Spencer, but he didn't speak to me and I didn't speak to him. It was just business. I didn't get it at the time that it might make him look bad if I became the starter and he didn't recruit me even though I was from Ohio and especially from Northeastern Ohio which was producing so much Division I talent. I didn't even care. I was just cool with Tressel, which come to think of it probably also bugged Spencer because I had a relationship that jumped the chain of command.

CHAPTER EIGHT: STARTER

The night before the opening game, Spencer wasn't even pretending to support me. The relationship was just bland. He never offered anything to me other than a bland relationship. He didn't reach out to me and try to let me know what it was going to be like playing in front of 100,000 people and in fact nobody did, not even Archie Griffin, the greatest tailback to play at Ohio State and maybe to ever play in college football. I don't know if it would have helped me or not though because I might not have been ready to start maturing outside of football.

I can't remember who my roommate was that night. It was going to be a noon game and I didn't sleep the entire night. My mind was racing and I could not fall asleep. I was listening to a song in my CD player on repeat, a song by Lil Flip called This is the Way We Ball. I probably listened to that song 500 times that night. My roommate was sound asleep and I literally didn't go to sleep and kept on visualizing the game. Just visualizing.

I still use this technique to this day. I just sit back and play things through my mind over and over, how I want things to go. I knew the first fifteen plays in the first few series. We got a list that Tressel called the First Fifteen. But I wasn't even thinking specifically about those plays I was just thinking about myself having success. I still think that way—visually—and it's actually a lot stronger now that I am an adult.

I think this is where belief comes from. I don't think people understand the power of belief and just minimize it. But even as a kid I could control my subconscious mind by saying this is what I'm about to do and I think that if you can think and give conviction to what you think and you can put action in the direction of where your mind is going, it is like the world opens up to you.

With football, I just kept on visualizing myself and believing I was going to go out there and have success. I was nervous but I was trying to visualize success in order to minimize the doubt. I was seeing myself breaking tackles, making big runs, making big plays, hearing the crowd roaring. I was seeing myself that night just having success the next day and not being able to be brought down by one person and really believing it.

I remember feeling like this is something other guys might not always feel but I could always visualize it and confirm it to myself and I would come on the field and before we ran the play, instantly, I knew I was about to break a tackle. Or I would make a decision that not one person was going to tackle me. I make these small affirmations to myself, no matter what I am doing. I just believe the world isn't how other people see it but how you can create your own world by visualizing it and affirming this to yourself. I just think the more you really, really believe, in some way the world just opens up to you. It's the power of belief.

Game 1—Texas Tech, August 24 (Pigskin Classic)

As I was putting my uniform on in the locker room, I just felt like I was ready to go. I had knocked the nervousness out like before the game you do these hitting drills and once I got the first contact in the hitting drill I was ready to go. I got hit in one of those drills, just the RBs hitting each other about 60%, and then I was ready to go, expecting to go out and get 15-20 carries and at least 100 yards. I was taught in high school that at a bare minimum, in an offense featuring the tailback, I had to get at least 100 yards.

I don't remember the details of whether we won the toss, I have no clue. The first two series we didn't really move the ball. We got a few yards here or there and that was basically it. Then Coach Tressel told me on the sideline if I don't make anything happen, I'm going to have to give these other guys a shot. There were no points getting scored, and we weren't moving the ball. Nobody was doing anything. The crowd wasn't really into it because it is boring. The game was actually pretty boring at the start.

Then I got my first break on the third series. The call was 46-Dave. I was already in tune to the game and had been thinking, Damn, I have to make something happen. I was already functioning with a sense of urgency because the game wasn't unfolding how we wanted it to.

The line opened up a hole, Bryce Bishop came and pulled around and I got through the line from the left to the right and I took off behind him after I waited for the blocks to develop.

CHAPTER EIGHT: STARTER

I went 59 yards for a TD and the crowd went wild and after that, it was over. I got hit with the fame bug. I got injected with a massive dose of the almighty fame. Then I scored the second TD two series later, and scored another touchdown later on a 45-yard run—that's when the fans went wild. They started chanting my name, MAUR-ICE, MAUR-ICE, MAUR-ICE... and when you hear that from 100,000 people, that gets you a little bit high.

I don't remember how many yards or TDs I had at halftime, I was just having fun running. I never paid attention to stats during the game.

Nobody was saying much to me during the first part of the game. Some teammates were congratulating me, like Ryan Hamby from Cincy I remember for sure. Me and Ryan were always cool and he ended up making the block that got me in the end zone in the second overtime of the national championship game. The defensive guys were also pumping me up, and Mike Jenkins, so there were a few guys. After that point, with the first three TDs, it was under control.

With every kid, what they're trying to do when they're coming to a major Division 1 university is trying to recapture that fame they had in high school, because that's how we got there. So, I think most kids become frustrated when they don't experience that same level of appreciation from fans or they feel like they're not contributing in the way that they would like to. And that's tough. Just about every guy on Ohio State's team, even the walk-ons and the guys who never start, was the best player on their high school team.

Every one of us was trying to fight to get into that space where they matter to the team. They don't just want to be another body on the sidelines. Everybody wants to be a star. Even though it's a team sport, everybody individually wants to be a star. Everybody wants recognition. You don't put in all that time lifting weights and everything else I did just to be one of the 100 guys on the team.

By the 3rd quarter, the game was out of reach and in the beginning of the 4th quarter, they took me out. We kicked their ass and Lydell went in as 2nd string. I think he must have been fuming on the sidelines because he couldn't do anything and I wasn't making things any better because there was no level of humility on my part. That's a nice way of saying it. By the end of the game, all of the guys on the team were rallying around me and I was making success look fun.

After the game, Tressel congratulated me and Spencer gave me some sort of basic congratulation but nothing special. I still wasn't his guy and never would be even though I had 175 rushing yards, 30 receiving yards, and 3 TDs that game. If there was acknowledgement, it came from the guys in general on the team but not from the coaches even though a few days later they announced I was named Big Ten offensive player of the week for my performance.

When I came out of the locker room, I gave my mom a hug, and she was so happy. And I had a whole crew from Youngstown. These are street guys. I was done with the street but I was still hanging with these guys. I wasn't ripping and running the streets and selling drugs or doing anything like that in Columbus but let's be realistic, you live in the same neighborhood and I still had a relationship with them even if I wasn't doing all the same activities. These were just friends from the neighborhood and friends of my brothers.

I was having success on the football field and then after the game I didn't expect my brother and all the guys from the neighborhood to come down but they came down for the game and when I came out of the locker room they were there. Cars were everywhere and when I came out I had 30 people all over me.

At this point, I was hungry and I had to eat when I got back to the condo and eventually my guys came over about 7 or 8 and we went out that night. We went to a place called Studio 69, which I'd never been to before. I wasn't usually going out at this time. I was 18 years old.

This was a black club and there were live performances going on. The bouncers let us in through the back. Someone with us knew the club owner. We got in there about 11 or 12 and there was champagne and alcohol everywhere. We didn't have team rules about alcohol but even if there were, I wouldn't have cared. I didn't feel like I was going out to get drunk or get high. This all had to do with women. There were women everywhere, all around

CHAPTER EIGHT: STARTER

us. At this point, I was drinking and having a great time. Not smoking weed at this time but I was drinking champagne, liquor, everything they threw in front of us. They comped us everything at this point.

When we went to the nightclubs and I was on stage with rappers and in the VIP room, that's powerful. I had immediate success on the field which translated into parties off the field, too. I was having legendary times and partying with a lot of women—at 18 that shit really meant something. Fame was infectious.

I wasn't identified as an OSU football player at first but word just spread. I was in the VIP area with the guy who performed that night and we were just having a good time. It was Fabulous, who was a nationally-known rapper. We stayed there until 2am and then went to Waffle House. There were probably 30-40 people with us at this point. It would be the 7-8 guys that I knew and then the people that they know and the people that they know and we filled up the entire Waffle House.

There was a bunch of people, still a lot of girls around us. Nobody was asking for my autograph but a lot of people were coming up to me and saying Congratulations. Black guys, white guys, everybody.

As a matter of a fact, we went to hotels after that. All my guys were staying at the hotel right behind the Residence Inn and went there and partied a little bit and left after that. I went back to the condo about 4 or 5 am and it was lights out.

I slept in Sunday morning and then went to watch film and get some treatment for some minimal stuff where I was a little banged up. What that partying did for me, personally, was in the simple way it made me out of control. I went back to that party lifestyle pretty easily.

You have to think about this: my motivation to play football was really first, to have a chance to be somebody and make a lot of money, and second, to get women. And everything I had experienced that night was a part of this fantasy that I had in my head when you become famous. When you become famous, you get rich, you get a lot of women, you have fun in life and party all the time. So what I experienced that night was a fraction of what was to come.

Even after that big first game, the light still didn't go off in my head that I could go to the NFL. It was still like let me see, even if it went through my head maybe in subtle ways it was still like is this success real? Maybe that was just against Texas Tech. You have to go out here and convince yourself that you can have this level of success more than just once.

The rest of the week after the first game, I didn't wake up with any aches or pains. It wasn't like I'd had a game with 18-20 carries. Football doesn't hurt unless you take clean hits but if you run behind your pads you are going to minimize the impact.

Monday of week 2 we started getting ready but the motivation was totally different. The motivation before was to just be a great football player but now the motivation was to really be famous.

Actually, I had fans waiting outside the practice facility following me home pretty much immediately. I had more girls on campus who would know who I was once the quarter started. If you are balling at Ohio State, everybody knows you.

Game 2—Kent State University, September 7

We had an off-week after Texas Tech and by this time, my confidence was through the roof. The team was now ranked in the top-ten in the country and I knew we were going to beat Kent. Classes still hadn't started, because OSU was on quarters, so as for practice, it was still the same deal—I was getting there before everybody and staying later. I was still out-working everybody. That lasted until after Washington State, when I broke out for 230 yards and then all my behavior started to go wrong.

I had a short game against Kent State. We beat them 51-17 and I had 2 TDs and probably only 60 or 70 yards. Tressel wanted to get Craig and the receivers a bunch of passing attempts because in the first game Craig didn't get into much of a rhythm because we were running the ball a lot.

I didn't get any sleep before this game either. I don't think I slept before a game until we went to Chicago for the Northwestern game. I was still nervous for all these games. It didn't sink in and start to feel normal until

CHAPTER EIGHT: STARTER

the middle of the season where I got comfortable and felt like, Ok, I'm cool, I can calm down, relax, and sleep before a game.

After this game, the partying started to get out of control. I was using all my tickets and getting some from other players. Every week the entire season, my entire group of people from Youngstown were coming down on Saturday and after the game it was a party.

We went to Studio 69 a lot and went to all sorts of clubs on Route 161 and Morse Road. That whole area was a place to go. Downtown wasn't really a place to go yet. We would always end up at the Waffle House at the end of the night, just having a good time like college kids but it was me and all these guys from the south side of Youngstown.

We were partying but it was just weed and alcohol. We didn't need no guns, just partying and trying to get women. I wasn't trying to get women for myself—I was just the attraction. At this point, people were getting my autograph. I was feeling great, but it wasn't actually until after Week 3 that I was feeling like I was a star or anything.

Game 3—Washington State, September 14

This was a top-ten matchup. We were #6 and they were #10. I got 230 yards and once you do that, your mind changes to, Oh Shit, these guys were great too but we just beat them. The first two quarters I was getting hit harder than ever and I actually hurt my knee in the first quarter. There was a big difference in the level that WSU played at than we'd seen in the first two games. This was just a dogfight. I didn't even gain 40 yards in the first half but there was no doubt that I was the starter anymore. There was a wide gap between me and Lydell at this point.

In the locker room at halftime, the coaches sat us down and said this is what we're going to do based on what we saw in the first half. We were losing 7-6 and I only had 36 yards. We just flat out didn't have much offense. The coaches figured out what to do to make the running game work though and after that it was just on.

If you ask anybody about me they'll say two things: I'm the most casual aggressive player. I'm not jumping around and slamming lockers, I've never raised my voice or hollered. I don't listen to super aggressive music. I just relax and focus.

In the huddle, I was more of a director. After my runs, I would tell the linemen, make sure you get this guy or that one. I would say, Hey look, the last time you pulled around the guy was aggressive so I'm going to slow down and you make sure to kick him tight. Or I'll start my path running wide so they could get up under him and then I'll run behind them. One thing I was very good at was understanding blocking schemes.

If I didn't understand anything else, I understood who was supposed to block who and where the point of attack was supposed to be. Understanding that allowed me to adjust and know my lanes for running. My biggest runs were always to the right, behind Shane. Shane was a helluva run blocker. Look at the yards LaDainian Tomlinson gained running behind him for the Chargers. Shane was a big aggressive collision waiting to happen. He's a Mack truck. If you need shit cleared out, Shane is going to clear it out.

So in the second half against WSU, the first series I just ran wild on them. We started on our own 9-yard line. We got to the 17 on the first play and then coach called 47-Dave. I ran it and the end crashed down and I just bounced on him and took off. I got 44 yards on that play and 73 of the 91 yards on that TD drive. Actually I ended up with 194 yards in the second half alone and that was on a hurt knee.

I got hurt for real in this game though—I tore my meniscus. In fact, it happened in the 1st quarter and I went into the locker room on a cart and they shot some painkiller in my knee and I went back out there.

I don't remember what happened on the play when I got hurt. Something happened I guess and a guy blasted my knee. I felt it and I couldn't bend my right knee. I hobbled off the field and then I went to the locker room and they basically just shot me right in the knee. At first I was on the sideline and my right knee was messed up and they said, Let's go to the locker room. I didn't know what they were going to do. I think I rode the cart into the locker room and I wasn't thinking anything other than it was normal just to get away from everybody and see what is going on. I wasn't thinking my

CHAPTER EIGHT: STARTER

season was over. I was still mobile. It felt like it was hurt and something was not right but I didn't have a severe injury. The pain wasn't too intense.

I went into the locker room with a trainer who had been there forever and knew exactly what to do. There was no option—it was just like, Hey we're going to shoot you up and I was like, Okay, cool. They didn't tell me what they were going to put in my body and even if they had I wouldn't have understood what it was. To this day, I don't know what it was and it wouldn't have mattered—I was young and dumb and would have taken any shot to get back out on the field. That's the point. The whole notion of informed consent is out the window when you've got a guy like me who wants to get out on the field.

The needle must have been about 6-8 inches. It was a long-ass needle. It went in the top of my knee. It was the longest needle I'd ever seen on a human—like a needle you would use on a horse—and they just jabbed it in there, through the kneecap. The whole needle went in, up under my kneecap. I was in pain from the injury but I had so much adrenaline. Imagine it, this is the middle of the game and you got like sky-high adrenaline. I didn't even think about it.

After the shot, there was instant relief. The trainer put a little knee brace on me and I went out of the locker room on my own power. The crowd went nuts when they saw me jog back out of the tunnel because they had seen me go in on a cart and now I was jogging out. I don't think they know what happened in there—like they for sure didn't know I got stuck with an 6-inch needle full of some serious painkiller. They never think about stuff like that.

All the fans were going crazy because I was like the savior at this point. I had some more long runs in that game and a couple more TDs and we won 25-7.

Even after the game, my knee didn't hurt. My whole group of guys was there outside the locker room like clockwork. I knew all of them very well. I had been hanging with this whole crew of guys from back home and they were all in Columbus with me. Some of them would have been playing basketball with me the day when I was 10 years old and saw that young guy get shot and fall dead right there on the court. We were all a long way from the south side of Youngstown at this point.

My guys and I partied all night at Studio 69 and ended up at Waffle House, and I went to bed early the next morning. But when I woke up a few hours later, my knee hurt like hell. It was swollen. If they gave me pills for the pain, I don't remember taking them.

So at that point, I went to the facility and they were like cool we're going to get an MRI of your knee. Everything was like get this guy an MRI, get the shit in his knee repaired, get him his physical therapy, and when is he coming back?

The MRI showed that I had a torn meniscus and needed arthroscopic knee surgery which was scheduled for Tuesday. This was September 17th, we were 3-0, and ranked #6 in the country. I was named Big Ten offensive player of the week for the second time in my first three college games. Classes still hadn't started and weren't going to start until the following Wednesday. So, the timeline was very condensed and quick…bang, bang, bang, bang.

If you want to know the truth, this was my fourth surgery already from football. I had had two ankle surgeries, thumb surgery, and this surgery. This was the 4th time I'd had surgery from football and I was 18 years old. Think about that. The way I ran was punishing to the defense, sure, but also to me.

At this point the doctors and trainers told me it would be 30 days until I could come back but I didn't believe them. I said I'm going to rehab the hell out of this and get back sooner. I was only on crutches for probably about a week after the surgery and then it was just rehab, rehab, rehab.

Game 4—Cincinnati, September 21

I sat out the UC game. I didn't practice that week. It was just a bunch of rehab for me at the facility. I remember doing intensive rehab and working with a woman who I guess was a specialist in knees. I was doing balance drills, negative resistance, ice and stimulation and all that stuff and it was actually a little bit more intense than practice even though at this point, I was happy to give the rest of my body a break. The grind of a college football

CHAPTER EIGHT: STARTER

season on a body is serious business, with each game like a series of massive car collisions and then hitting in practice during the week and another round of serious collisions in the next game.

Actually, I had never heard of a meniscus before. I knew it wasn't a major surgery but I didn't know what a meniscus was. Even if they explained it, it would have gone all over my head. I was just trying to feel my way through it. This is weird, but most of the time, I never even wanted to hear how long an injury takes an average person to heal. I'm a 100% feel guy in terms of how the healing goes.

At this point, they were only giving me ibuprofen but not serious pain pills. I didn't need those. I was helping out at practice when I wasn't in rehab and was just around but the other guys were getting pretty prepared.

We didn't expect UC to give us such a tough fight. During the beginning of the game, we struggled a lot to get into any rhythm. I think maybe the offense turned it over a couple times but I just don't remember too much about that game other than we just weren't moving the ball on the ground. I was on the sidelines and getting pretty frustrated with what I saw.

The frustration came because any kid when you go to a game you want to play. I couldn't make anything happen if I was hurt. At this point, my confidence had grown because we had 3 good weeks in a row and I was thinking, Man I could go out there and ball with those dudes, even though I was hurt. Of course I felt that way—I came to Ohio State to win championships.

Eventually, Chris Gamble—who went in on defense—ended up picking the ball off in UC's end zone in the final minute to seal the victory. One of our cornerbacks, Richard McNutt, had gone down with an ankle injury and this is the first time we figured out Chris could play defense. He was a receiver but had been messing around in practice going as a cornerback against Mike Doss, who was joking around with the coaches that he wanted to have a shot as a receiver. After this game, Chris started playing both ways which just about everybody does in high school but nobody even tries in college. And eventually Chris got drafted in the first round as a cornerback and had a Pro-Bowl career in the NFL. Like I was saying, that's what a supreme talent he was. He was just gifted athletically.

One thing I remember clearly after the UC game was being on the bus home. This victory was a big deal to me even though I didn't play because in football or basketball or even in track I had never gone down to Cincinnati and won anything in high school so I was feeling pretty happy about finally going down to Cincinnati and winning.

After we got home, it was a fun time. My mom would come to all the games she could and afterwards she would hang out in the apartment and cook delicious food. Of course when it was time to go for the nightlife, she would stay home. She would be there at the house, with me, before the partying started, cooking for all of us. My guys would all be staying in hotels off 161 and they would come over to the house, watch highlights, eat something, then I would get dressed and we would go out. Some nights I just didn't come home and left from wherever I ended up at and went to watch film at the facility.

I don't remember being on crutches when I was on the sidelines of the UC game or even using them for more than a few days. This whole knee injury was over for me in 10 days. I was injured on a Saturday, had surgery the following Tuesday, out for Cincinnati, and I played in the Indiana game the following week.

Game 4—Indiana, September 28

I didn't even wear a brace when I went back for Indiana. The trainers just put a sleeve on it, a basic bandage and a sleeve and it was like, Bye, see ya later—I'm gonna go ball. Well, of course they gave me a shot in my knee with another 6-inch needle. They stuck it right in before the game, and then, Boom, it was like let's go.

As far as what I now know those are pretty heavy-duty painkillers, like maybe Toradol. This situation is pretty much like you've got a young kid who would swallow nails to get on the field and the trainer says, Hey come over here, I've got something for the pain.

CHAPTER EIGHT: STARTER

Even though I didn't have much pain before kickoff, they still shot me up. It was more like a protective, or preventative thing, I guess. I didn't think anything about it because I was just a kid and I wanted to play and would have done anything they said to play. I wasn't thinking about long-term health effects or wanting to play with my kids when I was 35. I was 18 and stupid.

I had practiced at 100% during the Indiana week and I wasn't scared. I just put ice on my knee each day after practice. There wasn't any contact for me that week though. I remember we won 45-17 but other than that, all I remember is that it was a slow game at first. Nobody was that excited about the game, nobody cared too much. Even though it was the start of the Big Ten schedule, we were just going through the motions, beating another opponent, going 5-0.

The amazing thing about this game is that the wound from my surgery still hadn't healed and on my last carry of the first half, which turned out to be a TD, I got tackled in the end zone and my knee actually started bleeding. When I went in the locker room, they told me I needed to get stitches or I couldn't play the second half because my knee was bleeding. I hate stitches but I would have done anything to get back out there so I let them sew up the wound and I played the second half.

At halftime, we were leading 21-10 but I only had 50 yards and wanted to get my 100. I almost got there with 40+ yards on the first drive of the second half and I finished with 105 yards I think and 3 TDs. I already had 10 TDs on the season and was well on my way to 1000 yards, with almost 600 at this point.

As usual, all the guys from Youngstown came down for this game. It didn't matter who we played because nobody really came down for the actual game. Every single game they came down. Every week. After WSU, the partying had gone through the roof and after Indiana it was still through the roof.

Party, party, party, party—all night long, Saturday night into Sunday morning. It was the same every time—staying at the club until 3 or 4am, going to Waffle House or Steak n Shake and hanging out there with women, hanging out at the hotel, all that. And I would have film study at 1 or 2 in the afternoon so sometimes I had time to go home for a few hours and sometimes I didn't. As a kid it didn't even matter if I had enough time to go to sleep, rest up, and watch film. I was just rolling.

When we partied, I was just drinking champagne, just having a good time. I was still only 18 years old. In the early-2000s, it was a joyous time. Everybody had some money, everybody was partying, everybody was happy. We were happy that we won, happy we were undefeated and climbing in the national rankings, so everything was celebratory.

These guys from Youngstown were definitely from the streets and some of them were dealers. They had money and they wanted to party. I don't think they were carrying guns. There were never guns that I was aware of. Nobody was going to get on the freeway from Youngstown to Columbus with guns with a possibility of getting pulled over.

That's a rule, when you're coming to Columbus from Youngstown and you have flashy cars, there's a likelihood you might get pulled over. So nobody is going to be drinking and drugging and having guns on the highway. They would just get the drugs and alcohol once they got to Columbus.

Even when I look at it from their perspective, I don't think my friends were doing anything malicious trying to damage my career. What else did we know how to do. It was just like, he's from our neighborhood, we happen to know him, he's one of the famous people in Ohio right now. So they were just happy for me and happy that someone from the south side of Youngstown made it the hell out.

We were just having a good time. Looking back on it, I wasn't going to extra film sessions, wasn't going to extra conditioning that I could do after practice, and not going to class as much. The more women you get in your life, the less important school and everything else becomes because all these things that weren't in your life before you are who you are now, these things are at your fingertips now. So my focus at that time was just football and partying.

Classes had actually started right before the Indiana game. I was in African American Studies 101, remedial English, and basic college math.

CHAPTER EIGHT: STARTER

I was also enrolled in Varsity Credit which gave the players 2 hours of academic credit for being on the football team and a 2-hour independent study. I had 19 credit hours but I ended up withdrawing from math and finished the semester with 14 hours and a 2.5 GPA.

I don't think anybody in class was asking for my autograph until later in the season. At this time, I would only drive onto campus for class and then get off campus and get over to the facility. I was driving an old 2-door Cadillac Eldorado I had owned since high school.

I was becoming more well-known because during fall quarter at Ohio State, it seems like everything is about the football team until that first loss of the season and the bubble bursts. But we weren't losing and had got past our only tough non-conference game and were set to roll through the Big Ten until the Michigan game.

It wasn't like I was accessible to many people though. I wasn't walking across the Oval or hanging out at the student union like a regular student. Some players went to places like the Hale Black Cultural Center or the Union where they were going to be seen. But guys like me, if I know there are going to be places with lots of people, I am going to avoid those. I enjoyed playing and enjoyed people appreciating me, but I never wanted to be the guy wearing a letterman's jacket and wearing a class ring and saying this is what I did. I just enjoyed the training, I enjoyed the game, and I enjoyed being on the big stage.

Game 6—Northwestern, October 5

There was a different focus in practice heading into the heart of the Big Ten schedule. This was a night game, in Chicago, and they had experienced some success in recent years. Once we got into conference opponents, there was just a lot more familiarity with the schemes our tougher opponents were running and older players were remembering people who did certain things the previous year. It just felt more familiar.

I didn't even know Northwestern was in Chicago. I hadn't ever been there so that was cool—it was a chance to go to Chicago. I had been thinking it was just another team. We got in late Friday night but we didn't get a chance to explore the city. We stayed in a hotel and I was sleeping great after that first sleepless night and this was a 7 o'clock kickoff anyway so we could sleep in.

The anticipation was great and everyone—the players and the fans—were all wearing purple so what I remember is that everything felt really bright. At OSU everything is grey and more of a dull color, but everything at Northwestern was bright purple, almost like Cincinnati Elder the year before and we lost that game, so maybe I was having some flashbacks when we took the field.

I remember there were more cameras there during warm-ups. Cameras were following everybody around. I think it had caught on that we were sort of good. A 5-0 start for Ohio State means things are going good and can keep going that way. We had climbed all the way to #5 in the nation and our plan was to keep climbing.

There was just a heavy interest and then the game started and we were rocking and rolling but in the second series, I fumbled the ball. I was coming through the line and I was tripped up and, Boom, a guy busted the ball out. I was trying to maneuver to the right and this guy hit the ball and I remember coming to the sidelines and Tim Spencer said, Hold on to the motherfucking ball. Damn, that put me back. His favorite word was motherfucker. And I was like, all right, I get it, and I sat down on the bench feeling like shit and thinking, Damn, I screwed up, I fumbled. Teammates were coming up to me saying don't worry about it, we're cool. The feeling in the air was no big deal, we're cool, we're going to get this back.

I hate to talk about them like this but it was Northwestern and we felt pretty confident. So we weren't moving the ball for a couple series and a few series later I fumbled the ball again. I was coming up the middle and I didn't have the ball secured. That was totally on me—I get that.

But then I came back over to the sidelines and Spencer was going crazy and I don't remember what his initial words were to me but he was yelling at me, motherfucker-this, motherfucker-that, and at one point basically he kept coming after me and I said, Shut the fuck up. I just got tired of him

CHAPTER EIGHT: STARTER

yelling. I didn't need that sort of verbal abuse. It's not what I signed up for when I decided to come to Ohio State.

This was the tipping point after months of a bad relationship between us because no matter what I did in practice or no matter how successful I was during the season, there was never anything positive between us.

I always knew I wasn't his guy. I wasn't his first choice. We weren't the same. He didn't recruit me. So, even though I realized that he was happy we were succeeding, he wasn't happy we were succeeding behind me playing running back. When I went out there and fumbled the first time, he cussed at me, and then when I did it again, and he cussed me out some more, and worse this time, of course I'm going to tell him to shut the fuck up. Of course. I was just tired of hearing his tirades. I told him exactly that and we got to arguing on the sidelines and I just kept telling him to shut the fuck up. I was tired of him. I was tired of hearing his shit over and over and over again because I was balling whether he wanted me to or not and I wasn't going to stop balling.

In fact, he would give everybody a hard time during practice, playing the tough guy role. But I always thought it was so fake because deep down he was a nice guy and not hard at all. It's not a bad thing to be a nice guy—but if you are, just be nice. Don't try and be hard.

The truth is that I grew up around a lot of seriously tough guys. Like real tough guys, on the street. So Spencer cussing me like that on the sidelines wasn't going to work with me because I wasn't intimidated by him. He was my coach but I wasn't scared of a single thing he could do to me.

If you look at my body language during the argument with him on the sidelines, you can see by my posture that I wasn't backing down. It wasn't the most professional thing I ever did and I look back on it and say, Damn I wish I hadn't done that.

It was the first time I'd ever stood up to a coach like that in my life and it's no way for a player to act but we shouldn't ever be in that position where we're getting cussed at. It's unprofessional but for some reason most football coaches get a free pass and in fact think that's how they're supposed to act because that's how their coaches acted. It's a vicious circle.

But it's just my personal feeling that a coach doesn't have to cuss at a player to motivate him. Verbally abusing a football player in practice or on the sidelines has no more place in football than it does in your home with your kids. I don't have to say to my daughter, Shut the fuck up, or, Go do your fucking homework. When you learn responsible adult culture, you can just articulate things in a way that is more polite and there's no reason football coaches can't be held to some standard of common decency in how they treat players. If you feel like you have to browbeat guys or diminish somebody all the time, well, Yo, you don't have to do that. Not everybody is responsive to somebody just cussing at them.

A lot of these guys playing bigtime college football, they may come from places where you have to take into account the social dynamic: he's a black man and I'm a young black kid and I don't even have a father who talked to me like this. So in the environment I grew up in, no man talked to another man like that because it is territorial and disrespectful and talking like that leads to bad things that nobody wants. But Spencer grew up in St. Clairsville, not in the streets, and the way he was talking to me was incredibly disrespectful but he couldn't have understood that, because he didn't grow up in the streets.

Nobody had ever cussed at me like that before. When you're growing up, to cuss at somebody is supremely disrespectful. Like to even direct a cuss word at another individual or to use a homosexual slur—well guys don't take that lightly and usually there's severe consequences when it happens. That was the first time, absolutely, that anybody ever directed this sort of language directly at me. I just snapped back at him, out of emotion. I can see now that a lot of that response is derived from ego and now I have the skills to overlook verbal abuse like that if it happens, but only because of personal development courses that I took in prison.

You have to psychologically know that I wasn't going out there screwing up on purpose. I wasn't going out there and fumbling the ball intentionally or even carelessly. I was doing my best not to and cussing at me to get me to stop ain't the way to go about it.

CHAPTER EIGHT: STARTER

You get more out of somebody when they mess up by encouraging them instead of intimidating them. It was just poor leadership on his behalf but absolutely also a poor response on my behalf. I'm not going to deny that. I don't think I'd react to that today because I understand more about responsible adult culture and how to de-escalate a situation when people are getting in your face. I learned that in prison in a class called Cage Your Rage.

After Spencer backed off on the sidelines, Tressel eventually came to talk to me and then it was easy as could be to cool down. He was saying everything is cool, just calm down with this stuff on the sidelines, and hold on to the ball. Simple. He didn't even seem upset or raise his voice. Tressel was super cool, super classy. He was all about respectful and dignified communication. With everything you do in life, the essential part is how you deliver a message to somebody. Do I say to my daughter when the doorbell rings, Hey will you please get the door?, or Hey, go get the motherfucking door?

Actually in the Northwestern game, I fumbled a third time, in the fourth quarter, too, but the momentum of the game had come around and even if the offense wasn't getting it done, the defense wasn't going to let them win. They weren't going to move the ball on our D.

I'll tell you something, though, this is the first game I got a concussion. I got the concussion right before halftime. This safety, Dominique Price I think his name was, hit me so incredibly hard, the absolute hardest I've ever been hit in my life. Helmet to helmet. It was a head-on collision without any seat belts or air bags. I was running off the right edge and I don't remember anything except he caught me head-on with a full head of steam.

He just hit me so unbelievably hard. I had the edge and some green in front of me and then this guy hit me right upside the head. As I was falling, I thought to myself, Damn, this guy just knocked me out. I could picture myself falling and picture myself passing out, as I was doing it.

I hit the ground and I did everything I could to get back up. But I had this thought, Oh shit, I really don't want to get up. I just knew in my head, if I didn't get up, Northwestern is going to look at me like they got me. They are going to look at me like they messed me up. Football isn't just a physical game—at the highest level it's also a psychological game. And I didn't want them thinking they hurt me.

So I got up and I walked back to the huddle but all I could see was bright purple everywhere and I got into the huddle but I couldn't see actual people. So I was talking to Craig and I was like, Hey look, whatever you do, don't give me the damn ball, because I can't see. And I'm like telling him, I literally can't see because this dude just hit the hell out of me.

I actually had a little more time than usual to recover between plays though because the guy hit me so hard he knocked himself out. He stayed down and took awhile to get up. But eventually they got him off the field and we ran the next play.

I think Craig held onto it and ran a quarterback sneak but didn't get the first down. When we got over to the sidelines, the coaches asked Craig why he didn't give me the ball like he was supposed to and he said, Yo, Reese's got a concussion—his head is screwed up. I was still seeing stars and I guess they gave me some ibruprofen or something. It was like nobody knew it was a concussion at the time because I got up and was on my feet.

In the context of now, football in the early-2000s was still all about hitting people with your head. Of course they had taught us throughout the 1990s to see what you hit and keep your neck up. I had learned see-what-you-hit since I was a kid but it was widely known that people would run with their heads down and aim at someone to hurt and intimidate people. This was a big part of football when I was in high school. There's no denying there's people out there trying to hurt their opponents on every play. That's just fact.

In the locker room at halftime, I was just sitting there trying to get myself together. I told the trainer I was messed up but the fact that I walked off the field under my own power made it seem like less of a big deal. There wasn't nearly the sensitivity to concussions then that there is now. No concussion protocols, no requirements about sitting out plays, nothing. If a guy is on his feet, he could get out there and play.

CHAPTER EIGHT: STARTER

I came back out after the half, rocking and rolling, playing the entire game. We won 27-16 which was closer than we expected but a win is a win in college football and our undefeated season kept rolling.

We came home from Chicago that night on a flight and I had my car at the facility and I drove myself home. My brain was fine until the next morning. I woke up the next morning with a pounding headache. Pounding. I grabbed some Advil and laid there until I had to be at the facility in the afternoon to watch film.

Tressel sat me down after film and told me how I could have handled the situation differently with Spencer. He was talking about having more self-control and saying it was a teachable moment. I think he probably talked to Spencer separately. But I never talked to Spencer again the rest of the year.

I didn't know anything about Spencer as a player, but you have to put that in context, before I came to Ohio State, I didn't even know who Archie Griffin was. I didn't have any clue who he was until I got to Ohio State. Just think about this, I was from Northeastern Ohio and Archie had left OSU in the mid-70s, after he got his Heismans. He was out of the NFL before I was born. I guess if he'd dominated in the NFL, I would have heard of him, because Cincinnati was in the same division as Cleveland and Pittsburgh, but as it happened, he didn't, so nobody in Northeastern Ohio was ever talking about him.

Actually, the first time I ever even heard about Ohio State was when Eddie George was playing against Notre Dame in 1995 when I was almost 12 years old. This was the first time I ever heard who they were and I didn't hear much about Ohio State after that until Tressel got hired there.

We live in a town where it's all Steelers or Browns or the YSU Penguins. When you're a kid, college football is college football to you. You don't even know the difference between Division I and Division I-AA or Division III. So when we played in the street, nobody was trying to be somebody from Ohio State. We were trying to be one of the Browns or the Steelers.

The first time I remember meeting Archie was maybe him passing through the facility or through the locker room. Even now, as an adult, when I see Archie, he is just a real quiet dude. He never said too much.

During the season he wasn't talking to me about anything. He never came and found me at practice or talked to me about the pressures and things that might come my way. Tressel tried to sit me down once or twice and talk to me about things that might come my way but that was the extent of it in terms of mentoring. Nobody really took me under their wing or anything—there was never any real intervention about what I was experiencing. I was pretty much on my own.

The nature of one of my conversations in mid-season with Tressel though was that boosters might come up to me, and girls might come up to me. Just simple basic stuff. The best way I can describe it is that, and this is just my take on it, but I think Ohio State was phenomenal in the mid-90s and it seemed like they might win National Championships in 1996 or 1998. But then there was a let-down for a few years. They hadn't had a national championship for decades.

And then we came along, the Youngstown boys. We burst onto the scene—here's this young guy in Coach Tressel, wearing a sweater vest and getting everybody else in the city to wear sweater vests for some reason, and then me, who's coming to ball. And now the profile of the program jumped really quick. So for both of us, there wasn't like a level of understanding of the issues that we might face at this level. We knew what was up in Youngstown, but this was a totally new level in terms of fans. To show you how crazy things were at Ohio State, I even had an Assistant Athletic Director come into one of my tutor sessions once asking for my autograph. Everybody wanted a piece of me.

The irony of all what happened later with getting suspended is that I didn't ever meet any real Ohio State boosters in Columbus. Maybe that existed in the Earle Bruce or John Cooper era, but any benefit I may have received was from guys I had always known from being around Youngstown. So those aren't really boosters to me—those are just guys who are around town and may not even like Ohio State but may want to help me out if I needed something in some capacity.

Even once we got to be 6-0, I was sheltered during the season: going to school, going to the facility, playing games, going home. I really don't remember me getting out into the community and meeting people until the months after the championship. That's when I remember life really changing for me.

Game #7—San Jose State, October 12

I don't even know why we played this non-conference game in the middle of the season other than to make money. We certainly could have used another bye week and maybe someday college football will eventually realize that young bodies need a week to recover after each game and playing each week just tears up our bodies, not to mention the damage to our brains. Luckily, I was cool after the concussion by the next game. No more headaches and I could see fine.

But before San Jose State, you better believe we did so many drills in practice about holding onto the ball. I'd never had any problems with fumbling in high school and in fact, part of the smear campaign against me after I got suspended was the rumors that the fumbles in the Northwestern game had to be related to gambling.

That was the smear campaign about my friend Bobby Delimutti who I had worked for in Youngstown. I guess I'm a lot more conscious now of how these things work because I certainly didn't understand it then. OSU and Andy Geiger were just throwing everything they could at me to discredit me. With their massive resources and influence in the local media, they could take any story and build any narrative around it.

I mean Bobby gambled on games but I didn't know nothing about it. He wasn't calling me up and saying like, Yo, why don't you fumble. That's stuff you hear about on TV and in the movies and some guys might have done it in the past with point shaving in basketball, but I certainly wasn't doing it and for the media to run all those stories was reckless and unfair. It used to be they had columns and inches to fill but now it's all click-bait and sports fans—especially ones who hate Ohio State—will click on anything like this and that's advertising revenue for a news outlet or website with no regard for the truth or the player.

But I get it, I made headlines and they've got a 24/7/365 news cycle they need to fill up. Even still though there's guys out there like saying on sports radio shows that they represented me in my lawsuit against the NFL when they didn't. It should make you question everything in the media, for sure. I know I don't believe hardly anything I read about a player anymore until I talk to that guy myself and look him in the eyes.

So not surprisingly, we beat San Jose State 50-7 in front of 104,000 people which is a lot of tickets and programs and concessions. I had 130 yards and three more TDs. But I also took a lot more hits. The game was on ESPN so that was more money for OSU and more hype for us. I was leading the Big Ten in rushing with 850 yards and 15 TDs and talking heads on cable sports shows were already blowing smoke about the Heisman and me challenging the NFL's rule about entering the draft early.

Game #8—Wisconsin, October 19th

The next game was fun as could be. We were #4 in the country and Wisconsin is always tough. Their stadium had a much younger vibe because I guess most the fans seated close to the field aren't older alumni and boosters in the high-priced seats. Their stadium was just so rowdy. I heard Ohio Stadium get loud plenty of times after a big play or something, but it was never rowdy for like a sustained period of time like at Wisconsin.

This was another late-afternoon game that went into the evening and it was cold. But it was fun because they always play this song Jumparound and by the 3rd and 4th quarter the fans were going crazy. It was a close game all the way to the end and we only beat them 19-14.

I got 25 yards on my first carry but then they stuffed me pretty good the rest of the day and kept me out of the end zone. I ended up with 130 yards on 30 carries which got me almost to 1000 for the season in just seven games.

I remember one thing from this game as clear as hell though, and this taught me a lot even later on in life when I look back on it and this is the stuff I miss about football. This is one of the memories I have that gives me so much respect for Craig.

CHAPTER EIGHT: STARTER

We were in the midst of a tight game, and this is before Mike caught the big pass over the middle and before it was even clear we were going to win this damn game.

But this just shows you what poise does for people. With the game locked in a battle and everybody in the huddle kind of looking around at each other like, Damn, we gotta go down here and make this shit happen, Craig just opens his mouth and says, Man isn't this shit fun?

Then we broke the huddle and while everybody else is walking up to the line of scrimmage, he's still looking back at me and I'm like, What do you mean isn't this shit fun? And he says, Don't you just love this shit—the fans going crazy and here we are in the middle of it?

He was just describing the moment and what I remember about what he meant is this: this pressure doesn't bother me, this is FUN, and he couldn't wait for the next play.

But in my head I was just locked-in, focused on one thing, thinking to myself, Dude, we gotta score. But he was just out there having fun and then he threw that deep ball to Mike and it taught me later on in life that no matter how crazy stuff gets, if you remain with a level of poise and simplicity and have a state of relaxation in your mind then the game slows down and you have a better chance of doing what you need to do.

Craig was cool as a cucumber and he made it happen and obviously Mike made that catch. If you ask me, this was an even bigger catch to make than the catch Mike made in the Purdue game but everyone remembers that because of what Brent Musburger said, Holy Buckeye.

Even though we won, the Wisconsin game is where I messed my shoulder up which hurt me for the rest of the season. The last play that I carried the ball basically messed my shoulder all up.

It was in the 4th quarter, and we were driving down trying to hold onto the ball and run out the clock. I got 30 yards on this last drive and some key first downs, but on one play the safety tackled me and drove his helmet right into my shoulder. He hit me hard as hell straight on in my left shoulder. Safeties are usually the ones to mess you up because they have like a free shot—they see you but you don't see them. It felt like a guy stuck a knife in my shoulder—that shit hurt so bad. I came off the field with my arm just dangling at my side.

In fact, I fumbled the ball in the pile but the ref didn't see it because there were so many people around. I was going down and getting tackled and people were all around and I fell to the ground and the ball came out. If there was a better replay and challenge protocol back then it would have been a fumble and Wisconsin was mad as hell because they knew I fumbled. But at that point, after that carry I think all we had to do was take a couple knees and the game was over.

As time expired, I knew for a fact that I was hurt. That shit hurt. Nobody knew what it was. The trainers put some ice on it and we flew back that night. When we got back to Ohio, I still had an ice pack on it.

The trainers just thought it was a stinger, when you pinch nerves in your shoulder and neck. That was a popular thing, even when I think about the advancements in medicine and treatment with athletes, everything was still very primitive in 2002 and they couldn't tell me what was wrong with me. If your shoulder hurt, they just said it was a stinger. And the only thing they thought was a concussion was if you were straight knocked out, so the method of diagnosing our injuries was pretty backwards even then.

Even now, I still don't know what that injury was. I don't have a clue. I never got an MRI or anything. I was still only 18 and I had already had 4 surgeries and I was hurt again, seriously, and I was absolutely thinking football wasn't going to be a long-term thing for me.

It was already on my mind that I couldn't just keep getting pounded for 3 years of college, which is very relevant because the ESPN Magazine article about being "one and done" came out right before the Wisconsin game. I remember this clearly because the Wisconsin fans were holding up the article when we were walking through the tunnel, screaming at me, Dude you're not good enough to be one and done. They had the article in the stands and on the sidelines and this is why that game was so fun to me because the article came out that week and fired up their fans.

From day one, I just thought somebody misdirected this entire article. I gave that interview the Monday after the Northwestern game. Steve Snapp,

CHAPTER EIGHT: STARTER

the longtime OSU media guy, came up to me before practice and said, Hey ESPN wants to do a feature story on you. He wanted to meet me after practice in the running back room. That's when I met Gene Wojciechowski who was a straight-shooting guy for sure. He's a journalist and I was a story that he was covering, plain and simple. That was his job. But Snapp was sitting there with us the entire time I gave that interview listening to our back-and-forth.

It was the first time I had ever met anyone from ESPN and my feeling was that it wasn't any different from regular media. I had done lots of local media in Youngstown and we were just sitting down, and Wojciechowski was congratulating me on my season so far. We started talking about my childhood and during the conversation we started talking about LeBron who was a senior in high school at the time. I don't know how we got on the subject of him but once we started talking about LeBron, Wojciechowski's questioning was all directed into whether I could see myself entering the NFL draft after this season.

Then the entire context seemed to shift for me and this became an article about whether I could you see myself leaving after one year and being one and done. He wanted to know did I think I had the ability and that sort of thing. As we were talking, I was thinking my body can't take that many hits and I'm thinking in the context of taking 300 hits and they used to have charts that RBs usually last this many years and they take this many hits and I'm thinking absolutely I'd jump straight to the NFL the next year if it was possible but it wasn't possible and I didn't really understand why the conversation stayed on this so long.

Absolutely, I wanted to start making some money because I wasn't making any as a college football player. Ever since I was in high school, everybody was making money but me and it was my body that was getting totally destroyed.

At no point during the interview was I worried I was getting set-up. Wojciechowski was likable, I had a good feeling, and I think he was asking questions just as a curiosity about whether this could really happen—could a 19 year-old play in the NFL? I'm not sure if people had really thought about it before.

I don't think he actually had the intention for the story to come out in a bad way so looking back on it now, I don't think for a second that I was getting set-up. All the questions were just in the context of LeBron and his money and the amount of hits a running back could take and the amount of money that was possible to change my life and my family's life, which is something I understood very clearly already. It's something that every inner-city kid starts to understand the minute he begins to excel even in junior high. There's money behind athletics, big money.

After the interview at the practice facility, we went over to the stadium with a photographer. And the whole entire time, I was going around smiling, laughing, joking, and we're going through all these photos—hundreds of photos. And at the very end of this happy-go-lucky photo shoot, where I'm smiling the entire time, they ask me can you act like you're angry, and you're throwing your jersey on the ground after a game or something, which didn't even make any sense to me.

Steve Snapp was standing right there—in fact, I'm actually throwing my jersey to Steve Snapp because why would I really want to throw my jersey on the ground? Ever since I was three years old and would put on my cousin's jersey, all I ever wanted was my own jersey. All my jerseys, even my junior high jersey or my jersey at Austintown where I only played one year were a highly valuable treasure to me. A guy's jersey is sacred. I wore every one of my jerseys with pride and no player ever throws his jersey on the ground. That's a sign of serious disrespect and every athlete understands this.

But that photographer was saying, act like you're throwing your jersey down, act like you're walking off the practice field. They're saying, We need you to act angry, we need you to act like you're tough. Steve was saying, C'mon, give 'em a tough face and while he's saying this, I'm actually thinking, Man, I don't act tough like this. I'm not that serious unless it's game-time. That isn't me.

Then we go to walk out of the stadium and they say, Hey how about we take one more shot as we're walking out of the stadium: you standing on the

CHAPTER EIGHT: STARTER

wall, put your foot on the wall, cock your head back, and look directly into the camera with a mean face. So they directed me to do that and they take that shot and I thought nothing of it.

I went about my business and a few days later they use that mean-faced, angry shot as the cover of the national magazine and then they use all of these pictures throwing my jersey away in the story. ESPN manufactured this story and it seemed like Hey, he's one and done and on the cover it looks like I'm a thug and I do whatever I want to and don't care at all about OSU which couldn't be farther from the truth. I was killing myself in practice and in the games for OSU because I like to win championships wherever I'm playing. Period.

Then, combine this with the fact I was just very publicly on TV with this confrontation with my coach during the Northwestern game and all of this makes me seem very ungrateful for this opportunity. It was like basically I was saying to hell with you and kiss my ass, like I was some super bad dude. But I didn't even intend to convey this message at all. I just thought I was doing a regular old interview. This wasn't even my intention and that's how the entire story got screwed up. It was laughable but also like, My man, Snapper, he was tripping letting it all go this far.

I never talked to him about it later. Of course he kept apologizing because he was one of the truly nice guys but he didn't have to catch the wrath of it. Absolutely, one, from the Wisconsin fans I caught the wrath but two, it was a distraction to the team. And even when I went around town it was like I had to answer questions about whether I was going to try to be one and done. Nobody on the team confronted me but they had to deal with the questions and nobody wanted to talk about that shit. We were winning and climbing in the rankings and all we wanted to do was beat Michigan, win the Big Ten, and if we were lucky, play for a national championship. Me being one and done wasn't a thing until ESPN made it a thing.

I also remember the spirit of OSU fans turned on me. They were wondering why would I want to be there? Basically they were saying I didn't belong here. I even started getting email saying I didn't deserve to be a Buckeye. That's when shit got real. I saw how fast things could turn on you in Columbus. It's easy enough to figure out anybody's email at Ohio State and I was getting some nasty shit.

I speak from this perspective when I say this: as a kid, I didn't even know what national media was. I knew what ESPN was but like it was funny that everyone took this shit so seriously. Even if I had been that badass dude in the article who didn't care about Ohio State or being a Buckeye, it wasn't that serious to me. If I happened to see a kid on the cover of a magazine or Mike Weber or JK Dobbins had said they were going to be one and done, I don't see how anyone could even care enough to get so passionate about that to figure out my OSU email address and send me hateful messages. Put it this way—I've come up from real life. I've come up from the streets where I've watched people my age get murdered, executed gang-style, and I had to figure out how to survive. I watched guys get executed and beat down for real. So football to this day is a vehicle but it's also just entertainment. It's not life.

Game #9—Penn State, October 26

After Wisconsin, I was practicing but with no contact. I'd never had a stinger but I wasn't worried and I just thought this pain in my shoulder was a normal thing and would go away if I put ice on it after practice each day. The pain never went away though. I was held out of contact as we prepared for Penn State.

I played the first series but on my fourth carry I got hit and landed on my shoulder and I came out. I managed to get past 1000 yards but I now knew I had a serious injury.

Going into the game, I thought I was going to be able to play but then I got hit and that shit hurt and I said, Man, I'm done with this. I remember my shoulder felt like it was about to fall off. As I came off the field, I just let my arm hang limp. Basically my body was just beat up. It had taken so much destruction and I was only halfway through my first collegiate season.

I went into the training room during the game but it was more serious than just giving me a shot of Toradol. During the rest of the first half and halftime, they were doing ice and stimulation, ice and stimulation, so I could go out on the sidelines for the second half in case they needed me I guess. I never got my shoulder x-rayed though because it wasn't broken. They were trying to put extra pads on it but nothing was going to help this time. I couldn't have any contact on it. Zero.

We won but it was another close game, 13-7. Chris saved the day again with another interception that he ran in for a touchdown. He was just dominating on both sides of the ball and special teams. The local news even made a video where they had him selling programs before the game, marching with the band in the halftime show, and sweeping the stadium out after all the fans went home.

Chris and Craig and the #1 defense in the country were carrying the team and we kept winning. Craig was so tough and smart and didn't make mistakes. Chris was just the most gifted athlete on the field. And the defense, well, most of those guys ended up playing on Sunday which shows how good they were. Actually most of the offensive line played on Sundays as well, so that shows how stacked we were.

My birthday was October 29th, a few days after Penn State but I didn't celebrate my birthday this year, everything was chill. My mom was still coming down every week after the games and it was still fun though. I just look back on this season and the only thing I think is that it was just a really fun time in my life and I was fortunate to have the chance to play with those guys and enjoy the kind of success we enjoyed. It was the result of hard work for sure, but it was absolutely a fun ride.

Game #11—Purdue, November 9

I missed the Minnesota game the week before, which was no big deal because we beat them handily, 34-3. Some teams ahead of us lost though so we moved up to #3 in the country, which was a big deal. We knew if we could win out and run the table, there was a good chance we'd end up in the top-two in the country and play for the national championship.

The next game was at Purdue and I played in the first half. We were just trying to move the ball, but I got injured. The only reason I tried to play against Purdue was because it was on the road and they were pretty good. The coaches knew the offense needed a spark that Lydell and Mo Hall couldn't give them so I tried my best but I was seriously hurt and not getting better.

I don't think I was ready for Purdue but in football you just get beat up so it was me trying to push myself. I had 14 carries for 52 yards against Purdue but the way I was falling in certain ways, I wasn't really myself.

I went into the locker room in the first quarter to get a Toradol shot and played the rest of the first half and had a couple carries in the second half but then I was done.

I was running in a protective manner, trying to protect myself. I wasn't prepared mentally or physically to run people over. I wasn't ready for high-speed, head-on collisions, and you could tell from the way I was running.

We won though, on a gutsy pass from Craig to Mike Jenkins that went 37 yards for a TD on 4th and 1. Unbelievable. Those guys were just professionals, already, in the way they went about their business. It would have been less dramatic if they had put more points on the board early, but when they absolutely had to, they did and we escaped by a score of 10-6.

Game 13—Michigan, November 23

I didn't even dress for the next game at Illinois because even though it went to OT and we won 23-16, we certainly didn't think it would be that tough.

It was freezing cold in Illinois and they took us all the way to the limit. Our offense wasn't getting it done and I was frustrated that I couldn't play but I'm an optimistic person on a lot of levels and I just knew we would win.

Let me put it this way, if I walked into any bad neighborhood and if someone told me I had to live in this neighborhood, in my mind, I would figure out how to take over this neighborhood or make this neighborhood work for me. I don't look at the bad side of shit. Sometimes I still get depressed and beat myself up but usually when I'm on the right side, I'm an optimistic person.

We were 12-0 at that point, with only one game left, against Michigan. This was the game everyone had been looking forward to all season.

CHAPTER EIGHT: STARTER

At first, the outlook on the season was let's just get out there with this freshman running back and this tough defense and see what we could do for the season. We started at #13 in the polls which was good but not that promising.

Then we got into conference play, and the further we got into the season we started thinking, Oh shit, we could go to a real bowl. And the further we kept winning, it was like we could really make something happen and do something.

So, I was just thinking I had to get my shoulder together. I was a 19 year-old kid, who basically in the last year had played 13 high school games as a senior, some of them while banged up. Then I got to Ohio State early, had surgery on my thumb, did conditioning, played spring ball, and then I went through summer conditioning which was hell because I had to get there first and leave last and out-work everyone.

Then we did camp in August and I got my ass beat up on scout team trying to get a starting spot. Then I was playing the entire season, starting as a freshman and had knee surgery during the season and was dealing with this serious shoulder injury that nobody could even explain to me.

So right around this last week, after the shoulder injury, I started taking things more serious. I had cut out the partying after games a few weeks earlier and I was really thinking hard about my future.

When my shoulder got hurt, I got serious and started to really handle my business. We had a lot of close calls when I wasn't playing much against Penn State, Purdue, and Illinois, which might have got my teammates thinking I wish we had Reese because these other guys were barely getting it done.

During the Michigan week, outside of the facility I didn't hang with any guys on the team. I was at the senior tackle but I wasn't into the whole rivalry thing, it wasn't a big deal to me. I didn't know anything about it. I hadn't grown up on it, even watching it on TV.

My shoulder was still strengthening and it was all ice, stimulation, rest, ice, stimulation, rest. I was telling myself all I needed was rest. As we neared the end of the season I was just thinking my body hurts, but there was no way I wasn't going to play at home against Michigan. Just no way.

I had been training the last 4 years for this and if we were going to beat Michigan, I knew I had to be out there to help get it done.

I was focused during Michigan week. I wasn't doing contact in practice but I knew the game was a big deal for the town and I had to be ready mentally even if I wasn't 100% physically.

At this point, everything had blown over from the one-and-done article and it was very clear that if we won we would go to the national championship and the significance of this was starting to sink in. We had been #2 in the nation the last two weeks and everybody wanted to play for the national championship.

At first, I didn't differentiate much between the bowl games, but as the season went on, I heard the other guys talking, and I learned a lot more about how college football worked and I knew if we went to the BCS national championship, that was the biggest stage to play on. So all during Michigan week, I was watching film, using lots of ice and stimulation, and I wanted to win so bad.

Let me frame this up: I just love to dominate big moments. I don't get caught up in the significance of what teams are playing but I place a lot of emphasis on big moments and championships. We could have a city-wide bridge tournament here, and I don't usually give a damn about bridge but I would want to win just because it was big and I wanted to win.

I'm a huge competitor and I just always wanted to seize every moment. I wanted to own this moment on this big stage against Michigan and this became a big deal to me, to the point that one night after practice in the middle of the week, on my way back to my condo, I went over to the middle school track in Gahanna and jumped the fence and ran sprints just so I knew I was training every chance I had before the game and knew in my heart those dudes from Michigan weren't out-working me.

But I'll tell you what really did it for me before the Michigan game and this is serious stuff and this went through my head during the game. For whatever reason—and if Coach Tressel did this on purpose, he's even smarter than people think he is—but me and Cie Grant roomed together the night before the Michigan game. I hadn't ever roomed with him before

CHAPTER EIGHT: STARTER

because I had always roomed with running backs. But before Michigan they put me with Cie Grant and to this day I'm not sure why.

After dinner, when we were back in the room before going to bed, he was describing to me what the Michigan game meant to him. I was sitting on the chair with my feet up on the end of the bed and he was sitting on the other bed up where the telephone was and he was describing to me not only his 4 years at OSU but his whole life story.

He was saying, I remember playing at Iowa and Purdue and I remember this and that and I'm not kidding but my man Cie must have told me about every game he played in since peewee football but then he said, and this really got me: he said I just never had a chance to win anything. He said, I was never in a position to win the national championship and he said to me, You're a really big part of that and you have really given us a chance to win.

I always knew what I brought to the team but to hear it from him, this senior, who was killing me during camp, just killing me by tackling me into fences and shit, and he was now saying how they depended on me. This brother needed me and he depended on me. It was like a switch flipped on in my head. I had always lived in my own world, even to this day, but on that day, I got into Cie's world and it just struck me that he wasn't the only one who needed me, the entire team needed me, and I needed to go out there and help the team win this game.

If you still don't believe me that I could be a humble guy, or that I just didn't think I was that big of a deal, and that a lot of my life I went through thinking I was this anonymous black kid from the south side of Youngstown, think of it like this: when I robbed those people in downtown Columbus a few years later, I robbed them without a mask on because I didn't think anybody would know who I was. Can you believe that shit?

Sometimes I'm naïve about who I am. I'm naïve about how other people perceive me. Put it like this, some people get caught up in themselves and how big they are, but I wasn't caught up in myself at all. I didn't know what I meant to Cie or anyone else before that night. The message that I was somebody just wasn't sinking in. I might have felt important at a club, hanging out in the VIP section, but what's that? That's nothing really in the grand scheme.

Even though I knew 100,000 people cheered for me, I also knew that they would turn on me in a second like they had earlier in the season.

So before talking to Cie, I just didn't know that he and everybody else felt for me. Coming from him, that meant everything for me. When I went onto the field for the game the next day, I was locked-in, laser-focused.

To tell the truth and bring it back to reality, another reason I was locked-in and laser-focused was that actually, a day or two before the game, Coach Tressel had told me I wasn't starting because Lydell and Mo had played all those weeks prior and he was sticking with them to start.

So first I found out I wasn't starting, which was a low-point but also great motivation, and then all that stuff Cie said, which meant the world to me, so on game day, I was like, BOOM. I was like to hell with all these Michigan dudes and watch this shit—just wait until I get out there because not starting burned me up and I knew when I got my chance out there I would be balling.

In the locker room, the trainers had given me another one of those serious painkiller shots from the 6-inch needle in my shoulder and they put that circle donut pad on and then they put another pad on and another pad and like fifty pads and I just said, to hell with it, I just told myself I don't give a damn if this shoulder falls off today. It had got to the point that this was how I felt. I wasn't mad or resentful—I just couldn't wait to prove to the entire world what I could do and do what Cie told me the team needed me to do.

Mo Hall started the first series but in his first two runs he didn't have much room to run and they put Lydell in for 3rd and long. That was an incomplete pass and we punted and the next time we got the ball that was it. I was in.

For the second series, I went out there and they gave me the ball and I took off running. I had a 28-yard run down to our 10 and the whole crowd knew I was back and playing hard. I was definitely in the mode that I didn't give a damn if this shoulder fell off.

CHAPTER EIGHT: STARTER

I have always had a great ability to hit the I-don't-care button. I can flip this switch in my brain either in a positive or negative way that I can say I don't give a damn. When it's time to play, you give it all. That's what I believe. I live for big moments and you can't ever worry about getting hurt even if it's inevitable in a massively violent sport like football.

In the first quarter, I scored our first touchdown on a 2-yard run behind my man Shane to the right and that made it 7-3. They kicked a couple more field goals in the second quarter and it was 9-7 Michigan at the half.

The game was a dogfight but I was taking the opportunity to notice everything I could about their D and what guys were doing. At halftime, guys were keyed up and some of them were going crazy in the locker room to motivate each other, but I was just keeping to myself, like I always did, thinking things through and trying to figure out what we needed to do to win.

Nobody scored in the third quarter and I went over to Tressel about halfway through the 4th quarter and told him I should run a wheel route and have Craig hit me near the left sideline. I could see how they were adjusting and lining up and what they were doing and what the linebacker was doing and how he was getting lazy after he read his keys.

Some football players are just lazy. A linebacker is supposed to read the fullback, tight end, QB, and then get his eyes back around to maybe a crossing route. A lazy guy will just look for one thing then look for another and then sit still and be lackadaisical in the middle of the field actually waiting for the play to develop.

What the linebacker is supposed to do is check if anything is coming back side and try to re-route it or get up under a route with a corner or safety or even check to see what the running backs were doing. So we were running all these plays and I'm watching what this linebacker was doing and I had figured out that this dude wouldn't even know if I ran the wheel.

I know the plays throughout the week that we're putting in, so I'm constantly thinking about what can I do, or what plays can we run. I'm thinking like the offensive coordinator: what plays can we run that will be to our advantage, how are they lining up, etc. And based on what I was seeing from Larry Foote and Cato June is that those guys were real active but the lazy guy was just playing around and not doing his job. So I went over to Tressel and said Yo, let's run the wheel route because that dude is falling asleep. The wheel route is traditionally one of the most sneaky routes even with active linebackers doing their job, but with this guy, there's no way they would stop it.

After the play was called, I started off like I was going to break off in the flat so this linebacker made a beeline to me because he thought he would stop me there if Craig threw to me. But then I turned it on and headed downfield and it's too hard for that guy to turn back around and just like I said, the wide receiver from that side had cleared out the defensive backs and I was wide open and Craig hit me right between the numbers. It was a 26-yard pass and got us to the Michigan 6 yard-line.

I thought when I caught the ball somebody might come and crash into me so I turned around and dove out of bounds on purpose. I absolutely threw myself out of bounds. The moment was so big that I caught the ball and I just said I'm going to turn around and go out because I don't want to get popped and have the ball get jarred loose. My back was turned and I didn't know what was going on or whether a safety was going to come over and destroy me.

After the play, I just hopped up saw Mo Hall coming onto the field so I knew I had to get my ass out of the game and I ran up to Tressel and said, I told you so, I told you so. I just knew from being a student of the game that it was going to work and he believed me which was just like him, because I was the one who was out there between the lines. It was an incredible moment for both of us because he trusted me.

I was on the sidelines the next few plays. I absolutely wanted to go back on the field and get the touchdown but two plays later Mo took a pitch to the right and ran it in from the 3. He was a lot faster than me and had some experience throughout that week running that play to the outside.

We went up 14-9 and I was happy as hell, just standing there next to Tressel. He calls the plays, but Spencer says who goes in. I try to stay out of the ego space in my head about whether Spencer didn't want me to get that

TD. Only he knows but if I ever get into a bad headspace, I might say there was some level of resentment and even jealousy and he didn't want me to get the game-winning touchdown against Michigan because of who I was, that kid from the streets.

People are not always very kind. Sometimes they love using dudes like me who come from the 'hood to their advantage, but they don't like promoting us or they don't like if we get the success, like we don't deserve it because we just come from the streets.

It's weird but I see it in bigtime college football and basketball all the time. Coaches like using guys who don't care if their shoulder falls off during a game, but they don't like seeing us on the cover of magazines.

I can give you an example of this outside of sports that is almost the same thing. Recently, I went to Canton City Schools to speak to a behavioral health agency who booked me with the intention of me bringing kids of color in to their agency. They wanted me to be marketable for their organization. They were pimping me out. I was cool enough to be used to be pimped out but I'll never forget the uncomfortable look on their faces when I told them I owned a behavioral health agency of my own in nearby Youngstown. They looked at me like, Oh shit, he could be our competition someday.

So when I look at a guy like Tim Spencer, I think I'm good enough to work for my success, I'm good enough to run the ball, and catch the ball, but when it comes to having any level of advancement or stardom beyond that, sometimes people want to control that because they don't want kids from the street to reach a level beyond what they think we should have.

It's a weird funky space to be in and I was feeling that then. This dude, think about it, I came onto the scene and didn't talk proper and I'm from the 'hood. I was young, raw, and acted like a young Mike Tyson. But dudes like me are the ones who win games. Dudes from the 'hood win championships. It's cool to be with rough dudes when it comes to winning championships, but when it comes to promoting them outside of running the ball or catching the ball, it's funny, because they won't always do that.

I am 100% sure that Spencer was the one who said Mo Hall would start the Michigan game. But it got to the point where I didn't even care what kind of cage they put me in, I was going to escape it. I don't think people realize that when they put up barriers they actually make the individual facing the barrier stronger because now we have to fight to get over it. Listen to me, this gives me a tremendous amount of motivation.

We partied all night after the Michigan game. That was the biggest party, we partied all night. Everybody came down, there had to be about 40 people. The whole city partied. It was like a dream when the fans took the field. We celebrated on the field, we celebrated in the locker room, we hung out in the locker room, we went to do interviews, we were eating the food they laid out for us. There were people everywhere. It was a beautiful time and after we got done partying in the locker room, I got together with all my guys from Youngstown and we partied all night at Studio 69 and the Waffle House.

An interesting detail I remember so clearly is that Juan Bell had come down that night. This was the first time for him coming down. He was like a brother to me—one of the guys who I'd grown up with, one of the guys I was always playing in the street with, and he was the one who got murdered right around Christmas that started all the trouble with Andy Geiger.

These were all my Youngstown boys. There were pictures of me and Juan from that night on the 30-for-30. We partied all night. I was drinking champagne because Juan probably bought 30-40 bottles of it. He must have put out 3 or 4 thousand dollars that night. This was a great time for everybody and he had a wad of cash on him that was obviously from him selling drugs. I don't know what he was selling but he was hustling for sure.

After the Michigan game, we had a mandatory meeting on Sunday. They were telling us that the day after Christmas we would fly out to Arizona. There was a long gap of 6 weeks between games so there was just a lot of conditioning and lifting and making sure that my shoulder was 100% by the national championship.

Not long after the Michigan game, I was named the Big Ten freshman of the year and was the first team All-Big Ten running back. I was also on the USA Today freshman All-American team.

CHAPTER EIGHT: STARTER

I had 20 carries for 119 yards against Michigan and broke the freshman rushing record with 1,190 yards and 16 TDs basically in only eight full games and change. It was a helluva season, including a knee surgery and a tough shoulder injury, but I got through it and we were 13-0, Big Ten champions headed towards a national championship game.

CHAPTER NINE
CHAMPION

FALL QUARTER ended the week after the Michigan game. I just had some exams and papers to turn in and otherwise I was conditioning for a few weeks and then I went back to Youngstown.

Juan got murdered on December 21st. I found out from my older brother Michael. I can't pinpoint where I was because all I remember is practicing after Michigan, conditioning, and then going to Arizona.

This sounds crazy but I had dealt with so many people dying prior to that. Not that this felt like just another murder, because obviously this was someone I knew well, but life still went on. He was close to me but Brandon Peete, getting murdered when I was in high school, was the guy who was closest to me before that who got killed.

It was the summer of 2001, before my senior year at Harding. Brandon was 2-3 years younger. He didn't live on my block but he would always be in our neighborhood. He always wanted to be around, just like young dudes act, always wanting to be near the action. He got shot with an AK-47. When you're that young, to get shot with an AK at 14 or 15 years old, it just tears your body apart. He had left a neighborhood club and the gentleman who murdered him, they just caught Brandon walking home and they were targeting him but I don't know why he got killed.

Honestly, I want to say that there were more than a hundred people we actually knew since we were 8-9 years old who got murdered. If you check the statistics starting in the late-80s and early-90s, there were plenty of people who got killed. All through the 90s and early-2000s you were just dealing with mass amounts of murders. There were young black teenagers all over Youngstown who were getting killed. It was per capita a ton of murders. Youngstown at that time probably had 80,000 people and maybe there were 20,000 young black males and 100 of them at least got murdered. That's a lot for a small town.

I don't remember getting the call about Juan. I don't even remember where I was at and I don't remember crying or not crying. Most people don't cry when you get those kinds of calls, it just happens this way: you get the call and they say, Hey have you heard what happened? And it becomes like, Man, that's messed up. Then you try and find out and get the details of what happened and where it was and just try to piece together what happened.

This was a major thing for me. Juan was somebody who I had known since we were kids. My grandma lived on the bottom of the south side on Overland and we had a unique situation where my mother worked out at NEOUCOM and for the majority of my childhood, probably until about the age of 10 or so, I spent a tremendous amount of time over there.

This is where I played football with the Braves and the majority of the people at the bottom of the south side lived around my grandmother and we all knew each other and grew up together and my uncle lived down there and this is where the original relationship happened when we played for the Braves.

Juan was my older brother Michael's age, three years older than me. I just heard that someone tried to rob him and he got killed. I guess some way, somehow and even to this day I don't know and I'm just speculating but it must have been something in regards to drugs and the other guy shot him.

When Juan came to Columbus to party after the Michigan game, he dropped thousands of dollars on that champagne. Everyone in Youngstown must have known that he had a lot of money which made him a target to people in the streets.

I got the call about Juan and it didn't immediately go through my mind about the funeral. First we just wanted to figure out what happened and deal with the shock of it all.

CHAPTER NINE: CHAMPION

But then in the context of us about to play for the national championship I wasn't even thinking about when the funeral was going to be. And then we finally got to Arizona and I was like, Hold on, his funeral was in a few days so I put the wheels in motion in regards to trying to attend it.

The team flew out there together on the 26th and the funeral was going to be on the 31st. The game wasn't until January 3rd so I thought I had plenty of time to go and come back.

We got settled into the Scottsdale Princess hotel and I was in my room, maybe the 27th or 28th and I started trying to make arrangements to get back to Youngstown.

I remember talking to someone out there from our Compliance office. I let them know I needed to go back and they said they would try to make it happen. I was also talking to Tressel and anybody who was in a compliance role. But all I heard from them was a lot of, We'll-try-to-make-it-happen talk.

Here's the biggest part I remember—I went up to Tressel's suite and he referred me to the compliance folks and they said they could make it happen using the NCAA Hardship Fund. They said they had to check on this form or that form but they could make it happen. Basically at that point they were willing to help me out. Then a whole day passed and I didn't hear anything. Nobody was like, Hey, we don't have that form on file so let's hurry up and fill it out.

I went to practice the next day and I was back in the room that night and I was starting to get confused because I'm like, Yo I haven't heard anything from these people. So I was calling to everybody—we had this entire phone tree of some sorts when we were out there to tell us who to call if we needed something and I tried everybody but got nowhere.

This went on for another day and by the time I go to sleep on the 30th and wake up the day of the funeral, I know it ain't gonna happen. We were two hours behind and the funeral was at 11 o'clock and it was a 4-hour flight. The next thing you know, we go into media day and I get asked about it, tell my side, and then the whole thing just exploded.

Ever since I got to Ohio State, I had filled out every form that I had ever been given or knew about. Maybe there's a chance Andy Geiger wasn't lying when he said they didn't have the form on file they needed to use the hardship money, but as soon as they figured that out why didn't they print it, have me sign it, and fax it to the NCAA? They just didn't want me to go, plain and simple.

But what we were dealing with and this is just my personal belief—I understand that there's rules and regulations but when a man has to get home for a funeral, they should be able to find a way to get him home.

Just put it like this: would it have been different if this death was different—if this were like a sister who died and this was anything other than a drug-related murder?

Throwing up all those roadblocks to me going home—all the nonsense talk about the forms—they just changed the narrative and got the media to buy into this being a question of whether he filled out the forms or not when that wasn't the question at all. Ever. That was never the question. The question always was, do they want this guy to go home to be at the funeral of a gangster who was murdered in the streets? Is that the image they want for the program and for their first possible national championship in 30 years.

You have to remember, nobody had any football championships around Ohio State in the last few decades. Not Earle Bruce, not John Cooper, and certainly not Andy Geiger. He wanted that championship more than probably anybody and wasn't going to let his star running back fly to Youngstown just because some gangster got shot in the street like a dog.

In fact, bringing up all those forms was consistent with how OSU acted after the NCAA investigation started. It was consistent with them asking me to come and do punishment runs at 6am the next three months. It is that whole mindset that I'm not going to tell you that you can't be here but I'm going to create the circumstances so you won't want to be here.

It never should have been about the form. It should have been about basically a guy who was like a brother to me dying, me wanting to go pay my respects to him, and me not having the money to do it on my own. And oh by the way, my teammates and I are generating tens of millions of dollars for OSU, the entire Big Ten Conference who each got a share of the $13.5 million dollar bowl payout, and the BCS.

CHAPTER NINE: CHAMPION

So instead of the question being did I complete the form, it should have become, Can we help this kid figure this shit out and do something that's vitally important to him?

At this time, I was very aware of the fact we were generating a whole ton of money for the university. I was 19 and my performances on the field sold jerseys and sold tickets and I'm not saying they should have bent the rules for me but now that I'm an adult and I've experienced the best and the worst of life I've also realized that in life, if you want to make something happen, you can make it happen.

If they wanted me to be at that funeral they could have made it happen. If this was an 8 year-old super huge Buckeyes fan with leukemia who I had visited in the hospital all season who had died, they would have chartered a damn plane to send me to the funeral and sent a cameraman to livestream me playing the hero. But this was a gangster who was brutally murdered.

I've seen everything you can imagine in every position that's highly regulated and I've been to the most highly regulated place in the world, prison, and I've been in courts, and whatever you want to make happen, you can make it happen. And if you don't want to make it happen, it won't happen.

This is what they were thinking: we've not been to the championship in over 30 years, our star player won't be at Media Day, the narrative will become Maurice Clarett goes home for funeral of his friend killed in a drug murder. That's the thing they were trying to prevent. So if I don't go home, they're thinking he just does media day and this episode fades into the sunset and everything proceeds like they want.

But I was like, Hey, people are trying to control narratives and stories that promotes them. Like you know what I'm saying, let me fix this narrative that makes sense for this position or promotes or glorifies me. That was the whole situation. If it was someone who was dying from cancer and on their deathbed, you better believe they would have said go on and go see about them—there's nothing wrong with that. But not for my guy Juan Bell.

That's where we get into the bigger issues, because if you want to take kids from inner cities and urban areas, who come from messed-up situations like mine, you have to take all of the shit that comes along with it. You can't just pick and choose like I want this from you, like I want you running and catching the ball and scoring touchdowns, but I don't want all that bad shit. Especially because this bad shit is what hardens someone like me and motivates me to perform on your field.

This is the shit that I was motivated to get away from and escape and become somebody. But there's a danger when coaches and athletic directors and general managers become people who say, I just want the parts of you that help my team or my institution or my brand. That's when it becomes total and complete exploitation. If they don't care about us as people and realize we have feelings like when someone close to us dies that's pretty screwed up.

All these things expand into larger conversations—all this stuff, the power between people and let me take the best parts of you and throw away the worst parts of you and it's all one thing. All of that goes into the decision-making of how people deal with each other and they need to do a better job dealing with hardass players from the inner-city who have real shit like this happening in their lives all the time.

Going to that funeral would have helped me pay my respects and if Geiger's close friend had died don't you think he would have wanted to go? Juan wasn't my best friend but we knew each other our whole lives. I grew up with him, interacted with him, hung out with him. Part of me died right alongside him the day he died. I mean, this person had just been with me a few weeks earlier celebrating after the Michigan game.

And then he passes away and you say you don't have a form on file so I can't go see him off? It wasn't like he was sick and in the hospital. Once you're dead and they put you in the ground, you're gone, brother. You know what I'm saying? And that's the thing, I just felt like it was disrespectful.

At the end of the day, it became like Geiger had the power and he could do whatever he wanted to and I was just like, You don't have the power—I'm going to call your shit out and say you're lying. What difference did saying that mean to me? I wasn't going to bite my tongue for that guy. It's

CHAPTER NINE: CHAMPION

not like I was ever going to be the director of the Alumni Association or in commercials for the local grocery store. I was never going to be that guy.

It keeps coming back to me that, still to this day, football isn't that important to me. I don't live and die for it. And I probably would have said that stuff even back then at the national championship game. This was the first time I realized I had a national platform. Not only did I make comments about the hypocrisy of the university not letting me travel to the funeral but I also brought up the issue of homelessness that I witnessed in Columbus. That level of despair, in such an affluent city, just didn't make any sense to me.

The entire week before the game, our whole team and the coaches and the Board of Trustees and about a hundred other people who none of us even knew were staying at the Scottsdale Princess, a ridiculously luxurious 5-star resort, and there's all this suffering back home in Columbus? I think our team expenses for that trip were like $1.5 million. These sorts of inconsistencies which I was trying to make sense out of were more important to me than who wins a football game and it was nice to show the country I wasn't just a football player and thought about deeper things. I mean college football players you see on TV are real people.

I wasn't the only one thinking these things and saying these things either. Shane gave an interview about how it's a shame everyone is making money off us and how the players were basically being used and he was right.

The exploitation of college football and basketball players by the NCAA is the greatest system of human exploitation in the United States since slavery and it absolutely doesn't need to be that way. There's more than enough money to go around.

College football and basketball could be the greatest system to uplift especially poor black kids if everyone weren't so damn greedy. There's no shortage of money. The NCAA makes a billion dollars a year, every year, off of March Madness. A billion. And how much do those players get?

Do head coaches need to make $5-10 million/year? Do assistant coaches need to make a million? Do athletic directors need to make millions? Does Mark Emmert, the president of the NCAA, need to make $2.5 million?

Some of that should be trickling down to the players if not in cash at least in terms of worker's compensation protection for future health problems and tuition reimbursement programs with no time limits so we can actually get an education when we're not lifting, practicing, and watching films 50-60 hours/week.

Everybody associated with college football is getting mad money but the players. Even the bigtime college scholarship athletes are getting crumbs off the table and this shit needs to stop. The entire system is a fraud based on the lie that college football players are students when in fact they're gladiators violently beating each other all fall long in coliseums all over the country.

An even bigger part of the fraud is that you've got so many outstanding black football and basketball players earning the money to support entire athletic departments—through sweat, broken bones, and other lifelong injuries to their knees, backs, and brains—to finance scholarships for huge numbers of mainly white kids playing non-revenue generating sports like volleyball, soccer, tennis, golf, swimming, and fencing.

OSU has over 30 non-revenue generating athletic teams listed on their website, including the Spirit Program, which is cheerleading, I guess, and other than the track team they're almost all white kids on these rosters. It's another massive transfer of wealth coming from black labor to subsidize white opportunities. The average annual profit of the OSU athletic department the last three years was $75 million—from football and basketball—and money from that covers all those scholarships for non-revenue generating athletes. You can't make this shit up but tons of people don't find a single thing wrong with this and keep saying black collegiate stars who want to make money should just be grateful for the chance to go to college.

If you had told me that the national championship game would be my last time playing for the Buckeyes, that wouldn't have hurt me nearly as much as my friend Juan dying. That's real loss and there's real grieving when close friends die. In fact, my tutor came to see me at the hotel after media day and I told him this would probably be my last game as a Buckeye. I was done. I didn't believe the institution had my best interests in mind and cared

CHAPTER NINE: CHAMPION

about me as a person and I've never been able to sacrifice my body and my brain for something I didn't believe in.

Even though I played football at the highest level, it wasn't that important. Football was always just a vehicle. I just happened to take it serious then and happened to be talented but it was just a vehicle to get elsewhere. My initial thought was just to get out of Youngstown—not to get out and never return but to get out in the sense of surviving and doing something else. I couldn't even see anything farther than that down the road then. I was just trying to survive and not get murdered, which sounds crazy to say now but I was trying to live and not die, that's all.

A lot of times kids screw up during their developmental years because they can't see that far down the road. They don't have a roadmap to succeed. They are just like I want to get the hell out of my situation—that's a task in itself. When you think about it, now that I'm older, when I think about the school system I came out of, and the neighborhood I came out of—it was a completely inadequate social environment.

When you come out of that, just to survive and escape it is like a full-time job. It's traumatic. That level of stress is literally causing trauma to your brain. You're dealing with so much hate and tension and dysfunction and death that you don't realize how dysfunctional it is until you go and try to live a normal life.

Then you look back and realize this shit you grew up with is not normal and other people aren't dealing with this level of dysfunction. Now I think about if my daughter grew up in half the shit I grew up in, as an adult I'd probably go crazy if my kid was living that reality. I could never let my daughter grow up in that, even though I grew up in it.

When you got kids battling through all that shit and constantly knowing that they have to get out of that shit, it becomes a full-time job for 100 social workers just to help them, which is exactly what the Red Zone is trying to do now in Youngstown and Columbus. We're trying to teach young kids that when they finally do get out, they are going to have to build an entire new life because they don't have the foundation for a successful and productive life in a sphere other than surviving the streets.

It doesn't surprise me that I'm getting so involved in the school life of kids now even though I didn't take school that seriously. I think that's the natural progression after you get past the part of your life when you just want to get money to collect things. Then you start going through life experiences and you start to realize that the collection of possessions to make your life or to have more resources is important, but to have meaning you have to feed positivity back into the negative space that was in your own life.

I'm giving back now into things I was negatively impacted by. Even in my own evolution in prison when I started to read and started to connect the dots, it was like, Oh this is why I was such a dummy because I didn't know or have any understanding of anything but the streets.

Then you start to travel the country and speak in different venues and hear more information about how early childhood education affects a person in their life and then you start to look at your peers and your friends and you start to see how messed up these people are and you start to realize everybody didn't have football to save their lives or give them some sort of privilege in life.

Then you're like okay but the people who did make it, these people took school seriously so how do you make school cool or how do you get involved to just change the culture in the community. I remember being a kid and thinking there's nothing ever to do except play sports. So how do I now become the guy who creates the events for these kids so there are things to do and they see there are people who really truly care about them and want to make sure they have a better life. That's what I want, for all these kids my agencies work with—a better life.

When I was a kid there wasn't nothing to do but get in trouble and run the streets. In urban environments you just don't have the infrastructure. Every activity in urban, or even rural, environments has to be organized or put together by someone. You don't have gyms and batting cages and well-manicured football fields; you don't have volleyball courts and basketball courts and all these facilities for kids to go to.

The biggest difference in urban and suburban settings is the infrastructure. They have the resources to develop the kids in the suburbs.

CHAPTER NINE: CHAMPION

In inner cities you just have dilapidated parks and playgrounds that are real old and you can't really get access to it or you just don't have it at all.

So now you say we just need to create the spaces that we didn't have. We have to do it on a consistent basis, which is a ton of work but that's what we're doing at the Red Zone.

It doesn't surprise me that it feels natural for me to be doing all this stuff for these kids. This feels more important and I hate to say it but it gives me more fulfillment or more gratification than football ever did. Working with kids is rewarding. I guess there's a pleasure in actually seeing people appreciate your efforts and what you're trying to do for them.

Now we have our own space and have started to host activities and it doesn't surprise me at all how natural this feels for me to be doing all this stuff for these kids. Then there is an amount of appreciation from parents who might not have the resources to put this stuff together themselves. To actually see them saying my kid came, my kid had a nice time, and the kid says thank you. To see them express themselves early, that's a thing and you can carry that thing and create some sort of presence in their life. That's when you start to tie into better grade and attendance reports and incentivize that stuff and now you just have better kids coming out of the system. You might still have problems but you have more kids graduating, more kids caring about themselves, more people just paying attention to how their life unfolds.

I might be doing this stuff if I had gone to the NFL, but I wouldn't be doing it with the same perspective. I might be throwing money at things but money isn't a cure. It's a tool to recruit the appropriate staff and the people with the skills to make it happen and some resources you need but I don't think I would have done things with the same perspective if I had been successful in the NFL. I also might not have stuck around as long—maybe I would have just donated some money and moved on.

The NFL has a way of jading guys. I've seen guys who come from like super struggles and horrible situations and then when they get financially stable the transition into a higher social class starts. I see guys thinking like, Damn, I'm living in Upper Arlington now—forget the 'hood. Or I'm living in Dublin now or some prominent suburb and my friends are all prominent businessmen and my importance comes from going to the get-togethers and luncheons and golf courses and there becomes a disconnect from their roots.

So it's totally opposite in my situation. Going to prison gave me a deeper connection to the community that I'm in. I think four years, man, of being inside a prison and being active in prison amongst men gave me like an education about issues related to personal development you couldn't get on any college campus.

I learned so much more in regards to what I'm doing now. I can see how guys turn out and how girls turn out and how different experiences cause what they end up doing.

I saw all that shit first-hand and I wouldn't have learned it in the NFL and I don't know if my life was destined to go this way but all the dumb shit in my life definitely put me in a position now to try and benefit a lot of people.

As crazy as it is to say, all the stupid shit actually helped me. It helps me realize that people think of me differently, in a good way, not just like I'm talking to Maurice the football player but now I'm talking to Maurice who had a bunch of success, went through some seriously messed-up times, got himself together, and is just a regular guy now trying to help people get their lives straight.

Because I wasn't allowed to go to the funeral, the night before the championship game, I was just not interested in the whole thing. I didn't even care anymore that this was the biggest stage. There was a total disconnection. I still had motivation to play for Tressel and my teammates but the motivation to want to succeed and do this for Ohio State was gone.

The older I get, the easier it is to see that everything is interconnected. People just look at life like it's a bunch of random events but I think everything is interconnected and I was grateful to understand this a long time ago: everything you do in life, I think the guy who has the advantage is the guy who has everything in perspective.

CHAPTER NINE: CHAMPION

And the best perspective for college football, or probably all athletics really, is that there's no fear of losing. There's no fear that something bad is going to happen to me if we lose. There's a comfort in just not basing your identity or life on winning a game. The guy who can do that is the guy who always survives. The guy who is loose, cool, and comfortable. The guy who could lose but still live with himself, that's the guy who wins.

I had always been one of the guys who would just run recklessly. Even though football players are supposed to love collisions, usually they love organized and structured collisions. But when you run the ball and you are just absolutely reckless and you're 235 or 240 lbs. and you just recklessly run into guys, well, not everybody can take that shit.

And then you just get right up after being tackled hard and it's like sometimes in football you just run into a guy and you might be hurt but you get up and act like you aren't and you just run into them again and again and eventually other players just get out of your way because they don't want to deal with that. In junior high I was like that, in high school I was like that, and up to this point in college it was like that. But I was not ready to do that in the days leading up to the Miami game.

My attitude going into the Miami game was just wanting to get it over with. I was the starter because of how well I played against Michigan. I wanted to play hard and play with spirit and passion but there wasn't like anything extra driving me.

My motivation was just the people. Even if you start the season not even liking guys, you get into a system where you're practicing every day, running together every day, going to film every day, eating together, it becomes like a respect for yourself as a human being to play hard for them. That's what I felt before the Miami game. These dudes appreciated me, too.

You know when you come off the field and guys were patting your head and guys were looking to me to succeed. When I ran onto the field, and TV probably can't capture this very well, but lots of times your teammates are saying in the huddle that we need you, we need 6 points, we need you to put it in the end zone. Guys were always saying this to me in the huddle and it meant something to me.

Everybody knew I was just fearless and that brought something extra to the huddle. Everybody knew when I was out there. Once I gave that impression to people, that I was always ready to go, that was real comforting to my teammates. They appreciated that getting hit doesn't bother me.

If you had asked me warming-up for the national championship, I would have said that I wasn't feeling as reckless as usual but I still wanted to win. I wasn't giving 110% even though I was giving 100%. I guess I was doing enough to compete but I wasn't all-in.

One of the worst things people can do is make you feel like you're not appreciated. So when they didn't send me home for the funeral, it was like they didn't care about me as a person. All of my animosity was projected onto Geiger and the compliance office, but not to Tressel or my teammates. I was going to try and lead them to a championship and they knew it.

As soon as the official blew the whistle for the kickoff, competing and winning was all that mattered, 100%. It was game-on, and I was going to do more than I'd ever done, on the biggest stage I'd ever been on, to win that football game for my teammates and Ohio State.

Looking back on it, I guess I was conditioned that way, the same way that soldiers in the old days were conditioned to go over the top when their captain blew the whistle. I guess there's a reason why football coaches and drill sergeants use whistles. They're just classically conditioning the hell out of us, so that when that whistle blows, we go over the top. And that's what happened to me.

In the first few offensive plays, I realized that Miami was, as a team, probably the fastest team that we had played. We didn't realize that looking at the film going in. We had heard they were fast but some of the things they were doing to our guys up front were impossible to stop. Some of the linebackers, the way they moved, they were physically faster than what we had been playing the whole season.

So, it became like, Oh shit, they are faster than us and we don't have any way to adjust to this. We realized that early on. They were so fast and a lot of the plays we ran were slow developing, down-blocking schemes, runs that developed slowly and they were beating us to the point of attack. It was like

CHAPTER NINE: CHAMPION

a boxer beating you to the punch. They were punching us in the face before we could get our gloves up.

We were big underdogs, like they were 12-point favorites, but I went in 100% expecting to win. Even when we ran into Frank Gore and some of the other Hurricanes a few days before the game, I was talking shit. We saw them in the mall and I was like, To hell with these guys.

Not everybody was like this though. We had guys on our team who were literally fans of them. The Miami Hurricanes were a big deal at that time, like a brand all to themselves. I'm serious. But I didn't care if they were the defending national champions. I didn't care if they were undefeated. I didn't give a damn about who they were as Miami Hurricanes or what that meant.

But some other guys on our team who were from Florida knew some of their guys so some of them were talking to them like they were happy to meet these dudes and I'm like, Look, we're getting ready to play these dudes for a national championship so let's not be so cool with them.

It just felt like too much of a bitch move to me to be cool with them and shake hands and hang out. I was like, Nooo, I want to fight these dudes. Maybe it wasn't like I actually wanted to physically fight them but it was more like, we are nowhere near cool. It's hard to want to kick someone's ass when you're cool with them.

So, during the first quarter, we couldn't even get into our offense to see what was going on. But if you look back by the 3rd or 4th series, we had adjusted. If you look at the whole season, Craig hardly ever ran the ball. He had only 287 yards rushing during the season. But at the end of this game, Craig has the most rushing yards of anybody. That was a wrinkle we threw in during the game. Tressel came to me and asked me to be the lead blocker because he wanted to run Craig. This was decided early on because they weren't prepared for us running Craig.

Actually, there was a lot of panic in our huddle in the first quarter. The bottom line was that Miami was real good and we didn't have an answer early on. If you just want to be blunt we had no answer for what they were doing.

Just think about this: you studied your opponent for more than a month and created a game plan and all the plays that we tried to throw at them, none of it was working. We didn't put in any new stuff—we just tried to execute the plays we had already ran as well as we could. But all the things that we thought would work didn't work.

I was getting some carries and the biggest thing on the offensive line was that you need movement and we weren't getting any movement. Our guys were getting blown up before they could even pull around and go to where they needed to be to make blocks and open holes. Defensive guys were all pushing up in their face. Miami's defensive line was balling.

We thought that they would be, but we just didn't think they would be as dominant so early. I want to say it without disrespecting my guys who were doing everything they could and most of them went to the NFL too, but most the guys on Miami's defense were All-Pro NFL guys: Jonathan Vilma, DJ Williams, Jerome McDougle, Vince Wilfork. They all got drafted in the first round.

So Tressel came to me early on and we changed our basic running game. I became the lead blocker because everybody has a match between the offense and the defense and the QB is matched up to the free safety. Since he's the deepest person, it takes more time for him to get to the line of scrimmage. My match on whatever side I was on was that linebacker. If I'm lead blocking, DJ Williams has to come to me and Craig can get 3-4 yards before the free safety can come to hit him. It was just a numbers game. It was just a basic adjustment for me to become the lead blocker.

This was real strap-up-your-shit football, just like in camp. Especially my first touchdown. That was an inside run, between the tackles, just like I'd shown in August that I could do. For better or worse, my brain was just hard-wired to want to blast my way through a defense and score even if it was like a head-on car crash.

I scored my first touchdown from the 7 yard-line. I just strapped it up and knew I was going to get hit but actually I got through the line clean and bounced off their weak-side linebacker on the 1 and into the end zone.

Surprisingly, we were leading and then it was just a matter of holding on. It was 14-7 at the half and in the third quarter, we were in the red zone and getting ready to score again so things were looking good for us.

CHAPTER NINE: CHAMPION

This is the play that everybody remembers when they think of the OSU-Miami national championship game because people had never seen anything like it before.

Craig was trying to throw a touchdown pass to his roommate Ben Hartsock. In the huddle, Ben had said something like throw it to me because I want a TD. It sounds like something that would happen in a schoolyard football game but it happened in the national championship game. Tressel can call any pass play he wants, but Craig can go through reads and try and throw it to his roommate if he wants to. If you look at the film, Craig was trying to force the ball into double coverage and Sean Taylor picked it off.

I was off the right-hand side of the line of scrimmage when the ball was picked off, protecting the edge. So I'm blocking the defender and I didn't even see the interception but I could tell from the crowd reaction that something bad happened and I looked and I saw Sean Taylor running the ball out from our end zone.

After the interception, Taylor just took off and when he was running I noticed he wasn't protecting the ball. The funniest thing is that the only reason I recognized it was because ball-security was the first drill that I'd done as a running back every day in practice since I was in the 8th grade.

I'm a running back and I know how to secure the ball and I saw immediately that Sean didn't have the ball secured. There's just different things that individual people notice and because of my background and training, it was obvious for me to notice this guy had the ball flying around everywhere. So, I just thought if I took the right angle I could reach him and take the ball.

There was another thing, too—Sean didn't see me because he was wearing a visor. When you're wearing a visor, your depth perception is off. He had a dark visor on. I love how visors look but the biggest reason I stopped wearing visors when I tried to wear them in high school is that it screwed-up my perception of how far someone is away from me when I'm running. You can't actually see them. It's just like wearing glasses—when you're wearing them, you see things differently. The visor is just a piece of cheap plastic and it looks cool but it messes with your vision of the field.

So I'm thinking first he isn't keeping the ball secure and second he won't realize how close I'm getting to him because of his visor.

I created my angle, thought to myself I was going to go steal the ball, visualized myself stealing the ball, and then I did it. I hadn't ever seen anybody do it before but I saw myself doing it before I did it.

In fact, Sean didn't even know I was stealing the ball until halfway through the tackle. I just stuck my right arm into the spot where the ball was going to be and I grabbed it and clutched it to my gut and let my weight drag the ball away from him. Then Vilma grabbed me and popped me. He was the first one to see that I had the ball so he made sure I was down. I got up and was going crazy because we got the ball back but then I realized my neck hurt. It was a weird tackle with Vilma kind of grabbing me from my waist and dumping me. In football you can fall in weird ways that hurt you and that's what happened.

After that, we stayed on the field and went three plays and didn't move the ball but we kicked the field goal to go up 17-7, which was the most important thing.

The rest of the 3rd and 4th quarter, the game was so long but I don't remember too many details about it. I don't remember the moods too much, just the plays. I think I finished the game with 17 carries and 64 yards. It was just back-and-forth, short running or passing plays. Nobody was going anywhere, just a few yards here and there.

The game was tied at the end of regulation so I'm thinking, Damn, we gotta go out there and win. What happened off the field with me and Andy Geiger was ancient history at this point. For me, it was all about winning and how the hell do we win this game. That's all I was thinking about, 100%.

Everybody was in like a shut-the-hell-up-and-play mode. It's no different than if I walked outside right now and there were 11 people waiting to kick my ass. There's no time to think. Competing with Miami made us give every effort we had and the game was happening so fast we didn't have time to think. We just had to put everything we had on the line right there. Those dudes were that good that we just had to fight.

In the first overtime, Craig scored on a quarterback sneak. Then Miami came back to score. Both teams scored pretty efficiently and I don't even remember anything about our drives.

In the second overtime, I went back down and scored and all we had to do was hold them. My TD run was 46-Dave. We were on the five yard-line and I made a jump cut and dove into the end zone with the ball out. This was strap-it-up, smash-mouth football. I was going to get into the end zone and there was no way they were going to stop me.

Actually, there was a great photo of my dive that was on the front of the Dispatch the next day and eventually got painted onto the wall of the Buckeye Hall of Fame Café before Andy Geiger had them paint over it a year or two later in an attempt to erase me from the history of that game.

We went on defense after that and on the last play, Miami actually called the wrong blocking scheme. They called the wrong protection and that's how Cie got in to Ken Dorsey, their QB. The obvious thing is that whenever you have a linebacker coming off the edge you always have to shift protection on the line. The only reason we won is that Cie came down to the edge and the center was supposed to call the protection and they used the wrong scheme. The center was supposed to call protection towards Cie Grant's side, but they called it the other way. We knew that as soon as the ball was snapped. It's called Jet protection and they called their protection the wrong way.

The game was over, the fireworks went off, but reality for me had set back in within a few minutes. It was a celebratory moment at first but then pretty quickly the pre-game stuff hit me and I didn't really feel like celebrating. I was super-late off the field, super-late in the locker room. I was one of the last people off the field because I didn't want to celebrate. I wasn't even talking to anybody on the field. I was just roaming around chillin' by myself. There's a notable picture if you go back—I'm sitting on an equipment cage on the sidelines, and I've got a visible expression on my face like I just didn't want to be there. My friend had been buried, I didn't get to say goodbye to him, and no crystal trophy was going to make up for that.

ACT II

CHAPTER TEN

OUTCAST

I don't remember if Geiger was in the locker room, and I don't remember getting congratulated by him or anyone else.

After I finally went into the locker room, I just got undressed, showered, got on the bus and went back to the hotel. All I did was save my jersey.

Let me put it this way—this victory was important to me, personally. The national championship was important to me on a personal level. I was glad we did that and I was glad to be a big part of the team's success.

I just chilled that night at the hotel in my room while everyone else partied. And the next day I went to Las Vegas by myself. I had booked that trip before the game to hang out with my Youngstown buddies who went out there to watch the game.

These were just regular guys—Bobby Dellimuti was there, Antonio was there. There were 8 of us. My mother went to Arizona for the game but she went back to Ohio after that.

My mood the next day was relaxed. It was the first time I'd been to Vegas and I was staying at the Bellagio which was great. I remember meeting Jay Z out there—everything was a blur after that. He was at a blackjack table and I walked up to him and introduced myself to him. I don't think he knew who I was but the people he was with did for sure because they had watched the game. They were probably Miami fans but gave me respect for what we did.

It was cool just walking around Vegas. Some of my teammates were there celebrating but I wasn't hanging out with them. After I met Jay Z, the trip could have been over for me—that's all I cared about.

I stayed in Vegas for a couple days and came back to Columbus after that. School started and we had some down time to get treatment. Basically, I was just letting my body recover because I had gotten majorly beat up during the season.

I didn't hear anything more about the issue between me and Geiger. It was such a tender issue because I had called him a liar but the coaches were hitting the recruiting trail and also nobody wanted to say anything about it because we had the joy of getting the championship.

I was just having fun, thinking maybe I could win the Heisman the next year. I was planning on staying at Ohio State.

My mindset was more that I had been pissed off in the moment but that was behind me now. It wasn't like I had given up on OSU or given up on my team. Of course I still wanted to win more championships with Tressel.

I thought the celebration in the Horseshoe was great. Of course politicians like Governor Taft and Mayor Coleman were there trying to bask in the reflective glory but the best part for everyone was hearing Cie Grant sing Carmen Ohio and even now, hearing him sing it is really powerful to me. It's nostalgic. Being there with my teammates celebrating made me feel like I was there with the guys I accomplished it with.

I think life comes down to who you put in work with. The purest things about sports are fan appreciation and the work you put in with your dudes. I signed a lot of autographs for fans that day and was happy to do it.

There had been an autograph-signing event for the team at City Center Mall after the Michigan game but before we left for Arizona and actually I didn't go. I thought we were being used so I didn't go. I told them to tell the media I was at the dentist because it just seemed they were using us. I was always happy to sign an autograph for a kid who would keep it but not at some event where autograph brokers were getting us to sign shit they could sell.

CHAPTER TEN: OUTCAST

Maybe I was naïve or maybe I was right to say we should be compensated for signing autographs at those events. Sometimes it hurts when you're dead broke and you see people auctioning shit you've signed on eBay.

After we won the national championship, things changed around Columbus big-time. The only way I can describe it is like going from a Cadillac to a Mercedes Benz. You were already doing good but somehow now you're doing even better. It felt memorable what we did. Historic. Going 14-0 was epic. It felt like it was significant to people because winning the national championship hadn't happened in their lifetime or they were too young to remember it if it did. Looking back on it, this would have been the right time for some behavioral interventions with me. I could have used some people reaching out and giving me some advice around this time, even though I can't guarantee I would have listened.

There's a lot of people who could have reached out and, who knows, I might have listened to them. I thought maybe Archie Griffin, who is OSU's most famous running back, would have reached out after I broke the freshman rushing record, because he knew better than anybody what I was going through.

But Archie never got involved with me or congratulated me. You have to remember, I represent something different than him, much different. I represent the streets. Archie has to be cool on a different level with a different group of people. I think he was the head of the Alumni Association or something at that point, dealing with a half-million people who'd graduated from OSU and wanted the football team to win but didn't want nothing to do with kids from the streets, for the most part.

Even now I don't know modern-day Archie. But as a man, we represent two different things. I'm on the tail end of the Mike Tyson era and I grew up in the origin of hip hop gangsta rap era. I was just totally raw, from an absolutely violent background. I wasn't doing violent shit myself personally, but I grew up in it, 100%.

I wear my passion and pride for Youngstown on my sleeve. If you look at it, that's not a corporate Ohio State reputation. But it's the shit I loved and people didn't know how to take me being so raw. It's not good or bad but as a younger man I didn't understand how raw I was and how uncomfortable that made people. It was just how I felt toward the world. I didn't even know how to relate to people back then—I had no clue how to push out my message in a way people could understand it.

It's important to realize though that the whole point is that how raw I was is what made me play better or made me who I am and that's the issue for big billion dollar universities getting paid big money by exploiting kids from the streets who they don't know how to handle outside of the athletics sphere.

I just don't think Archie even cared to be involved with me and my shit and I don't blame him. He would have just thought we should keep winning games, making the university more prestigious, making more money, and that sort of stuff. That was his job then and a man has to do his job.

So, winter quarter is going along and I'm enrolled in a couple African American Studies classes and an English class and working with my tutor making sure I can pass them.

As far as football, I'm just working out trying to get ready for spring ball, conditioning all the time at the facility and that's where my car got broken into. Even though the car break-in happened in the spring, nothing happened then. Nobody even knew about it and it didn't become a thing until summer.

But when that break-in happened in March, before spring ball, it was no big deal. There wasn't an insurance claim filed and that's maybe the one thing that pisses me off to this day. It wasn't even my shit that got stolen and I never even made an insurance claim about it and eventually the OSU public relations machine used that to come after me when they were kicking me to the curb.

I got the car from a guy who repossessed the car and the CDs were with a bunch of stuff in the back seat when I picked it up. I never cared they got taken and for sure didn't intentionally file a false police report about them. I didn't know nothing about them and they weren't even mine. They just happened to be in a car that was loaned to me. That was the extent of my understanding about them. Period.

CHAPTER TEN: OUTCAST

When it happened, I called Tressel. He told me to file a police report, so I filled out a police report and told them exactly what was in the car and guessed how much it was worth. I didn't know so I just did some simple math and came up with a number, put it in the report, and forgot about it.

Actually, I didn't play spring ball. Tressel didn't even want me to get hit in spring ball. He just wanted me to take care of my body. I didn't even play in the spring game, which was very normal. I had to take care of myself.

During spring quarter, I took another African American Studies class, Nutrition, and Rural Sociology. That was a course that lots of football players took. It might have been interesting but couldn't have been less relevant to me and I failed it. I was just looking forward to the school year ending. I finished that quarter with a 1.5 GPA but still had a 2.1 overall so I was straight with my grades.

Once they told me the summer conditioning was voluntary/mandatory, I was like to hell with that. Listen to me, I was almost 240 pounds during the season and I was thinking if I really wanted to make a run at the Heisman I had to be lighter and take my training to a whole other level.

That summer, I went to train in Cleveland with Eric Lichter. He had his own gym at the time up in Cleveland and within a few years, Ohio State hired him as their director of sports performance so I guess I was ahead of the curve but it still pissed people off.

It was me, Nate Clements, LeBron, and a guy who played for the Patriots. OSU criticized me so much for taking off and not training at the facility but then they hired the guy themselves because he was that good.

LeBron had already been drafted but he had trained with Eric when he was in high school and whenever he was still around Northeastern Ohio. It was about a 45-minute drive for me because I was living at my mom's house in Youngstown.

Eric was on the front end of being a trainer with his own personal facility. I hadn't seen independent trainers open their own gyms yet. He had a high level of understanding about dieting, the use of sand pits to develop speed, etc. To have one of these and a whole weight room and a training facility of 40,000 square feet in 2002 was revolutionary.

I had been introduced to Eric through LeBron because I just thought our training program at Ohio State was the bare minimum. The guy who ran it under Cooper had left and what I was looking for and what I was getting at the facility were two different things. I needed someone who was going to push my ass.

And at this point, me and LeBron were real tight. We were always talking on the phone and hanging out. Even when I was down here at Ohio State, I was driving up to Akron for his games and just chillin'.

I trained like hell that summer and got down to 230 and I was in the best shape of my life, 20x better than I was freshman year. I was really trying to make a run at the Heisman. In fact, Sports Illustrated, in their college preseason magazine, named me as the Heisman favorite and picked us to repeat as National Champions.

But at some point, in June I think, I got a call from OSU's compliance office, Hey, you have to come to Columbus. They said I had to come down and answer some questions about the car break-in and the police report I filed. I called Tressel and he told me to go in and tell the truth and that's what I did.

As unlikely as it sounds, I've always wondered if Andy Geiger got the NCAA to investigate the break-in—whether he used them as a way to get back at me for calling him a liar. There's just no other explanation for how they even found out about it because it's not like it was in the news. Somebody threw me under the damn bus, that's for sure.

The whole basis of this was supposed to be that I had under-valued the CDs that got stolen, saying they were only worth a few thousand dollars. And then during the NCAA investigation, they inflated that value. They calculated there were 800 CDs worth $15 so they said I lost 12-thousand dollars worth of shit and made a big deal out of asking me where I got the money to buy all of those CDs.

I tried to explain to them over and over that I hadn't claimed this shit, it wasn't mine, and they belonged to the guy who the car had previously belonged to.

CHAPTER TEN: OUTCAST

But the NCAA kept saying back to me over and over that I falsified a claim. They were trying to get me to admit that but I didn't falsify anything. If anybody went back and listened to the tapes of my NCAA interviews, they would hear how this was complete nonsense. The interviews were just bizarre. Some grown adults locked in a room badgering a kid about where he got the money to buy CDs that he didn't buy.

None of that shit even made sense in a context other than Andy Geiger was serving me up to them to cut long, wide, and deep because he was still pissed, half a year later, that I had called him a liar before the national championship game.

When my attorney and Jim Brown said this was bullshit, that's what they were referring to. This was some bullshit. And this is where it was obviously personal. Geiger called for the investigation. He called the NCAA about this. He gave me up.

Eventually I think Geiger even told the NCAA to turn over the tapes of my interviews to the OSU police so they could charge me with falsifying the police report that I never made an insurance claim on. That's how vindictive he was. I got prosecuted for that underhanded shit.

I didn't realize it at the time but this was all totally personal for Geiger. I had tarnished his shining moment as an athletic director by calling him a liar. He'd never won any championships or performed on a national championship stage and you better believe athletic directors want the glory from what players do. And not just the glory, the money.

A couple years ago, OSU's athletic director got a $18,000 bonus when a badass wrestler won an individual weight class at the NCAA championship. You tell me what Gene Smith did to deserve that. Logan Steiber probably trained his entire life for that and he gets a plaque or a medal around his neck and goes back to his apartment to eat ramen noodles and the athletic director who was already making a million dollars gets another $18,000? That doesn't make any sense.

It was just absolutely personal for Andy Geiger to try and make me say I lied about the value of the CDs. I had called him a liar but he wanted to show that I was the liar. But I was like No, people, I didn't lie. I didn't lie,

I didn't try to get any money off the shit that was in the car—I didn't do anything to try and profit off this.

Geiger started the entire investigation of me but once we got inside it, I don't think he realized how bad it was going to be. At first, he just wanted to try and damage Maurice Clarett. This is when Jim Brown got involved and was saying, Yo, you're not trying to save this kid from the streets—you're trying to kick him back out into the streets. Jim Brown knew from the jump that this shit was a sham.

Whenever we would have conversations in private with Jim Brown and my lawyers there wasn't anything like let's figure this out because there wasn't any figuring it out. There was nothing to figure out. You can't make sense out of something that makes no sense, you know?

This was more like a big slap in the face to me. This is when Jim Brown was like screw you too and called Andy Geiger a slave master because he was acting like he owned my ass and could whip me himself or have me whipped by the NCAA.

But as amazing as it sounds with me losing my career at Ohio State, I'm totally cool with it. What else was I going to do, carry the football a few more times? Maybe win the Heisman? I've got bigger goals for my life than carrying a football and being known as someone who won a Heisman or even two. I'm doing everything and more than I ever hoped to do for other people now in Columbus and Youngstown by working with kids in underserved communities. That means more to me than saying I won a Heisman when I was 20.

Right now, I've got a hundred social service professionals providing resources for kids growing up in the streets like I did. We're trying to show them that their lives matter. And I'm supposed to regret not carrying the football a few more times? A few more concussions? A few more surgeries? That shit isn't going to happen. We're making a difference in these kids' lives and what difference would a few thousand yards have made? Maybe a few more knee surgeries or shoulder injuries—that's about it.

As for the first investigation interview, I just went with my mom and a local lawyer. I had met him in the fall before I even got big. He had

CHAPTER TEN: OUTCAST

represented my close neighborhood friend, so I called him and said, Yo, can you help me out.

I just thought a lawyer was a lawyer, and I didn't understand personal injury lawyers and all that shit was so different and specialized. He was a lawyer and Compliance had told me I could bring a lawyer. So I brought him and he did the best he could.

The interview took place at St. John Arena. I showed up there just planning to tell the truth and I didn't have a clue why they were coming in to talk to me. I didn't even know the police report about the car was a thing.

When they started asking questions about the car, that's when I realized what this was all about. These people were just asking me my whole life story in a two-hour window and then they go out with everything on the tape and on their notes and they go investigate and call you back in two days later and they don't leave town. They ask you questions and they investigate them. This is what we did for 2 weeks. They interrogated me five times trying to get me to throw the entire program under the bus.

They were under the impression there were these boosters who were just passing out money to us. So they came at me with every star player's name—asking me did this guy or that guy get benefits. They wanted me to rat out the entire team or some shit. You can't make this stuff up and the NCAA should be ashamed of their tactics. It's unprofessional.

I think college football has this mystique from the 80s that there are boosters hanging outside of the locker rooms and shit saying, Hey Maurice, nice game, here's 10 grand. If it happens in the SEC, I don't know. But at Ohio State you better believe it didn't. Around Valentine's Day, you'd have guys on the team—starters and stars—borrowing $20 from each other to take their girl out for dinner. So, hell no, there weren't bags of cash floating around that I ever saw.

I called Jim Brown after the first interview, when I saw things going south. I had met him after an awards banquet in Cleveland. Me, Jim Brown, and LeBron all got awards at that banquet and he said if you ever need me just call me. So I called him to say things are going left. They were asking me all sorts of questions and it comes to a point you don't even know if you're in trouble or not.

When the NCAA comes after a kid, they just start asking questions and you don't even know if you did things wrong but I was just trying to answer in the safest way possible to protect my teammates instead of just telling the entire truth.

Put it like this, you know teammates might have done something wrong by taking some things but there may be other things that you don't know if they're wrong or not and I was just trying to protect everyone's ass.

Everything in Columbus involving OSU is so unbelievably complicated. It got to a point with my lawyer, and this is probably just local politics, but it got to a point where I knew he wanted to defend me but he didn't want to be portrayed as the bad guy to the local crowd. He might have loved me but he wasn't going to sacrifice himself to save me because he had to keep working and making a living in Columbus long after Maurice Clarett was gone.

So Jim Brown was there for the second meeting. People were telling me Jim Brown was a troublemaker and I shouldn't be talking to him. The second meeting was more of the same but Jim Brown was sticking up for me. Jim Brown was able to figure out all the bullshit that I couldn't pinpoint—especially all the bullshit from Andy Geiger. He could easily see all the intention behind what Geiger was trying to do to me and why.

Then the NCAA started asking me all the stuff back to my high school days. This didn't even make sense to me and this is where it got out of Geiger's control because if I was a dirty player then we should have given back the national championship trophy. I still don't know what the hell Geiger was thinking, to this day, other than he was going to show this kid from the streets of Youngstown he was the master on this plantation.

We had 3-4 meetings after that, and I was like, to hell with it because I knew it was going downhill. The wheels were off the cart and there weren't any brakes. I was being held out of camp and wasn't allowed to go to practice. I should have known it was all over when they didn't let me in the team photo at the start of preseason camp.

CHAPTER TEN: OUTCAST

At some point, they told me they were suspending me "indefinitely" and I didn't even know what "indefinitely" meant.

They put stipulations on me, saying I had to go to psychological counseling because I was lying about everything and I was thinking, I was lying on purpose to save their asses and save the university from giving back the trophy. And this is when the punishment runs came in and trying to make this an inhospitable environment for me to be in. They didn't know what to do with me and were just hoping I could go away.

They let me on the sidelines for the first game of the season but then they said the TV camera was focused too much on me, which wasn't anything I could control anyway.

Then they made me re-enroll in completely different classes without the help of my adviser and they took away my tutor and other support and required me to get a 3.0 if I wanted to get reinstated. Once they started doing that shit, I knew it was over and I was ready to get the hell out.

They brought me over to sign my separation paperwork at the Schottenstein Center. I had to go in and there were all these attorneys. I didn't even know that attorneys ran the university at that point.

Archie Griffin was there and I was just thinking he had sold me out, letting these people do this to me. I can't deny it—that's what I was thinking at the time.

Who knows, maybe he didn't even want to be there and maybe he knew deep down what was happening to me was wrong. I'm certainly not blaming him and I know he's a good dude but that's exactly what I was thinking then.

I would handle things absolutely different today, but I still take pride in the fact that as a 19 year-old kid who helped bring the university a national championship and then got kicked to the curb that I told Archie off that day. I'd never talk shit to anyone now but back then, I was standing up for myself. Powerful people expect powerless kids to go away with their tails between their legs but not me.

Archie was sitting on the other side of the table all the way on the right and a bunch of lawyers were trying to read all that shit in the agreement to me and I was like, Yo I don't need you to read this shit to me. I knew what

I did was wrong but they knew nothing I did warranted me getting kicked out of school. They had their championship, which they were protecting, and they were done with me.

So when they got done reading, I looked Archie in the eyes and said, Fuck you, man–how are you gonna let these motherfuckers do this to me? I was hurt, sure, but I knew justice wasn't being done here and I wanted to let him and everyone else know that I understood the hypocrisy of it all.

At the end of the day, when you really want to say what I did, I borrowed a car. I drove a car. Someone loaned me a car. In my mind, I'm thinking, I just made all you tens of millions of dollars. Tens of millions, going out on the field hurt, with swollen ankles, a hurt shoulder, and headaches. I took long-ass needles in my joints and had surgeries and there were like hours on end I killed myself training and conditioning and they let this happen to me.

Even as a younger man I knew sometimes you could stop shit and have a real conversation with a dude, like, Yo, this shit just ain't right—we've taken shit too far so like, let's just stop. And this is what I thought could have happened. This is what I thought someone like Archie could have done—stopped this shit and said we've taken it too far and let's figure out a way to save Maurice because I meant something to OSU and they were invested in my development as a human being who was going to represent OSU for the rest of his life. But that didn't happen.

Often times now I'll find myself in different white circles and I'll find myself being a black voice for other black people who don't have a voice. So I was looking at Archie like, Dude, you're supposed to be a representative of me, of us, in some capacity, because you're right there at the table. You're on that side of the table with all those white dudes and I'm over here by myself.

But at that time, I was just thinking that dude doesn't give a shit about me. So I told Archie off from across the table. They were trying to walk me through this entire process and I was like to hell with this process and I got up and told him how I felt and walked away. I told him you should have understood what I was all about based on where I was coming from and you might not like everything about me but to sit there on that side of the

CHAPTER TEN: OUTCAST

table with them and let them kick me to the curb like this forever and end my career? C'mon, man. That shit wasn't right.

Pretty soon after that, I left. At first, I stayed in Columbus, re-enrolled in class, and got a couple girls to help me out. I was reluctantly accepting the process and I still wanted to be here at Ohio State. I wanted to handle my business and play for the Buckeyes even though I can see now that it wasn't ever going to happen. They were satisfied to get their one championship with me and then have a separation.

Even to this day I still love Ohio State. I love Ohio State and the pride that people have and the enjoyment they had watching us play football. It's like anything else, it's like a guy puts so much time into making this a thing in their life and they have success, so they fall in love with that.

But the politics and the disdain for certain individuals wasn't sustainable. I'm not even mad at modern-day Andy Geiger, but in that moment, we were both equally to blame. I don't care about the rhyme or reason now, but even as a human being you get wrapped up in your ego and your emotion and you do shit you probably wouldn't do if you weren't so emotion- or ego-driven and I think a lot of shit came from that place. Like a lot of shit might have come from his thinking, Who the hell do you think you're talking to? I will screw you over completely and run you out of town.

But at the end of the day, I'm not mad at Andy Geiger and I don't need an explanation. In this present day, that shit from back then makes me think, Damn, I made it through that shit, so no matter what happens with everything else, I got this. I can do this, whatever it is. It helps me tap into shit and helps me recognize like who bad people are. I can recognize now when I see an Andy Geiger in front of me. I was just a young kid playing checkers and he was playing chess, but now I'm playing chess too.

After I left OSU, this is when depression hit, 100%. This is probably what guys feel when they're 25 and they're done playing football and they can't do anything else, that's what I experienced at 19.

This was a total separation of everything I had built up to since I got out of juvenile detention so I could train and play high school football. I was right back to being that 14 year-old who had broken into my neighbor's house.

I was adrift in the middle of the ocean. I'm talking about depressed. From day to day, I didn't have any mood changes, no nothing. For me, depression really just felt like being absolutely numb. It's not like life was hard all of a sudden or I couldn't function—my depression was more like I was numb toward everything. Nothing really resonated and I didn't feel anything ever.

I started forcing myself to party just to have some feelings in me at all. I was sensation seeking, 100%. Whether I knew it or not, I had been sensation seeking in the stadium every weekend when I was playing. Like I was trying to get some gratification—I was a thrill seeker trying to get yards or get in the end zone. And now I didn't have that and that thrill had been a part of my life since junior high, 12 or 13 years old, and I couldn't find that feeling anywhere else. The easiest way to find it was with drugs and alcohol. The thrill of pleasing the fans had become a drug sort of thing so I replaced it with actual drugs.

I was partying with anybody who would party. There were a few dozen guys from Youngstown who had moved down here. We had been partying so much during the previous season that they got places here and then it became a thing and so many Youngstown guys were here in Columbus.

All I remember from that fall was trying to have a good time because I didn't have a life. Whenever anybody saw me, the first thing they would ask me was when I would play again and I didn't have any answer for that.

I was drinking, smoking, and popping pills to alter my mood. Tylenol 4, Xanax, prescription drugs. All that fall during the football season I was missing, I experienced a gradual decline.

I was still living in my aunt's condo in Gahanna and I started working out at the Westerville Athletic Club but it wasn't like real training for anything. I was partying at night and working out during the day so I wouldn't get fat and this is the time that I started hustling again, picking up right where I left off at age 14.

CHAPTER 11

HUSTLER

ONCE FOOTBALL was out of my life, I basically had nothing positive to guide my orientation. In early-2004, I was still in Ohio and I went back to hustling and selling drugs. The same shit I was doing in junior high.

Think about it—I was the same person I was at 14. There hadn't been anything done to correct my behavior or the orientation of my thinking. The only thing that had changed since I was 14 was that I got really good at football.

So, I was selling dope and weed. In the process of that, I almost got robbed a few different times before I finally left for Los Angeles. The last time, when I was down here in Columbus I almost got robbed and I thought, You know what, I'm getting the hell out of here. Everything was happening too quick. This was like the 3rd time in the matter of a few months someone had tried to rob me because they knew I had a lot of cash around.

The first time I almost got robbed, I was pulling up in front of my mother's house in Youngstown and was just in the process of parking in the driveway. Some guys were in back of my mother's garage and I'm pulling up in my Suburban, and they were running from the back of the garage— through the small alleyway between the bush and the neighbor's garage.

They must have known I was coming back to Youngstown. You know, when you are hustling, you never know how you're going to get robbed. Nobody knows the person who is going to rob them, but it is always someone who knows they've got cash on hand.

When you're in the streets, people are watching you, whether you know it or not. If you're making moves and you're in the streets, somebody is going to be like, okay, how can I position myself to rob him so he doesn't know. This isn't a territory thing, this is just jack boys who want money. Jack boys are just people who are trying to rob other folks. You got people who hustle and people who rob. Jack boys are people who rob and I was somebody who hustled. So I always had to watch out for the jack boys.

I didn't know these particular jack boys. I was mainly hustling in Columbus but traveling back and forth to Youngstown to sell dope there too. I had guys working for me—distributors. So I pulled into my mom's driveway and the jack boys come sprinting past the garage toward my truck with guns out and I threw the car in reverse and I'm backing up as fast as I can. Luckily my mom wasn't home because I didn't want to endanger her even though of course I was by bringing this to where she lived.

I hurried up and motored away and they didn't shoot because they couldn't get me and they had to get out of there too. They were masked-up but they still had to get away and gunshots were only going to complicate that and weren't going to get them the money because the money was driving away.

After I left my mom's house, I just drove straight back to Columbus and hit the reset button thinking, Oh shit, this is how shit happens.

I called my mom and told her you can't go home—you have to go to a hotel and I'll pay for it. I told her the truth about almost getting robbed and she didn't know all the details of what I was doing but she knew I was out there in the streets but there was nothing she could do about it. That's the harsh reality—if you're a mother, you know your kid is doing wrong but there was nothing she could have said to stop me. I was a man on a mission and nobody could have told me nothing.

In fact, my oldest brother Michael was still in prison in Belmont, near St. Clairsville, at this point so she knew about the streets but she never really responded to this.

Even to this day, there could be something major and there's no real response she can give. Mom would go to visit Michael but she never talked

CHAPTER 11: HUSTLER

to me about staying out of trouble. She must have known when I got kicked out of OSU that I was just gone, mentally, and there was nothing she could say to me.

Just imagine, it felt like football was gone and I was grieving part of me that died—the biggest part of me, maybe the only really well-defined part—and there wasn't anything else I could do but hit the streets. I had lost everything. There was heavy depression at this point but I couldn't identify it. I was medicating myself with drugs and alcohol but I just called it partying which is a much cooler and more socially acceptable name than depression.

In retrospect, I was partying heavy and I enjoyed the partying because that became the convenient distractor. I wasn't isolating myself but at the end of the day, I was still drinking and getting high but it was inside the club so it didn't seem like depression because we're taught that depression is this isolating thing. This was depression for sure but it was one long party with a lot of people and a lot of music.

In 2004, Columbus had a thousand little bars and clubs all along Rt 161 and Morse Road and then there were a lot of scenes downtown so there were a lot of places to party. I could go anywhere and would be recognized for sure.

What should have been my sophomore year, when I was 20 years old and out of football, was like still being in the prime of my life. I was still a relevant person in Columbus. I was still somebody and I was just having fun and all of the women were there and I was with them and doing everything else but when I look back on it, I was totally abusing alcohol and drugs.

I wasn't getting arrested or having any close calls with the law at this point. There wasn't anything violent or super heavy criminal, either. It was just women and parties and hustling—that's what my entire life revolved around.

Trying to get to the bare bones of it, I was an alcoholic then. I was addicted to alcohol, pills, and weed. I was getting high on everything all the time and drinking probably 4 days a week.

When you feel like you lost something that you were attached to and it was ripped away, you absolutely give up. Football was that for me—at this point, I didn't care about consequences because the thing that I cared about most was taken away. I had never even dreamed of being 45-50 years old or an old man. I just wasn't imagining any future for myself.

When I was younger, all I had ever been thinking in terms of a long-range plan if you could call it that was from watching MTV Cribs. No joke. It got into my head that that was what life was about and that's what people were supposed to try and get. For me, this was the height of everything and I really thought capturing that lifestyle would be some cool shit. I was just thinking how could I purchase a cool car, a cool house, and my behavior was basically only driven by what can I do to pursue this vision for my life.

At this point, as the 20 year-old Maurice, I'm trying to facilitate this vision of a nice home and a nice car. That was success for me. There was no 401k or trying to have a family. Go back and watch MTV Cribs—ain't nobody working with underserved kids in poor communities or even sitting down paying bills on that show or changing diapers.

The only version of success to me at that point would have been through houses, cars, and women. Football had been nothing more than the vehicle for me to get where I really wanted to go to attain that.

So when football was gone, there was no understanding of how I could create a life through school to attain that lifestyle. Selling drugs became that vehicle because that's all I knew—football and the streets.

See, if I notice a guy rolling down the street, looking like he's got money, I can ask him how he got all that and get a roadmap for myself. People have the misconception that it always has to be drugs. It could be selling bottles of water if they sold for a high price in the streets. It could be selling anything really.

So the question just becomes, What product can I sell to facilitate the lifestyle that I want? Drugs were just the thing because in my whole life all I ever saw getting sold was drugs. There wasn't anything else I've seen from an entrepreneurial side in the streets other than drugs. Nobody was selling computer software or insurance. It wasn't that I wanted to abuse the community and make people sick, but selling drugs is what I had seen so this is what I knew.

CHAPTER 11: HUSTLER

After I almost got robbed the first time, I knew I needed to roll with some more people. I needed guys who could be my security or be around me to be my third eye. Knowing about or thinking about getting robbed wasn't abnormal on the streets. That's part of the program. It's no different than a manager at a Wal-Mart knowing that when you open the doors, people will try and steal and you have to deal with it.

The way I tried to deal with it was making sure I was protected and I was watching how I moved, watching when I was in my house, how I was protected in the house, how my doors were guarded and different things like that. I had to do this for where I was living in Columbus and Youngstown.

The second time I almost got robbed was at a friend's house in Youngstown. I went to pick up some money from a guy who worked for me and literally some jack boys were waiting for me. It was basically a set-up.

The guy who owed me the money was trying to set me up to get robbed. I figured out based on what happened that he told guys to come and rob me when I was getting my money from him. I didn't anticipate it at the time but looking back on it, it's no surprise. He was supposed to give me $7200 and I went there thinking I was just going to get it and go about my business. But after I pulled up in his driveway, these two guys in masks started running up to my vehicle with guns drawn.

The friend who owed me money had came out of the apartment complex and one of these guys was acting like they were tackling him and the other guy came at me. It was all just a big set-up and then they both started running toward the car. I took off and was thinking to myself well if they shoot him, that's part of the program—he's gotta die. If it's a robbery and they kill him, he gotta die but I couldn't go back and help him because I didn't have a gun on me.

I was coming from Olive Garden and I had my two cousins with me and I just thought I was going to go pick up this money and didn't take my gun with me. Even though my cousins were also hustling, we usually didn't go out to the suburbs to eat carrying guns because there was a possibility of getting pulled over. I was just supposed to be picking up money from a friend and I didn't think it was necessary.

Basically getting out of there was the same thing as at my mom's house the last time. I whipped my Suburban over the curb and took off before they could get any shots off. This was like a scare tactic robbery, not a real robbery. If a car pulls up and I'm going to actually rob somebody, I'm waiting on the side and I'm not going to run to the front of the car, I'm going to run up to the driver's door and I'm going to shoot you and take your shit.

But with these guys, they came to the front of my car and I could see the hesitation. If you're pointing your gun at the windshield and you haven't shot yet, you don't actually want to shoot and you don't want to rob nobody.

As I was driving off, we called my friend's brother and told him his brother was getting robbed and he needed to go check it out. So he goes over there and his brother was fine. This was what tipped me off that it was a set-up.

Nobody goes up on you robbing you and don't shoot you in Youngstown Ohio. So that was red flag number one. The other red flag was that nobody else knew I was going there except my friend. This had to have been planned in advance and I knew the only person who could have tipped off the robbers was my friend.

After this robbery attempt, all I could do was return to Columbus and just keep living my life. The third robbery attempt on me was at my condo in Strawberry Farms. I was at my house, hanging out with my guys, and we were getting ready to go to a nightclub. It was just a normal Saturday night going out to our favorite club. My mother was there and in fact, when she was arriving, with everything that was going on, I told her to call me from the end of the street so I could walk her into my apartment.

At this point, I was very paranoid because so many people were making moves on me and I knew I wouldn't get away cleanly every time.

So, not long after I got her in the house, my mom started cooking chicken alfredo and I remember this like it was yesterday. She was just coming down to Columbus for the weekend to visit me and cook for me and my buddies. They were there and my guys decided they would go around the corner to where they lived to get dressed and then come back and we would go out.

CHAPTER 11: HUSTLER

As they left, they got in their car and I heard my landline phone ringing, which sounds crazy like we were in the 80s but the phone was ringing and their horn was blasting so I got to the phone and my guy said, Go grab your guns, some dudes are in your bushes.

I was thinking, Oh shit. He said that as he was backing out of my driveway, he saw these guys hiding in the bushes creeping up on my house. It was 8 or 9 at night and just starting to get dark.

I got into the front closet after I told my mom to go upstairs. This closet was by the front door and I got my AR-15 in there so I'm sprinting to the closet thinking at least I got this gun so if they kick through the door I can try and defend myself.

I didn't want to wait though, so to make a long story short, I open up my front door up and as I'm doing this, these two dudes are sprinting away from my place like they're scared. Their cover was blown and the element of surprise was gone. I oughtta thank them because actually they could have grabbed my guy and pulled him back into the house with a gun on him. But that's a pretty personal, up-close, hand-to-hand way of doing it and I think that their plan was to just kick in the door and rob me.

So these guys took off on foot and I ran into the house and I went upstairs to where my mom was hiding and said, Let's get the hell out of here. But first for some reason I remember my mom went down to the kitchen and put the food in the fridge, and on our way out the door I grabbed a bag with more than a hundred thousand dollars in it. I had been making some real money.

Mom was nervous as hell so we went to the Hilton at Easton and shared a room. The next day, I took her back to the house so she could get her car and she went home to Youngstown. I gave my friend the keys to my apartment, money to pay the rent for the next month, and told him you can have the chicken in the fridge and everything else because I was going to California.

CHAPTER 12

PLAINTIFF

Before I left for LA, I got connected to Alan Milstein through William Wesley, aka World Wide Wes. He was the guy who was instrumental in LeBron getting the Nike deal and that's how I knew him. He said I had to get in touch with Alan Milstein about challenging the NFL.

I had only met Alan in New York once and after that we talked on the phone. He really wanted to take on the NFL. I had flown to NY at his expense with my mother and basically we made our case. He was footing the bill 100% for all this and he put us up in Manhattan and he was saying we could win—we could beat the NFL.

It all started by filing a complaint in federal court. We filed it in the Southern District of New York. It was an antitrust case, claiming that the NFL's rule that players had to be out of high school for three years before being eligible for the pro football draft was an illegal restraint of trade. I wanted to work, so why couldn't I sell my services to the highest bidder? It was as simple as that.

Alan and the other lawyers argued that the three-year draft rule violated antitrust laws, and wasn't sheltered by the nonstatutory labor exemption. This exemption shields certain rules from the antitrust laws if they affect wages, hours, and working conditions, are collectively bargained, and primarily only impact the NFL and the NFL player's union, not strangers to that relationship. Like, they can agree on certain terms that only impact themselves but not if they impact outsiders trying to get in.

In this situation, there was a rule that wasn't collectively bargained, didn't affect wages/hours/working conditions, and in fact only impacted strangers to the relationship, namely people like me.

Here I was, suspended by the NCAA and not allowed to play for the Buckeyes, and not allowed to enter the 2004 draft either, because even though I graduated on December 11, 2001, my high school class's graduation was June 2002. By the NFL's rule, I had to wait until 2005 to be eligible. This had been the rule since 1990, I think.

My lawyer filed the complaint, Maurice Clarett vs. the National Football League, Inc., on September 23, 2003. OSU had announced a week or two earlier that they were suspending me for the entire year, so I didn't have much choice.

I think OSU announced this to try and stop the NCAA investigation. It was pretty clear that if it had continued, it would be easy to figure out that I was ineligible the entire 2002 season and OSU would have to return the championship trophy. Not wanting this, OSU gave me up and this is when Andy Geiger even had that restaurant paint over the images of me in a mural commemorating the national championship game.

But this is how he thought and how the NCAA thinks, like when they have schools remove championship banners years after the fact or vacate wins. What the hell does that even mean? The guys on the field that day played those games and they know who won and who lost. The fans who were there or watched on TV know who won and lost, but the NCAA engages in some serious revisionist history.

They also engage in some serious inconsistencies, like how a NCAA wrestler can get tens of thousands of dollars from a "foundation" for winning a gold medal or a world championship in a sport they're currently competing in collegiately. OSU has a guy right now who got $50,000 for winning a World Championship and $250,000 for a gold medal in the Olympics in Rio and went right back to compete for OSU and won another NCAA national championship. Don't get me wrong, I'm happy for the guy—who seems like the baddest Buckeye of all time—but this shit doesn't make any damn sense either if we're all supposed to be amateurs and you got young black kids

CHAPTER 12: PLAINTIFF

getting kicked off college football teams for selling their jerseys for a few hundred bucks or trading them for tattoos. And the NCAA is going to kick their asses to the curb but allow a wrestler to make a quarter million dollars?

It doesn't make any sense what the NCAA did to Jeremy Bloom back in 2002 either, making him quit football if he wanted to train and compete for the U.S. Olympic ski team. That shit is expensive and the only way to do it is to have sponsors. The NCAA wouldn't let him have sponsors in skiing and still play football so he tried to sue them for the chance to play football his last two years but he lost. It's almost impossible to beat the NCAA in court unless you're Ed O'Bannon and that case was so straightforward that no judge could have screwed him over.

My case against the NFL was filed in New York and at first it played itself out all on paper. Milstein was filing motions and I didn't even understand what he was talking about. All the legal mumbo jumbo about labor law—I didn't understand that.

I got so many calls in regards to things I didn't know about and Alan was doing everything he could for me, but the truth is, I think I was just the right plaintiff at the right time for him.

In fact, Mike Williams from USC, who had hired an agent and declared for the draft, was also ineligible to play and wanted to fight the NFL. So there was some momentum that it wasn't fair of the NFL to exclude us.

I was 6'0", 230 lbs and Williams was 6'5", 235 and there were plenty of players in the NFL smaller than us. There are cornerbacks in the NFL who are 5'8" or 5'9" and weigh only about 180. I'm not sure why we needed to be protected.

In fact an NFL team should have been able to draft us and either keep us on the roster and only play us a little if they didn't think our bodies were ready for it, or keep us on their practice squad, which functions like a minor league baseball team almost. But the NFL doesn't want to have to pay to develop players because that means less practice squad jobs for guys chasing their dream.

My case was assigned to a judge named Shira Scheindlin. I found out later she had gone to Michigan but she must not have held that against me, because she granted me summary judgment in the case on February 5th, 2004.

The opinion of the court can be found online easily enough, just google 306 F.Supp 2d 379 (2004) and you can find it. It explains how my claim falls under the Sherman Antitrust Act, which is something I had heard about in high school history class. It was supposed to improve the economy by eliminating monopolies. Essentially we were arguing that the NFL didn't have the right to place this restraint on people who wanted to work in the NFL.

One thing that the judge noted in her decision is that I was bigger than some of the best running backs to ever play in the NFL: Walter Payton (5'10", 200), Barry Sanders (5'8", 203) and Emmitt Smith (5'9", 207).

In her opinion, Judge Scheindlin also quoted someone named Learned Hand, who said antitrust laws would never allow a contract which prohibited someone from practicing their calling. I would still never say that football was my calling, but it was my way out of the streets of Youngstown and it could also deliver me from a life of hustling which was probably going to get me killed if I stayed in it long enough.

Even when Alan called me to tell me we had won, he warned me that it still wasn't over. There was really never any celebratory moment for when we had won something. He knew it wasn't over. Actually I never stopped hustling, trying to take care of myself, and Alan never asked me how I was living or how I was paying my bills.

So the case wasn't over but at least for a short while it seemed like I needed to get myself back in shape and in the mindset to play football again. This wasn't easy, because I was in the streets for real now.

The draft was a little more than 2 months away and so I was trying to workout at a gym I had joined in Westerville, but this wasn't really training. I was just basically keeping myself fit.

First, I had to go to the NFL Combine in late-February in Indianapolis. This is where NFL hopefuls are poked, prodded, and evaluated by scouts. They are expected to run, jump, and go through drills. There is even an intelligence test, the Wonderlic, which players take and results are sometimes

CHAPTER 12: PLAINTIFF

leaked to the press to embarrass them. It's all a big show and basically like a slave market.

I wasn't in shape at all when I showed-up in Indy, and felt like I was missing my moment. I weighed too much, ran too slow, and had a chip on my shoulder during the interviews. I had a hustler's mindset and I knew a lot of teams were turned off by me.

In the meantime, the NFL was trying to appeal the original ruling. The 2nd Circuit Court of Appeals would make the next decision. On March 20th, they agreed to hear an expedited appeal from the NFL and oral arguments were set for April 19th.

I didn't go to those but my mom did. I knew they were happening and she told me how they went after they were over. I wasn't at all surprised when the Appeals Court announced, on the same day, that they were reversing the case. One of the three judges on the panel that reversed the decision, in favor of the NFL, was Sonia Sotomayor, who is on the U.S. Supreme Court now.

Basically, the appeals court said that the NFL was allowed to create any rules it wanted through the collective bargaining agreement with the union for the players. Like kids on a playground "locking" a game at the start to keep out other kids who come up and want to play.

I was out of luck but I wasn't surprised because there's just no way that a kid from the streets of Youngstown was going to defeat the NFL, no matter how unfair the rule was.

The appeals court decision, written by Sonia Sotomayor, was so bad that a consultant helping my attorney, a guy who was a law professor at Michigan State actually, said later that her decision was as results-oriented and poorly reasoned a decision as he'd ever read.

His name was Robert McCormick and he got involved because about twenty years earlier, he had written an article explaining how this rule, which was then that in order to be drafted we had to be four years removed from high school, was what was called a group boycott and was an illegal restraint on trade. He consulted with Alan but ultimately the appeals court rejected their arguments and sided with the NFL.

He would have his students read the decision from the district court in my favor and then the appeals court decision which went against me. Judge Scheindlin's decision seemed clear and fair to them but the circuit court's opinion was convoluted and made no sense.

The appeals court just did what the U.S. Supreme Court did to Curt Flood—slamming the door on both of us black dudes trying to fight major sports leagues.

In fact, Professor McCormick said the judiciary did a grave injustice to both of us and I believe him. What rationale could the NFL have for that rule that would honestly survive a common sense test...size? I was bigger than a lot of the backs who were drafted. Age? I was actually older than three of the guys in the 2004 draft. That shit doesn't make any sense.

If a 19 year-old has an NFL body and NFL mindset, why shouldn't he be able to make some money off it? That's the American way. The NFL rule is flat-out un-American. There's no other way to say it.

The way I ran was so physical, running dudes over, and getting into the secondary where safeties had open season on me, that I wasn't going to be able to play like that forever. I just wanted a chance to earn some income off my talent before I completely broke down.

This is going to keep coming up, too. Wait until that QB from Clemson, Trevor Lawrence, who started as a true freshman and led them to the national championship, does it again as a sophomore. He's 6'5" and 215 lbs as a 19 year-old and will probably be 225 by next year and the NFL is going to try to keep him out?

Eventually, Goodell is going to have to do what the previous commissioner, Paul Tagliablue, did in 1990 when he just changed the rule himself overnight from four years to three years. Barry Sanders had been allowed to come out after winning the Heisman as a junior and a bunch of other juniors, including Andre Ware, another Heisman winner, were ready to sue the NFL the next year. The NFL couldn't keep inventing special circumstances like they did for Sanders—that his team was going to be on probation—in order to preserve a rule that doesn't make any damn sense.

CHAPTER 12: PLAINTIFF

This is America and people with skills have to be able to sell them in the market to the highest bidder.

Changing this rule wouldn't even be hard—Goodell could just announce it. Otherwise, the NFL better lawyer up because you better believe Trevor Lawrence is gunning for them and I'll be right there for him.

CHAPTER 13

ANGELENO

I HAD STAYED at the Hilton in Columbus for a couple days after that robbery attempt and then I got on the plane and went to California on a one-way ticket.

The whole reason to go out there was trying to connect with Jim Brown. During the suspension, he had flown me out to Vegas in November for the Roy Jones-Antonio Tarver fight at Mandalay Bay. He was also having a big fundraising banquet for Amer-I-Can that he wanted me to attend.

While I was out there, he told me that I needed some structure in my life and I should come out to California. He had planted that seed and said he'd hook me up to some of his guys.

He didn't know I was hustling—or maybe he did. I don't know. It seemed like he just thought he was trying to help a guy who was scuffling and trying to get himself together and he was going to try and help me get to the NFL. He told me I had no structure in Ohio once football was taken away and I needed to come out there and get in shape. He knew 100% that I needed to get out of Ohio and get myself together.

When I got to LA, he didn't know I was escaping—he just thought I was coming out there to get myself ready for the draft.

First I connected with someone I met at the Amer-I-Can banquet in Vegas. She picked me up at the airport and brought me from the airport to the Sheraton near Hollywood and Highland.

I arrived there with about 10k in my pocket after stashing the rest of the money with a friend. I went there without any plan other than to connect with Jim Brown and I had a mild interest in trying to get my shit together. I wasn't thinking at this point that I could still have football. The appeals court ruling in my case against the NFL, in May 2004, meant that I wouldn't be eligible until the 2005 NFL draft, which seemed like an eternity.

My goal in getting together with Jim Brown was just to get some direction in my life. Just as a human being, the streets were basically going to take a huge toll on me, mentally and physically and I didn't plan on living my life in the streets. As glorious and attractive as some people may make the streets look, I was cool on that shit—that was not my deal if it didn't need to be.

At that point, I wasn't even thinking about getting sober because once I got to LA there was just a party all the time. I only cared about having that MTV Cribs party lifestyle and I guess I wanted to quit hustling because it was killing me slowly.

Looking back on it, for sure I would identify my drug and alcohol use as a problem, but then, it wasn't like I had a problem drinking. The drinking and drugging came from the crazy lifestyle because of the stress of the life I had been living when I was hustling. It makes sense.

So I let Jim Brown know I was there but he wasn't in town and wasn't going to be in town for a week. I remembered I had a homeboy from Youngstown out there, Rufus Blaq. I called him and said, Hey man I'm in LA, let's go out and party. I never knew there was just a whole other level of partying out there.

Rufus had grown up on Ravenwood, just down the street from me, and he was out there working as a musician. He has written for Beyonce and other heavy hitters. He had made it out of the streets with supreme talent, phenomenal talent.

Rufus had originally gone to NY then he went to LA as his career grew. He was probably 5 years older than me and my mindset was that we could just have some fun out there.

We had spoken before I went there in fact because we had mutual friends and we all kept in touch so it was cool for me to hit him up when I went out there.

CHAPTER 13: ANGELENO

I stayed at the Sheraton for about a week and a half just partying the entire time looking at the women and the party scene and I was thinking this was really the life. I went there by myself but I just kept meeting people as I partied.

Nobody out there had any clue who I was. I was totally anonymous and I loved it. I knew LA was a different scene but once I got out there I just started living and enjoying the Hollywood scene which is a party every night, on Sunset, Vine, and Hollywood. I mean every damn night I was partying.

Pretty soon I met a guy who took things to the next level—Hai Waknine. I met him at his beach party. Through one friend or another, some girls I had been partying with found out there was a beach party going on in Marina del Ray so we went out there. It was some of the craziest shit I'd ever seen.

He had a 7000 sq. ft. crib on the beach and beds on the beach and cabanas everywhere and it looked like his house was a hotel. I was partying there all day with those girls and later that night we were sitting around bullshitting and he was like, How the hell did you end up out here?

He just meant how did I end up at his party with those girls. He had no clue who I was and didn't know nothing about college football.

Just for some context, it was normal for there to be like 8 girls and 1 guy hanging out together in LA. People like me I guess just like to be around women and all these women ended up wanting to go to his house.

In fact, there must have been about 100 people at his party and after that night, Hai and I just ended up being cool. One thing I know about Hai is that he was just a fun dude with a good attitude and a big personality. He was a fun dude—always laughing and joking and just having a good time.

I think the synergy between me and Hai was this—he owned a tremendous amount of real estate and what happened was that he was going through a federal indictment for extortion and basically the RICO act.

He was already on trial and he actually had an ankle monitor on during this whole period. This was my new friend and there was no business to it—it wasn't like hey you're headed to the NFL. These dudes already had tons of money. Any contract I would have got would have been chump change to them.

He's already living in a huge house on the beach and has a half-dozen exotic cars. This was the MTV Cribs I'd always seen on TV but in real life.

I can remember being at his house and he'd send his driver to get five grand from Washington Mutual. From the time we got up, there'd be 20 people at breakfast, and 20 people at lunch. We were going to Katana for dinner all the time.

Just think about this, I remember a sushi bill at Katana was fifty grand for a month. I was just a spectacle in his lifestyle and I was with him every day. For him, it was like let me see if I can help this guy as something to do. Like a toy, almost.

You can say it became something fun for him to do. At this time everything is a party so this dude's whole life is a party, everywhere we go.

LA parties every day the way someone parties for New Year's in a place like Ohio. Everybody comes to LA to have the time of their life. Monday-Sunday there's always a major party.

So, in my mind, I had made it. I wasn't training or hadn't made it in the NFL. But if you are staying somewhere and there's a Bentley and a few Mercedes and a Rolls Royce, it becomes intoxicating in itself and even though it's not mine I was still benefiting from all of this, hanging out with all those women and being a celebrity with the people.

Hai was like a celebrity, a major figure in a major city, and he created this lifestyle where I didn't have to do shit except just go workout. And the money I had was enough to live on.

My brother Marcus was wiring me money whenever I needed it. I was working out just to stay in shape but not training to try and take over the world. This went on for more than a year in LA and in April of 2005 I get drafted.

I had gone to the Combine in February and I was in shape from a workout standpoint but I hadn't trained and I didn't do any skill work.

CHAPTER 13: ANGELENO

I wanted to go through the motions and have those experiences but there wasn't any huge motivation to go to the NFL. I didn't even think it was possible after sitting out for 2 years.

I wasn't really that into it because I didn't think I could get drafted. In fact, when I was at the Combine, I didn't even talk to anybody from the Broncos or Shanahan. So during the draft, I watched it out of curiosity but I didn't expect to get drafted.

When I was watching the draft, it started making me more depressed like, Yo, this shit hurts. I was seeing people I played ball with and those people are getting picked and I was like, I'm not.

So I got in the car and went for a drive. At this point, I got a phone call from Denver's front office when I was driving on the freeway. After I talked to the first person, Shanahan got on the phone and said, Welcome to the Broncos. He said they'd have someone from the travel department hit me up to arrange a flight to come go out there to do media day.

The Broncos had taken me 101st, with the last pick of the 3rd round, which is all they do on the first day. A few running backs got picked ahead of me but at least I didn't have to wait overnight to see if I was going to get picked on Day 2.

So from there, I went out to Colorado the next day. That night we celebrated and partied. I went to Hai's house but it might have been like passover or some shit. So the day I got drafted there was some get-together or party or whatever you want to call it so I told him I got drafted and the people I had made friends with, we went out and had a good time drinking and drugging and the next day I got on a plane to Denver.

CHAPTER FOURTEEN
BRONCO

Somebody met me and the other draft picks at the airport, and took us to their facility, and it was game time.

Denver didn't have a first-round pick that year because they traded it away. Then they took 3 cornerbacks in rounds 2 and 3 and then took me.

They didn't pick until #56, in the second round, and they took Darrent Williams, who only played two seasons before he was murdered.

He got shot and killed after celebrating New Year's just a few hours after the Broncos lost and their season ended without making the playoffs.

I guess him and his friends had gotten into an argument with the shooters at the club earlier in the night and they tracked them down and shot up the limo they were riding in. This shows you that even when you think you're out of the street life, it can find you.

I had a clear fear from the jump that I wasn't good enough to make the Broncos. That fear set in when I got drafted. My first thought was when I hung up the phone. I thought to myself, I can't do this shit.

It wasn't as much of a fear that I wasn't good enough to play in the NFL as much as it was I knew I wasn't ready. Take this into context: I had been the high school player of the year as a senior, and I knew the amount of physical work I had to do even to prepare to be a premier athlete at that level. It took an incredible amount of film study and a lot of physical training.

Then I got to college and we won a championship and I was the Big Ten Freshman of the Year. I knew the amount of work it took just to be that guy.

It was a full-time job literally for 12 straight months from the time I arrived at Ohio State the first week of January 2002 until I scored the winning TD in the national championship game on January 3rd, 2003. It wasn't just natural ability—nobody comes out of the womb ready to perform at that level.

Then to go to the NFL, I hadn't done a fraction of the work needed to be halfway decent. So, I knew the wheels were going to fall off the car at some point. I guess thinking about it more, I wasn't scared, but reality set in that I wasn't going to be prepared to secure this opportunity. I just knew it.

Right after the draft, we did the media day in Denver and at first, I stayed in Denver. I don't remember the first time I went back to LA but when I was in Denver, my lifestyle needed to change so much and to wrap my mind around being a responsible football player just wasn't there.

I had gone to the rookie retreat in Florida where we went to a bunch of classes but it wasn't of any value to me. If I were in charge of that now, I'm not even sure there's anything you could do with most guys to reach them but I'd like to try.

Actually, they should do a retreat for guys who get cut and are out of the league. That's when guys would listen because that's when shit is real and football is over for them and they need to start their lives. That's a massive transition because all they've known is football since they were 8 or 10 years old and now it's gone? It's like, who am I and what do I do now? That's when people will really listen.

After the draft, I had immediately started to workout 100% Monday-Thursday, basically like conditioning workouts before spring practices. They put us up in one of those extended stay hotels near their practice facility. They gave me a rental car and I was conditioning four days/week and starting to be friends with the other draft choices.

Just like with any rookie I was meeting people, starting to understand who they are, starting to get the feel for the team. They had 5 RBs at that time, Mike Anderson, Ron Dayne, Quentin Griffith, Tatum Bell, and myself so it was a full stable.

Even at this time, I understood the business of it. They were paying Mike Anderson $5 million so I was thinking there's no matter what I do,

CHAPTER FOURTEEN: BRONCO

he is going to be the starter. I still wanted to earn some playing time but I always had that reality. In my head, I started to get into shape but I knew it would take me an entire year just to get revved back up.

My contract was all motivated in order to try and get more money. I had another lawyer who negotiated it for me. He was a criminal attorney, but he understood contracts. So it got broken down to, you know, the third-round contract was $410,000 guaranteed but after paying your agent and your taxes and just your fees and everything it really dwindled down to not much money based on how I was already living.

Like now of course, four-hundred grand seems like a ton of money but back then, based on how I was living with Hai, my lawyer and I were trying to figure out how to get millions. So I had a contract that was trying to bet on myself. This was 100% my idea. I was prepared to bet big and win big or go home with nothing.

A lot of that was engineered because I was kind of getting it together. You have to remember Jerry Rice was on the team at the beginning of that season. I was #20 and Jerry Rice was #19 and I started for real looking at John Lynch a lot, following him a lot, paying attention to how he practiced and how he prepared and how he got himself together. I was trying to learn on the fly from these guys about how to be a pro.

It was sort of working and if I been going to practice for a few years in a row, gearing up for years, I don't think my body would have broke down the way it did. But when you're just partying and sometimes you go to the weight room and sometimes you don't and then you try to do strenuous activity, it's too much of a major jump.

Actually, I was still drinking and partying all through minicamp. We were partying from sundown to sun-up during camp. The vodka in the water bottle story was some bullshit but the hangovers coming to the facility were 100% true.

In fact, during rookie minicamp right after I got drafted, I was flying back and forth from Denver to LA on the weekends. I would leave Thursday afternoon, get to LA and stay there until Monday morning and I would catch a flight and get to Denver about 9 o'clock and be able to work out Monday-Thursday.

If I could say now what broke down, traveling back and forth to LA to still live the LA lifestyle, that was a huge breakdown. I was still partying and those habits that I had built the previous year or two caused that breakdown. I was having so much fun there that going to Denver was living in a completely boring place compared to what I had came from.

During the regular camp, in July and August, I would party in Denver with guys. Even though you see professional athletes on TV and you think they take care of things but the majority of them, if they weren't playing, they were partying or hanging out.

But I took it a little too far because I was hanging out a lot longer than I should have been. We would have practice at 7 o'clock but I would be leaving the strip club about 5 or 6 in the morning and I was either still messed up at practice or at least had a hangover at practice and that happened several times that I could remember.

The Denver folks tried to connect me with their sports psychologist between minicamp and regular camp but I pushed the lady away. She had an office inside the training complex and we had like one little small session but after that I was like, Nah, I'm cool. I think there was just a racial, gender, and age difference that made me not want to talk to her. She could have been the best but I just wasn't ready. It wasn't the right platform.

I was going out all night to the clubs, strip clubs, and rolling straight to the facility still drunk or hungover. This was just not going to work out because the lifestyle I had built in LA was totally the opposite of what a professional athlete needed to be doing.

Even though it was detrimental to my career, I enjoyed the lifestyle. I still enjoyed the women, the parties, the drinking, the drugging, the pills, and the weed. I just totally enjoyed it. I didn't feel like I was doing anything wrong because I was enjoying myself, if that makes any sense.

When I finally started to get things together in camp, I for sure wanted to make the team. 100%. Outside of the partying, when I was actually taking part in camp, I started realizing I could really do this shit.

CHAPTER FOURTEEN: BRONCO

I was enjoying the football and even to this day I think the NFL wasn't really as hard as I thought it was going to be. I was just so far out of shape when I tried to enter the NFL that it wasn't going to work.

But if I had been drafted just a few months after the national championship game, still peaking, still in my prime and still hungry—it might have been a completely different story.

Our pre-season schedule was Houston, Arizona, San Francisco, then Indianapolis. I was there for the home games but didn't fly to the other ones.

I think if we could be honest, and I had all the management from Denver sitting around the table, when I started to have success on the field in camp, they were like, We're not going to put him in the game because if we put him in the game and he has success, how are we going to cut him?

That became very frustrating. I got into it with the running backs coach and it was like here we go again with this shit. I was 5th on the depth chart but I was performing and should have been moving up.

I was having open discussions with the coach like this is some bullshit, you know I should be out there playing and getting some reps but they were probably already thinking we're going to cut this guy because he's too much of a headache.

It wasn't that coach's fault, it was my fault, 100%, for doing all the bullshit I was doing but now I see the political side of it. This feeling started as soon as I started getting better, lifting more weights, conditioning, and really getting into football shape. That's when I started feeling pushback.

I was trying to fight for space, fight for reps on the team, and it just wasn't happening. It wasn't like I was screwing up. Sometimes the folks in Denver say he was drinking and they show a picture of me dropping a football but the truth was the total opposite. I was balling—balling in practice, balling on special teams, but there was some other shit that overshadowed that to make it look like I was a total screw-up and it became easy to believe the narrative once you hear all the other shit that happened after I was cut.

It didn't help that I got hurt in the preseason. I hurt my groin during the second week, during the second game we were playing.

An injury was inevitable. Just the wear and tear caused it. There wasn't a big hit. I just don't think my body was prepared to take the punishment from the rigor of running and hitting all day long. Too much wear and tear and I wasn't conditioned for it especially because I was still drinking every night.

They kept me around after the injury but I got cut after the last game so I stuck around for four games. Being real about it, it got to a point in camp where I was doing great and people were like saying, Oh, Shit, I see what he can do.

It got to a point where Gary Kubiak, the offensive coordinator, was like I get it about how good he can be and what people see in him. But then you got five running backs, one you're paying 5 million to, one you're paying 2 million to, another is making 800 thousand, another is getting 700 thousand, and here's a guy who is actually a headache and we got nothing invested in him.

Gary knew that if I got my shit together, I could be competing with those guys. But my attitude and my isolation and not being a good teammate or professional really got me penalized.

They cut me after the 4th game. We played the Indianapolis Colts and the next thing you know I was gone. I never got on the field that day. They brought me in the next day and said, Oh man, sorry it has to be this way—we wish you could have made it, we gave you an opportunity and you didn't secure it.

Shanahan was the one to tell me and I wasn't even embarrassed about the fact I got cut because I thought I was good enough. The fact of the matter was I understood it. I wasn't like what the hell are you talking about, I was like, I get it. At this point, I was thinking 100% I could play in the NFL. In fact, I believed it even more more after going through this. I thought I could do this shit if I got serious.

CHAPTER FIFTEEN

CUT

After I got cut, I walked out of Shanahan's office, cleaned out my locker, and I was done. I flew back to LA and this was September '05. I went straight back into the party lifestyle that I'd really only left for a few months until I decided to get out of LA.

Back in LA, I felt a little bit bad at first but was just in a state where I had to get my shit together. Getting cut was motivating and humbling at the same time. I was only in LA for like two days before I decided to leave for good this time.

The first night I went out back in LA, I was at a club party probably with 500 people. This was the first time that I had been drinking and smoking and I neither felt high or drunk. It didn't have any effect on me. I was thinking this was not it. I was super disconnected from the environment. We drank and smoked before coming to the party but I was emotionless and numb and it just wasn't doing anything for me. There was no sensation at all, just a feeling of emptiness—nothing like I was hoping to feel.

To tell the truth, I had been in a club where someone from Destiny's Child, Kelly Rowland, was performing, and I remember in the midst of being in this massive party that I was just so incredibly depressed I was like, To hell with this—I'm done with this. I just felt out of place partying and hanging out—it just wasn't fun any more. I think getting cut was the most difficult time in my life. It was more difficult that leaving Ohio State because even then I knew I would get a shot at the NFL.

I got up and left that party and I realized I gotta get my shit together. I thought I could really play in the NFL so I wanted to go back to Ohio to reunite with Tressel and hopefully get myself together. That was the whole thing—at that point, I believed I could have football back.

So I left there and I was like, I have to go back to Ohio. One thing that I always enjoyed was instruction. My high school coach gave a tremendous amount of instruction and Tressel gave me a lot of instruction, so I was like let me get back to Tressel and just hit the reset button.

I called Tressel as soon as I got back to Ohio. They were just starting their season when I went to his office at the practice facility but the guy's door is always open for me. Throughout my entire life he's done everything he could to help me succeed.

I sat down with him and he gave me a roadmap for how to get ready to go down to Orlando in December for a training camp for NFL Europe. His idea was for me to get back into class and start working out and get into playing shape, go to the NFL Europe, and then try and get back to the NFL.

So I started to get in better shape but I didn't re-enroll in class because to be honest, I didn't have the money for that and I couldn't just slide back into my scholarship. That opportunity was long gone.

The next thing I knew I had a shitload of free-time on my hands and then I started to get into trouble, hitting the streets, hustling weed, going back to the bars, and hanging out.

At this time, I was living in Columbus near Little Turtle off of 161. I was working out at this performance training facility at The Continent. This was a bunch of former players who wanted to get back in the league or guys playing Arena Ball. I figured I could train and rehab my groin but I was bored as shit and I didn't have any money and the only thing I knew how to do to make money was selling dope.

I was trying to create the same system I had before I went to LA. I was still getting dope in Columbus and selling it in Youngstown. This is what happened between September and December.

I got caught back up in the life and didn't end up going to Orlando for the NFL Europe training camp and at this point, it was like I was done with

CHAPTER FIFTEEN: CUT

football for good. My big takeaway from my experience in Denver, that I could do it if I wanted it, got lost in the process.

On New Year's Eve, I was just hanging out with some friends and decided I would rob a guy I knew.

The whole idea this time was trying to move on an individual who I knew would have money because he owned a club and it was New Year's Eve so he would be flush with cash.

I was actually at home when I decided this but I had a friend inside the club. I told him to call me when he saw the owner start counting the money and get ready to leave.

I had been robbing people my whole life. This was the life when I was in the streets in Ohio. So in this time period when I was getting robbed before LA, I was also robbing other people or setting them up to be robbed. In the streets, you're either robbing or getting robbed. That's the first law of the streets and this is a pretty horrible space to be in.

This was the era too of the whole make-it-rain thing, with guys just throwing around thousands of dollars at the club and I knew guys would be spending money and this guy who owned the club would have money. I didn't have any animosity toward him—it was just business as usual.

I did have previous run-ins with him though that made me think he wouldn't do anything after I robbed him. So this made him a target.

A few weeks earlier, I had been in his club, the Opium Lounge, with a buddy who liked the man's wife. So when me and my buddy would come to the club, he would flirt with the wife and the wife would flirt with him, but the owner of the club was too scared to say anything to that guy. Instead, he would talk to me and tell me to say something to my buddy to get him to stop flirting with his wife.

I was cool and cordial and I liked the guy enough to go to his club and hang out. But even though I was cordial with him, I still wanted to rob him. It was just all about the money.

I was at my house and I got the call so I rolled down there and by the time I got down there and got to the alley, I thought I saw him come out the back door. It was a dark alley and there were two people walking towards me so I thought it was him and his wife.

I started walking toward them with my gun in my belt. When I get to them, I realized, Oh shit, this is not him. But I thought, Screw it, I'll just rob these two.

I didn't have a mask on because I was thinking I would intimidate him like, Don't call the police or I'll shoot your ass. So I was walking up to these other two and my head was down, and the hood from my sweatshirt was over my face. It was so dark, so they couldn't get a good look at me and I didn't think they'd recognize me anyway.

When I got near them, I said, Hey, get over here. They couldn't have known who the hell I was and I didn't have any clue who they were. I just said to them, Give me all your money.

The guy said, What is this?, and I said, Stand still—you know what this is and if you mess around, I'll shoot your ass.

I checked his pockets and her pockets and didn't find anything. They were smart and when they saw me coming, they hid all their money in their underwear. All I could do is grab their phone. Even though it had no value to me, I took it because I didn't want them calling the police immediately.

After I robbed them, as I'm walking back through the alley to my car, the wife of the owner of the club actually came out the back door of the club and was walking toward me. If you can believe this shit, she called out, Hey Maurice!

I grabbed her and said, Come here, don't go back there—I just robbed those people. She said, Oh shit, that's my sister. So she jumped out of my arms and I tried to grab her but she was gone.

I panicked and instead of going and giving them their phone back and apologizing, I got in my car and I left and the next thing you know, I woke up in the morning and it was all over the news that Maurice Clarett had robbed two people at gunpoint early in the morning of New Year's Day.

CHAPTER SIXTEEN
ASHLEY

I woke up on New Year's Day and my mom had called me asking what the hell happened. I was in bed with Ashley and she didn't know so I had to go to the other room to talk to my mom.

Ashley and I got together in March of 2005. I was living in LA, but I was returning to Columbus periodically. When I came back this time I didn't have anything to do from the street standpoint. I think I met her when I was in Columbus to do a pro day before the draft.

Two of my buddies and I ended up going out to a club called The Red Zone.

I went there the night I met Ashley with a guy, Preston, who was cutting my hair at the time and another guy. Preston's shop was on Morse Rd between Cleveland and Karl. To make a long story short, we ended up at the Red Zone and I saw Ashley's sister there.

I told her to call Ashley and say that I loved her and see if that would get her to come out that night. She started laughing but she called Ashley and the next thing you know, Ashley showed up and we all hung out in that nightclub.

I had known Ashley from being around campus when I was a student. Ohio State is huge but it feels really small if you're black. Something like 5% of undergrads at OSU were black. Most black students kind of run in the same circles and go to the same places.

After Ashley got there, we went to a private section of the club and partied all night, hanging out, having fun, going to the Steak n Shake at Easton after the club closed.

So the next day, I went to visit Ashley and we sort of hung out. I told her I was living in LA and invited her to come out and told her I'd send her a plane ticket.

I went back to LA and a few weeks later, Ashley came out to visit. When she came out, she stayed for about a week. She stayed at my apartment and partied the entire week. I was showing her around LA and making sure she had a good time.

She went back to Ohio, and then I ended up getting drafted and moving to Denver. We were still communicating and talking all around that time. She also came to see me in Denver sometime that summer.

When I get cut by Denver, I came back to Ohio and I ended up moving into the apartment that she had just moved into. I was coming back at the same time so I ended up moving into the place with her.

Ashley was still a student and finishing up at Ohio State. She was majoring in logistics in the business school. She graduated in December in fact.

I was hustling all that fall and I found out Ashley was pregnant probably in about January, right after I was arrested for the robbery on New Year's. We were headed to Red Lobster and her mother was supposed to meet us there and the dinner wasn't to tell her she was pregnant, it was just a regular dinner.

But when we were on our way there, we were at the Shell gas station near it and Ashley was like, I'm pregnant. So I thought we might as well tell her mother.

At dinner, we told Ashley's mother and a month after that she went to this doctor for prenatal care and then we just started the process of becoming parents. It was a combination of things—this was more stress than I ever felt. It was more indecision than I could handle and I was wondering what the hell was going to happen with me becoming a father because I had these charges against me.

CHAPTER SIXTEEN: ASHLEY

After the robbery, I had just gone home and went to sleep and turned off my phone but when I woke up on Sunday morning, it was already in the news and it had already reached Youngstown so my mother was calling me. Even though I had taken their phone, the people I robbed just went into the club with the owner's wife and called the police and said Maurice Clarett had robbed them.

But when I had gone to sleep that night, having run into the owner's wife after the robbery, I didn't think this would go to the police. I didn't go to sleep thinking I was in trouble.

In Youngstown, there are robberies all the time and nobody goes to the police. If you live a street life or if you've been in the street or you've been connected to the street in any capacity, robberies are the lay of the land and you might do a lot of things after you get robbed but going to the police isn't usually one of them.

I mean, if you're an upstanding citizen, tax-paying, American contributing-to-society-citizen, you can go to the police and file a crime report. But from being in street life, it's my experience that nobody goes to the police.

The story broke in the news the next morning, New Year's Day. I woke up and my phone was going off and my mother was calling me and everyone was calling me. I guess they were surprised, but looking back on it, this was just inevitable. It was an unavoidable step in this downward spiral. After football was gone, I didn't know anything else so now when I look back on it, I recognize the inevitability of it, 100%.

With me being all over the news, I knew I had to turn myself in. I didn't do it that day though because it was Sunday. I didn't want to sit in jail any longer than I had to. I thought I would get my things in order to prepare myself to get a bond and so the next day, late at night on January 2nd, I went down and turned myself in. Actually, I waited until OSU beat Notre Dame in the Fiesta Bowl because I wanted to see the seniors from my recruiting class go out with a big win.

A lot of lawyers had already been calling me and they didn't care if I was innocent or guilty they just wanted the publicity of representing me. My lawyer's plan was to take me down to the police station, let me turn myself in, and already have the bond money lined-up but regardless I was going to have to spend the night.

I got processed in because this was armed robbery, pretty serious stuff. I went to my cell, and there was a bond hearing the next day. After that, I posted the $50,000 bond, and then at that point I was released from the facility. All of this took place on January 3rd at the Franklin County Courthouse, not far from where the robbery took place.

At this point, my life was so messed up that this didn't even matter to me. I wasn't thinking this was a big deal. I got released and got back to life. Now I had to figure things out because Ashley was already pregnant.

I had gone back to her place after the robbery but even the next day, there wasn't much to say to her. You have to put your mind in the mindset of living in the streets. There wasn't anything to say at this point like everybody knows it's messed up. It's no different than seeing someone in a bad situation and there's nothing you can say.

Things were obviously very very bad. I was kicked out of school, kicked out of the NFL, I had a criminal case, and I had a baby on the way. So at this point I was in super-survival mode.

Ashley wasn't cool with this at all but she didn't know what to say. She didn't know what to do. A person came into her life and wrecked it right after she graduated. For a large part, I derailed her plans of one day going to get a job in corporate America and starting her path after 4 years of college.

Actually, Ashley's father was in prison for 17 years but she didn't have any experience with guys in street life even though he had been in prison her whole life. Ever since she was a little kid her father had been in prison.

He was in prison in Texas for 17 years but to this day, she doesn't mention it and I don't ask her. This isn't something we talk about. I don't ask her about it because it's her business.

She obviously wasn't cool with her dad's situation but there wasn't anything to talk about. She knows the situation with me was messed-up but she also knew she was pregnant.

CHAPTER SIXTEEN: ASHLEY

So, at this time I'm in this space where I have to make something happen because I had a criminal case. And when I say make something happen, I mean, make big money to give her before I get sent away.

This was the first time I had been arrested as an adult and my juvenile record was expunged and didn't exist but I knew I was going to serve some time because I had a gun on me when I robbed those people.

Ashley's mother never expressed it, but I can only imagine what her mother was thinking about me. And it couldn't have been good. Her mother had sacrificed a large part of her life to put her daughter in the position she was in as a college graduate.

So imagine my daughter. We're sacrificing a lot to put her in a position to succeed and achieve up to her potential and if somebody came, you know, kind of like at the goal line—you graduate, you score a touchdown, you're moving your life forward and then you get tied into a pregnancy with a guy, and you get tied into a criminal case with a guy. A large part was probably that the circumstances looked like the life she was coming from.

So I was thinking I had to make some money. I was thinking I had to get in the streets and put in more work and make more money, 100%. I know I'm going to jail at this point because it's armed robbery and I've never been a fool. One thing I've never been is stupid. I know when I'm wrong.

I was smart enough to say, you know, you're Maurice Clarett in Columbus, Ohio and I couldn't deny it was me and I wasn't about to lie and bring other people in my mess.

Even at 22 I knew that. Unless I had an alibi, I had to admit it was me. Pretty quickly, the court set my trial date for August 14th. So I was rushing against the clock, I had 7 months to get my life in order. I knew I was going away for a few years.

CHAPTER SEVENTEEN
BIG HUSTLER

I WAS HITTING the streets full-speed January to August. It was all hustling and robbing and it wasn't an everyday thing but I was looking for people to rob, looking for ways to hustle. Hustling dope, hustling weed, hustling anything I could get my hands on just to flip a dollar. Just to make some money. So I was making money, reinvesting it back into product, and taking care of myself and my family.

Ashley and I had gone and purchased the crib and all the supplies and were buying everything we could afford. It wasn't like I was making hundreds of thousands of dollars at this time. You have to figure, when a guy in the streets has a robbery case, the street says I'm not dealing with this guy.

Even in the business world, you have a reputation and based on that people do or don't do business with you. In the streets you have credibility and it's all based on what you've done in the past and if you're honest and credible.

After my arrest, the word on the streets was that Reese was out there robbing people. The street guys, who had never given a damn that I used to be Maurice the football player, now looked at me like is he going to rob me if I do deals with them. Will he do that to me?

So people started keeping their distance. If a person's reputation is shot, it makes it very hard to be in the streets. In the streets, you have to be inconspicuous. You have to make the world move without being visible. You have to be discreet.

So, now, when I had a case against me and I was on TV for robbery, now I'm trying to do deals with people and nobody wanted to deal with me. I was radioactive. I had a criminal case and people were even wondering if I was cooperating with the cops and only trying to do deals with people to set them up.

I was in desperation mode and I would buy anything I could get my hands on to sell. So if I got into a hustle today, there would be some rhyme or reason to that hustle. I'm going to put a lot of thought into what I do before I do it and only do things that make sense.

But when you're desperate, you will buy anything you can get your hands on to sell. I was just trying to make money—doing deals and robbing people. And of course I was medicating myself for the entire year of 2006 with drugs and alcohol. My life was in desperation. I was trying for big hustles but wasn't being smart about it at all.

If I had known the clinical term delusional, I would classify myself as delusional or temporarily insane. I was probably sleeping consistently only 3 hours a night. There was a point where I remember Michael Jackson dying from pills and the nature of it was that he couldn't sleep and I went through a period for all of 2006 where I could not go to sleep.

It got to be frustrating that I couldn't lay down and go to sleep for an entire night. I don't know how it feels for other people but it felt like I was crazy because I just couldn't rest my brain. My brain never shut off so I could relax.

I tried Ambien, I tried Melatonin and I just couldn't do it. So the only way I could knock myself out was the hard pills: Tylenol 4, Xanax, Vicodin. And I washed them all down with alcohol. This would just wipe me out medically.

I was so full of anxiety and depressed and confused about the criminal case. I was anxious and confused because my baby was coming and I wasn't prepared for that. That gave me a sense that I had to do something but I didn't have a viable way to get out of these hard situations so everything became primitive and animalistic.

CHAPTER SEVENTEEN: BIG HUSTLER

I was in survival mode. This is why I understand the work that my social services agency, The Red Zone, is doing right now. Because I needed help back then. I was gone, just like some of these people we're working with now in Youngstown and Columbus. They're gone and we're trying to bring them back.

When you're in the streets, your circumstances are so extreme. You got no education, no skills, no anything to apply to the world to improve your situation. Think about this: I played football my whole life and it was gone. I didn't take school seriously so a straight life was off the table.

Then I had this dependence on alcohol and drugs, which is the biggest deterrent for any human being. And now I had a criminal case on top of drug and alcohol abuse. So when it's time to navigate life and figure this out, I couldn't even figure out the first step.

The only thing that made sense in my head was like, with most kids, let me grab a gun and solve my financial problems. Let me sell some drugs and solve my financial problems and if I could solve that, I could begin to sort other things out.

But getting a gun spurred its own level of problems. I would be awake in the middle of the night plotting on people, waiting on people to come out of clubs, waiting on people to take out their trash to grab them, doing so much stuff that was just devious.

I was doing all of this between Youngstown and Columbus. It was open season at this point and Ashley didn't have any clue that this was going on. For a large part, she was naïve about what's going on. I was going back and forth a lot at this time robbing and hustling in both cities.

My targets were all people on the street, all stuff that I set-up in my head. From being in the streets, you know who has what or you're connected to somebody who knows what has something.

Then at that point, you're just plotting. At nightclubs you're plotting. Nightclubs are one of the most dangerous places to be because you get intoxicated and once you're intoxicated and you're in the streets and you got money and at the end of the day you're looking for a girl and you're either going to end up in a hotel or at your house.

ONE AND DONE

If somebody wants to rob you, it's not very hard. If it's the middle of the night and it's dark, as long as you have the courage to sit in somebody's bushes or on the side of the house or behind their garage, you just grab them and take what they got.

The streets are super dangerous and I wasn't doing the waiting in the bushes but I could set things up to have people do things. I could orchestrate. I wouldn't say I had a crew exactly working for me, but we were working together. Life in the streets is just super dangerous. People who rob people are always watching and observing everything. Just watching and watching and watching.

Once you're into the streets, everything is fair game. I was fair game for somebody else and somebody else was fair game for me. Once you establish you're in the streets, you know without a shadow of a doubt who has what.

Why do you think guys carry guns? You have like minor wars in people's neighborhoods that aren't identified as wars because we're not in Iraq and we don't have uniforms on but these wars are just as significant as guys fighting for the country.

So even though it may be trivial, like we could call fighting for oil trivial, these guys are fighting for respect and for their families and they're fighting for territories. The nature of what we were doing was just like a war.

We were trying to capture somebody's money. It was a power thing. Let me come and capture your treasure. Let me plot. Why do you think those pirates sit in the sea, just waiting. They want what other people got and are going to do everything possible to get it.

The pirates are thinking let me catch one of these boats coming over here with these goods: if I catch you out of place, if I catch you in a vulnerable spot, I don't really want to kill you, but I'm going to rob you. This is the streets. This is why guys align themselves with other guys. It's not a gang. It's more like a united front for whatever we can do.

So for me it was a combination of both, robbing and selling. I don't remember the exact guns I carried but I had a lot of guns that I was keeping at my mom's house. She didn't know too much though, and I was keeping other guns in Ashley's house, like the AK-47.

CHAPTER SEVENTEEN: BIG HUSTLER

* * *

Ashley had moved into my mom's house before she gave birth. So one night, we were driving around Youngstown and Ashley wanted something to eat. This was actually a couple months before the baby was supposed to be born.

The only thing open was Taco Bell and once we got there, she said something like, I'm in pain, severe pain. So we went to the Akron Children's Hospital in Boardman and they were like, Hey you're about to drop this baby, and she ended up having the baby the next afternoon.

When I held Jayden for the first time, I was legitimately scared. I was thinking, what the hell am I going to do? Now I got this baby in the world that I'm supposed to take care of. And this is when I decided I needed to make those witnesses against me go away.

First I tried to buy them off and then I thought I was going to have to kill them. In my warped way of thinking, that was the only way to stop them from coming to the trial to testify and talk about what happened. In my mind, at this time, this is what made sense to me.

I was thinking my life would always be in the streets, selling drugs forever or doing something criminal in some capacity. I wasn't thinking about getting my life on the straight and narrow.

Ashley couldn't have said anything to get me to stop. I was too far gone. I think my situation paralyzed her, in a way like, What the hell do I do?

Even if Ashley's mom had begged her to come home, I don't think Ashley would have done it. Even now, Ashley is sort of a caregiver. She has always been trying to help me balance myself out. Because of the baby, she must have felt like she was connected to me and she needed to help me get myself together.

This may be a blessing in disguise, but I realized early in our relationship that Ashley's really quiet. I've been to a million places and she just never talks. But post-prison, her attitude and her disposition has changed because she had to take on the role of the father and the mother, taking care of Jayden. She is more vocal about how she wanted things. But prior to prison, she was just super-silent. She was even more silent if something was detrimental, like the situation I was in then.

I was doing all this other street life and was also trying to do the deal with the people I robbed who were the witnesses against me. I offered them 15k not to testify against me. I was trying to get the owner of the club to broker the deal for me. I asked him if he would tell them I would pay them not to testify against me but they didn't want anything to do with it.

It may also have been that the club owner might have felt disrespected and didn't want anything to do with me. I was trying to pay him to help me make these people go away but I realized it was failing.

So I made the decision to make my move just based on the life I was living. This is a perfect example of street-life decision-making. It was go to court, go to jail, or kill them and it all goes away.

My lawyer had their address to serve them subpoenas or motions. So one day I was in his office and he got up from the table and there were still some papers there. I looked through them and saw the address of the people I robbed. I committed their address to memory and put the papers back where they were.

I had this address in my mind for a week or two and I was thinking that I was going to try and kill them. This wasn't anything I had done before, but for whatever reason at that time I was comfortable with the thought. It is a lot to talk about it now because I understand my mentality and my mindset from where I was in my life then.

I was desperate and I was vulnerable. I was mad and I had to try and get out of this situation. At the time, I thought I was a gangster—a guy who is supposed to eliminate his problems by killing them, not taking responsibility for what I did. There was no level of responsible thinking on my part throughout this entire deal. Even though I'd never killed anybody, death and dying and murder had been a part of my life since I was a kid and this is what I was thinking.

I'm not surprised when I reflect on it now. I understand where I was at mentally. When I was in the streets, my mind was in an extreme mode. My level of intensity and danger was at an all-time high every single day

CHAPTER SEVENTEEN: BIG HUSTLER

because of my circumstances. So, I don't believe I was a horrible individual, or inherently evil, but given the set of circumstances I was in, I needed to be dangerous to survive.

Somewhere along the line I figured out that you solve your problems by killing people. That was the level of thinking I was functioning at. I had been witnessing gun battles and executions from the time I was a kid growing up. That was Youngstown and people got killed all the damn time for a lot less than this.

I had pulled the trigger on my gun before but I had never shot anyone or been shot. Put it like this, only through the context of trying to rob people was I shot at. Or in the context of our house getting drive-by'ed was I shot at, but I was never in a gun battle. It was never me and other guys going directly at somebody to shoot at them.

So on August 8th, I went down to Columbus and tried to put my plan into action. I was caught by the cops for a U-turn which is the saving grace of my life. I don't know how I could ever live with myself if I had done what I set out to do. My life would have ended that day too, for sure.

It is the luckiest thing in my entire life that I got caught by the police that night and I was lucky that I didn't try and shoot it out with the police.

I might have thought I was ready to die back then when I was in the streets, but I look at my life now and what I'm doing for young kids all over Ohio, for their families, and for college football and basketball players who I spend a lot of time going all over the country talking to, and it would have been a shame if things had gone differently early in the morning of August 9th 2006. In fact, even if I had killed the witnesses and gotten away with it, I think my existence as a responsible human on this planet would have been over as well. God had his own plan for me and everything worked out exactly the way it needed to when I got pulled over. That was some sort of divine intervention for sure.

CHAPTER EIGHTEEN
DEFENDANT

There was a lot of unnecessary drama around my case and how much prison time I would serve. Looking back on it now, there was one unbelievable scene that showed me how messed-up what we call justice can be sometimes.

Actually, this happened in July, when I only had the first robbery charge against me. It was before the police chase in August.

I had a few attorneys when I was free on bond waiting for my court date on August 14th. In July, one of them called me and said I needed to come to his office for a meeting with him and my other lawyer to talk about my defense strategy. But when I got there, there was this third guy there, who I'd never seen before, and a 6-pack of beer on the table.

As a matter of fact, the other guy turned out to be the prosecutor if you can believe that. He was there but I didn't know who he was. Nobody had told me anything about a prosecutor being there, which made no sense anyway. And someone had brought beer, like to the law office, in the middle of the day, which also made no sense.

I was sitting down, in this office, and my lawyers were talking to me about my case. So I'm thinking, I understand who you are, and who this is, but I don't understand who this dude over here is. So my two lawyers each grab a beer and they are sitting back and they're talking and I'm like, hold up a second. First of all why are you guys drinking beer in the middle of the day and secondly who's this other guy? They were like, Yo, he's a prosecutor. So I look at them like, what the hell?

At this point, the prosecutor speaks up. He says, Maurice you can just tell me what went down and I can get you a year on the gun charge and a few years for the robbery but you will be out in like a year or two.

But I'm thinking, Man, what is this bullshit? This was some convoluted bullshit. My immediate understanding was that my attorney-client privilege was out the window. I figured that my attorneys must have told the prosecutor everything I told them and they were just making some sort of backroom deal so I got out of there as fast as I could.

After all this bullshit, I immediately called another attorney, Mike Hoague, who I got introduced to through one of my friends. So I told him what had happened and made a deal for him to be my lawyer.

Pretty soon, I had to go to the hearing. I went with one of my original lawyers but he had no clue about what I was going to do. We got to the hearing and my lawyer was sitting with me and Mike Hoague was sitting in the courtroom too.

So in open court, I say to the judge I have something to say: I want to remove my original lawyers because your guy, the prosecutor, came into a meeting with a 6-pack and he was trying to get me to drink with him and my own lawyers were trying to get me to do a deal.

And the judge was like, What the hell? To this day, the judge still probably doesn't understand what was going on or what they were thinking. Nobody does, certainly not me. The judge was asking me—was this dude on county time, this prosecutor who was trying to get you to drink and socialize with him and your lawyers?

I said it seemed like they were trying to serve me up like he's guilty and let's just make a deal with him and get ourselves a little publicity in the process. But at that time I was like to hell with it, I wasn't doing it.

The judge granted my request to have a new attorney and my lawyer was pissed off and left the courtroom and I never spoke to him again. It turns out he used to be a prosecutor himself and was probably friends with this other prosecutor and they thought it would be cool to tell their friends they drank beer with me while making a deal to send me to prison.

CHAPTER EIGHTEEN: DEFENDANT

This was all while I was out on bond before my second arrest, but after the car chase I stayed in the Franklin County Jail while the prosecutors were figuring out what they were going to charge me with. At first, I hoped to get out on bond but it was set for $5 million so there was no chance of that.

I was pretty eager to have my trial and hoped to keep the August 14th trial date, but the judge ordered a mental health evaluation and moved it back to September 18th. I didn't think I needed this at all but didn't have any choice.

Throughout the process, I had to decide if I would make a plea bargain or have a trial. The trial was going to be complicated because my attorneys were afraid the jury might be biased against me. There were just too many variables and the maximum sentence was at least 30 years.

I was facing more than 10 felonies for the robbery and the car chase and I soon started to realize that they had information where it doesn't make any sense for me to keep on trying to lie or convince them that I was innocent. Plus the people I robbed were dead-set on testifying against me.

When they brought me from the jail to the court on the day of the trial, I was with Michael Hoague. He ended up basically talking to me, saying Hey Maurice—they got everything they need. They had solid witnesses and there was no need to push this thing any further because if I gambled on a trial, I could end up getting 30 years.

Michael also told me that if I plea bargained, I would get some leniency on all of my charges. Whereas if I went to trial, it was a roll of the dice and they would be mad at me because I wasted their time and they could maximize my sentence on all of them. So I thought it was in my best interest to make a deal and plead guilty to two of the felonies and accept my punishment.

I pled to one felony for aggravated robbery, my original crime, and the second felony of carrying a concealed weapon, based on the car chase. I was definitely going to prison for a few years and there was no getting out of that.

All throughout this period, the discussions I was having with Ashley were very vague—being in jail was new to everybody. She had just had a baby at the time, and would be taking care of her on her own, so anything above a year seemed like an eternity.

I'm pretty sure this was all just surreal to Ashley. She had just graduated college and now she had a baby and she was involved with a person who was going to prison for several years.

With my mother, it was more of the same. She had lived through this with my brother Michael, who was currently in the Ohio State penitentiary in Cleveland at the time.

The short stints I did in juvenile were nothing compared to this. I plea-bargained to seven and a half years but the only thing that meant anything to me was the minimum I had to spend incarcerated was three and a half years with six months in a halfway house after that. Four years total. But I could wrap my brain around doing 4 years for one simple reason: I compared it in my mind to going to college.

CHAPTER NINETEEN

#529-720

After a while, after things slowed-down and I was in the county jail for a few weeks, one of the biggest things that was weirdly comforting to me, was that this time gave me a chance away from the world to figure myself out.

Even knowing I was going to prison, I understood this was a time to figure myself out. I was thinking I was going to plead guilty, serve the 42 months, re-enter society through the halfway house, and really use the time wisely to make myself a better person.

You have to rewind things to even begin to understand how almost optimistic I was about this.

I had known in Denver that I was a train wreck on a lot of levels personally. I knew the entire time that I was in California that I was a train wreck, and when I came back to Ohio I was a train wreck. I think most guys who have been in trouble with the law, you know, their actual crime is not the lowest point for them—it's just the resulting compounding event.

I had been making decisions and doing stuff that I knew would eventually lead to going to prison for a couple years.

I can remember vividly thinking about this at the time I was screwing up: there's no place in society that if you're having a hard time, or a rough time, that you could go to heal.

Just take this in context of my life in 2005 and 2006: there was no place in society to say, shit, let me have a break. There's no place other than prison where I could stop my life, actually be safer than it was on the streets, and get my head on straight.

There's a lot of dudes out here on the day to day grind, even today, there's guys who I guarantee if you spend enough time knocking on enough doors in enough neighborhoods, there are guys who would just like to get away because they are mentally grinding.

I'm speaking about it differently now for sure, because I understand what trauma, and loss, and grieving is now. I understand that all of the things that I experienced from a personal standpoint were all destructive factors in my mental health.

After the car chase, I got a new trial date—in September. This gave me about 3 or 4 weeks of being locked down 23 hours/day in county.

This was essentially solitary confinement, behind bars, and the point of that is to break people. To get them used to being still, to house them, basically break guys before they go to prison. Break them from being a hard, tough guy into someone who can be controlled once he gets to the real prison.

After I took my plea bargain, I went to the state-wide Reception Center which was at Orient. I went from Franklin County to Orient to Toledo. I was in the reception center for about 45 days. So I was at the Toledo Ohio Correctional Institute, as inmate #529-720, by October or November.

I was separated from everybody at Orient as well. The easiest way to describe it was that I didn't know what was next. I was walking into an environment where I didn't know what was coming. So there was a natural level of fear for everybody who is sane.

Now that I've been there, I can say that prison for me was no different than going onto the college football field for the first time and being full of anxiety. There's an anxiety about going to prison, the same as there was anxiety about performing on the field.

In prison you have to perform like every day is game day and you can't relax for a second in the prison any more than you can relax on a football field. If you let your guard down in either situation, there's going to be someone there to smash your skull in.

CHAPTER NINETEEN: #529-720

When I was first incarcerated, I would just sit there. They would bring me legal pads and I would write my thoughts down. I would write letters back and forth to Ashley, and I would return mail that people sent to me. Obviously, when you're receiving mail, you have nothing to do but respond to that and it becomes your lifeline.

I started receiving mail almost immediately. Nobody posted my address, but I imagine just from people being curious they would figure out how they could write me a letter and the next thing you know, I would just start replying to mail and it would go back and forth.

I started getting mail in the county jail. Sometimes it was hateful, and of course you have the homophobic comments about getting sexually assaulted in prison but the nonsense was usually in the form of postcards or mail that wouldn't have any return address on it. The real letters though were always more positive, uplifting, and encouraging and came from complete strangers most of the time.

I was acutely aware back then of people trying to provoke negative feelings from me, so I discarded the bad ones, and wrote back to the ones who were supporting me.

My only visitors were Ashley, my daughter, and my mother. They could come every Thursday evening from 6:30-7:30. I was also able to talk on the phone, but at that time calls were like $15. So it was just a lot easier to write a letter and wait a few days. I was buying my stamps from the commissary—people were allowed to deposit money for me there to buy my stamps.

In the county jail, that was the first time that I actually read. The first book I got was As A Man Thinketh. I was reading it and trying to get my mind going in the right direction.

There was a gentleman at the county jail who was being processed out after a long sentence in federal prison. I don't even know his last name, but his first name was Adam. He had gone to federal prison and he had basically just dropped the book off with an officer to give to me. He wanted me to have it because he thought I would benefit from it as I started my sentence and a new chapter in my life.

This was the first book I had read, probably, in my adult life, 100%. When the guard handed me the book, I would have read anything. At that point, I would have read the dictionary.

I could read the words, but to comprehend, digest, and understand the context—that level of understanding just wasn't there for me.

That book was written around 1900, so the language was very simple and straight-forward to the point a kid could read it and absolutely understand it. In fact, I think I will always remember this line in the book: until thought is linked with purpose, nothing intelligent shall ever happen.

To cognitively think of the linkage of a thought having purpose, it was like, Oh Shit, I didn't know a thought could have purpose. This one line absolutely changed how I was starting to think about my life. I wanted to orient myself so all my thoughts were aligned with a purpose—getting clean, going straight, becoming a partner to Ashley and father to Jayden. This is what I wanted and knew I needed to do.

I would describe it like this—reading felt like I was working out a part of my body that I hadn't worked out before. You're reading this shit, and your mind is starting to fire and you're like there's something else up here other than me wanting to play football.

The only things I had been thinking about before was street life or football—how to rob or how to break a tackle, those sorts of things—and now I'm trying to understand fundamental aspects of human consciousness?

There's a primitive level from operating in an inner-city environment, very animalistic, nothing deep or thought-provoking—it's just survival, on a daily basis, and that didn't take this same level of intelligence.

Even football, which I put a ton of brain-power into—watching film and studying defenses and learning blocking schemes—was never in the context of life or decision-making or figuring out what the hell I want, or what I had or didn't have, or what my thoughts were about the future of my life. I was never thinking about things of that nature—big things. So now I was reading books and thinking heavy thoughts and this was a side of me coming from inside my mind that was pretty cool to experience.

CHAPTER NINETEEN: #529-720

Also around this time, I got a dictionary from a guard. They had a cart with miscellaneous books that rolled through, and the dictionary was on there so I grabbed it. It was just some of the coolest shit for me to be reading books and looking up words and feeling my brain and intellect expand.

I remember reading As A Man Thinketh over and over again. I think through the process of formally reading, in the beginning you're just reading words and not digesting them but the more I read it, the more I could digest it and get different things off the page.

I would venture to say I probably read that book, and I am comfortable saying this—I read that book about 40 times, between the county jail and reception. I was literally reading it religiously. I was taking notes, making notes. It was exciting.

In fact, it was the only book that I had before I went to prison in Toledo. So it was the only book I had in Franklin County and reception so I literally had nothing else to do all day but read and digest that book

I was at Orient, in what's called reception, until January or February. This is sort of like a way-station as they're deciding what actual prison we should get sent to.

I weighed probably about 260-270 when I went into prison. I was out of shape. I only got out of my cell an hour/day when I was in the county jail: 20 minutes to use the phone, 20 minutes to shower, 20 minutes to workout. In reception, we walked to the mess hall, ate in a common area, and walked back. So I got out of my cell a little more.

The food throughout the entire 42 months was pretty standard—-boiled rice, green beans or corn, and a piece of bologna or turkey and a couple slices of bread and a carton of milk.

In the country jail, I actually started gaining weight from people passing stacks of food to me. Other inmates were saying Clarett, you need some food, so here's some cookies, here's some graham crackers, here's some you know, miscellaneous treats. The other inmates knew who I was but there wasn't any level of fame or anything. They just knew who I was.

The guards didn't say anything to me. I think they didn't want to make any sort of deal out of me being there. There's no treatment of any kind—

good or bad—because I was locked down all day, so when you're in a cell all day, all you do is get out and take a shower and just shut the hell up and get back in your cell.

Prison was a reality check. I went to prison with the idea like, Hey, I'm here—now what do I do? You got some decisions to make about your life when you're in prison.

I realized real quick that this wasn't for me for the rest of my life. I realized very quick, even in the county jail and reception, that prison just wasn't for me.

I can tell you emphatically just the transition from county jail to reception to prison, when they locked me up, with my hands cuffed to my ankles, was a tremendous shock and very dehumanizing.

I was sitting in the back of the police van during the transitions and when I got transitioned to actual prison, then I was handcuffed to 30-40 dudes and standing there completely naked.

That deters you right there. An this is no offense to any guy who doesn't have a reference point to basic humanity and dignity, who might not realize how far away from life that prison is.

But I knew that this was not normal. From there, I was like, Damn, I'm not going to keep on doing this shit. I was not going to lead a life of crime and be in and out of prison. I was young. I was just going to shut the hell up, do what I had to do to survive and grow, and try to get out as soon as possible.

Literally, I was counting the days from the beginning. There's even a picture of a paper that I posted on instragram years ago that I was counting the days and marking them off.

I was literally like, man, I'm getting the hell outta here and going somewhere else because this just ain't my life. This ain't the life I imagined for myself. My plan was to work on myself, come out a better person, and never go back.

Television has its own version of prison and makes people believe there's this big predatory environment where guys come in and get beat and it's this big madhouse. But these are adult men, trying to deal with their own

CHAPTER NINETEEN: #529-720

shit. For the most part, guys are doing their time and minding their own business.

If guys had something on their mind, I would not know about it because people mainly kept to themselves. Everybody is in a bad situation in prison. Most the world doesn't realize that everybody in there is in a horrible situation. It's mass desperation as much as it is mass incarceration.

If I'm being honest though, I think the scariest part about being in prison was wondering, What am I going to do when I get out? Think about it, I mark this football part of my life from when I started 9th grade, when I was 14, and I got drafted at 22. So the last 8 years of my life, I put in work to keep making it to the next level, to escape the inner-city.

For most black kids, to make it to the NFL was like everything. So everything I started dreaming of and wanting after I was successful in college, I didn't get to enjoy. The end result, the millions of dollars I thought I could reap from it never materialized for me and I didn't have any back-up plan.

In the space of slightly more than one year, I went from getting drafted to going to prison. So, now, it was like, Where do I go from here? So that's a challenging thing for a guy to think about in his early-20s…what do I do for the rest of my life when all I'd ever known was football and the streets.

Things really started to move in the right direction once I got to Toledo. In Toledo, I met Kellah Konteh, who was the warden, and he was the biggest change agent.

Almost as soon as I got there, Mr. Konteh sat me down in his office and told me about the work I needed to do in terms of getting my head straight. Mental health or mental wellness work you could call it. He was just like, you know, we have different programs here in prison, from a psycho-social-emotional support perspective. Trying to teach young men how to be adults and function in the world with some sort of mental wellness.

It was just me and him, sitting across the desk from each other, and he was offering me an opportunity to help myself. He was saying, I can give you the classes and I can give you the program to change yourself but it's on you to make it happen.

Kellah was an African guy, actually born in Africa, who worked his way up from basically being a dishwasher to earn the position he was in as the warden at TOCI.

After I met with him, the process started. I was getting up every day about 4 or 5 am, reading and writing, and then I was going to classes, going to the housing unit, and getting back into working out. I was in a regular cell, by myself. All the cells were single-bed cells so I had a great space to own and control my environment and put in my work.

It didn't take too much convincing to get me into this sort of program. I was ready for it—in fact I was hungry for it. I wanted to get my head right.

The curriculum was called *Thinking for a Change* and it was an integrated cognitive behavioral change program. There were classes like Anger Management, Responsible Adult Culture, Drug and Alcohol Abuse Awareness, and Cage-Your-Rage. They were all courses that were therapeutic. Obviously there were diagnostic codes for all of the individuals in there. Everybody in there could benefit from these courses because they could all be diagnosed with a few things probably.

There were social workers and counselors who were running the courses. We would go to a regular-looking classroom for classwork, there was group work, and everything had a book. We were just going through books. There was a curriculum for everything. This was a real program, very thoughtful. A lot of work went into creating the program and I was putting in a lot of work too.

I was going to class and group from 8am until about 1 or 2pm. In prison I had to have a job, so when I wasn't in class, I was doing my job. My job was as a porter, inside the block. I had to sweep the block, buff the floors, wipe down the ranges, tables, and telephones. I had to keep the common areas clean.

I got paid $17/month into my commissary account which I could use for stamps and other things. I did this same job the whole time I was in prison.

In addition to putting in work associated with my mental health curriculum, I had access to more books in Toledo through a small catalog called Bargain Books. We could order books, magazines, and newspapers for a discounted price and they would be delivered to my cell.

The first few books I ordered were anything that had to do with personal development, from that section of the catalog. I would order anything that had a cool or catchy title—also anything that had to do with business or entrepreneurship.

A book by a guy named Brian Tracy was one of the first books I ordered: Change Your Thinking Change Your Life. That was some heavy shit and it all just came back to me needing to change my thinking and then change my actions based on that.

From there, I just kept literally hammering through so many books—old books and new books like Ishmael Beah's Long Way Gone about being a child soldier. That inspired me because he climbed to the top despite his situation and it also made me realize that things might have been bad growing up on the south side of Youngstown but not bad like being a child soldier in Sierra Leone, that's for damn sure.

It was thrilling to consume information. Where a kid might get academically motivated in high school, or at some point in college, I got the fever in prison. In prison, the only thing that ever changes is the day on the calendar. So I was able to consume information and feel like I was changing myself from the inside, in an environment that wasn't changing at all. I hate to even use this word, but when I look back on it, that was a fun thing.

Now I was ordering newspapers and magazines and reading out of those and my vocabulary was starting to change, my words were starting to change, my ideas of what I could become were starting to change.

Just like anything else I was able to articulate not just my thoughts but myself as a person and give words to my feelings and thoughts and that was probably the coolest thing that I experienced in prison. It really was like going away to college or something.

It's so easy to trace the transformation starting from As A Man Thinketh, and then hanging out with Kellah Konteh. These things just got me rolling in terms of learning about myself—self-awareness and knowledge of self. Like who was Maurice Clarett? I hadn't ever really thought about who I was and who I wanted to be. It had always been about what did other people want me to be.

Academia hadn't ever intrigued me, but understanding why I was pissed off did. Understanding that the way I treated people had been wrong. Understanding the negative impact that drugs and alcohol had in my life and how that affected me and other people.

Learning about myself and this process of self-discovery was more interesting than anything in academia had ever been. But what happened was, once I started to gather myself and feel like I could govern myself, that pushed me to a space of thinking okay what could I do. What was my potential and what could I achieve in the world outside of running a football.

This stuff was all making me feel like a better person but sometimes reality would set in and I would struggle to figure out what can I do to support myself and my family. These were the toughest questions. How can I create a life for myself outside of prison that is consistent with this person I was becoming but allow me to provide for my family.

I was reading lots of autobiographies all the time in prison and this gave me a lot of ideas and I can say again that this was fun.

There was also Wisdom of Success: The Philosophy of Achievement which was an interview of Andrew Carnegie by Napoleon Hill. I remember being amazed that this was from the 1920s but was so personally relevant to my life. It was intriguing to learn about the details of Carnegie's life—coming to America as an immigrant—and it was inspiring to me, thinking this dude did this or that. All this stuff that I was learning felt relevant to my situation in prison in Toledo, Ohio almost a hundred years later.

The biggest question I had to figure out while I was in prison is how can I support myself when I get out. I would go to the commissary and get legal pads and write down notes from my books on these big tablets.

I would use these notes to identify things that interested me. I would go over the notes and look for things I kept repeating. One of the first themes to emerge was an interest in elder care.

So then I would write to state agencies and ask for help: how do you run an elder care business? What do you need to start with? What were LLCs?

CHAPTER NINETEEN: #529-720

I would write just basic letters to places down in Columbus and they would mail back some pamphlets or other literature to read. Literally, I would call Ashley and get the address of certain offices, get the information, write the state agencies, and they would write me back and I would get information that way. Let's say this was around 2007 or 2008 but my approach was straight out of the 1900s and it worked and kept my mind active and I always had things to read and think about.

One reason I think I got interested in elder care is that I had 5 or 6 elderly women reach out to me on a monthly basis. I called them my Golden Girls.

They identified with people who were incarcerated because they kept saying once they got older there were similarities with people who are incarcerated—your kids grow up and move away and they get isolated. Then your friends start dying and you feel even more isolated. And then finally when you get put into these nursing homes, it's no different than being incarcerated—you're just being housed in an institution.

So the golden girls were writing me letters and it was like normal conversation but I could understand it because they didn't have anybody to talk to. These were just old OSU football fans and they tracked me down and wrote to me from their nursing homes or assisted living.

One of them, Henrietta, lived with her husband in Canal Winchester, Ohio. She would send me cards and everything from her really touched me when I was in that cold environment that does a lot of things to make a person feel less than human.

There was a spiritually nourishing aspect to all my communication with the golden girls. I think there's a natural sense when you get older, you try and get closer to God, and you realize you don't have a lot of years left.

Now that I think about it, there was a lot of religious and spiritual information getting pushed on me from them but it was all in the context of encouragement. Everything from them was always encouraging me to be my best self. If this was part of a ministry, I never knew about that. They would just consistently write to me about once a month guaranteed and that was one part of being in prison that gave me a lot of hope.

For a while, Ashley and Jayden came and visited me in Toledo, but I didn't like how I felt after they left. So, visits were conflicting for me. I loved when they came and when they talked to me. I loved hugging them and all that stuff, but when they left, the realization of what I was missing was overwhelming.

So, if they didn't visit as regularly, it was more like out of sight/out of mind and I could trick myself into thinking their lives outside of mine didn't exist quite as much. I started to just deal with them on the phone in a limited capacity, so I didn't have to physically miss my daughter growing up.

They would only come about 4 times/year but I was cool with that because it made it easier to block out of my mind what I was missing. Ashley had moved in with my mother back in Youngstown because I had been the primary source of income for her in Columbus and she was taking care of the baby full-time and needed help.

Once she got pregnant she had to stop working and rely on me. My mother was back home and they lived together for 4 years. My mother was working and Ashley stayed home and took care of the baby. This was very beneficial to me because my mother was able to step in and do something I wasn't able to do myself.

Obviously the family dynamic was that her mother didn't have the means to assist her the way that my mother did. She didn't have that external support from her mother. When you're talking about helping somebody in prison, taking care of kids, and all this other stuff that comes along with it, I was just fortunate that my mother was there to assist. She still had her job in downtown Youngstown at the Mahoning County Courthouse.

After I'd been in prison about two years, I started doing The Mind of Maurice Clarett blog. I hadn't even known what a blog was prior to prison. But I figured out blogs were platforms for people to express themselves. So I think it's natural that the more I read, the more information I acquired, the more I wanted to share it.

The blog became a form of expressing myself but I didn't realize it would also be a form of therapy. I was writing down my feelings, how I felt about my past, how I felt about my present, writing the things that I could do, writing about how I felt about life in general.

I was writing the blog posts on a daily basis and then just reciting them to Ashley over the phone. I would sit down and write everything in the morning. I used to wake up at 6 o'clock because nobody else was up but they turned the phones on and there was an electronic system that opened the doors to our rooms and we were free to move around the housing unit.

We weren't free to roam throughout the prison but we could move around our own housing unit. I could go and call her at 6 and each phone call at this time had decreased to $1.

I would dictate my thoughts to her and she would put them on a blog and the blog got very popular very fast but I have no clue how. I was just posting the stuff and to be honest social media wasn't even big in my mind at that point so I don't know how it would have caught on and spread because there was no Twitter or Instagram and even Facebook was a new thing that caught on while I was in prison. I didn't know anything about any social media platforms at that point.

It was 2008 when I started doing the blog and then even more mail started rolling in. Different people would reach out to me, wishing me well and just in general connecting with me.

You know you get this consistently in prison: people don't know what to say so they encourage you. They say things like you should just continue to grow and stay on the right path.

But you don't have a reference point for life. You get up every day and live and other people are moving from one place to another but if a guy calls from prison, his life is staying in one place forever so it's not like you can have a regular conversation other than wishing them well and saying hopefully they continue to grow and that was the nature of the letters I got.

As I thought more about life after prison, I was really focused on senior care services but I didn't know how I would get the money to get into it. I was just dead-set into trying to get into some aspect of that and transportation for senior citizens was something I could understand.

I knew that seniors like the golden girls had a significant barrier getting rides to their appointments. This came from a entrepreneur magazine and it said that elder care business would be booming in the 21st c. and they had a How-To manual which I ordered and received for how to start a senior care business.

The whole future for me at this point was going back to Youngstown. The only dots that I had to connect were what do I do to make money because I hadn't done anything in my whole life other than playing football or running in the streets. So I had to bring a skill or service to the marketplace. I was just trying to figure out Step One.

At this point, the psycho-social-emotional development classes for me had ended. I graduated from the classes about 2 years into the process, but the learning didn't stop. There wasn't a ceremony but I got a certificate that went in my file and I moved forward. The certificate said I had completed those courses but there wasn't any sense of accomplishment like I could go do whatever I wanted with the rest of my life—I still had to figure that shit out.

I got really heavy into Dr. David Hawkins. He was one of the most influential authors for me in there. He wrote Power vs Force, Transcending the Levels of Consciousness: The Stairway to Enlightenment, Truth vs Falsehood, and many other books. I took a lot of understanding from those books.

One of the biggest things he was talking about was how we create illusions from hypothetical situations. And as much as I would use visualizing in my life just walking around, I didn't realize how much those hypotheticals were driving me negatively. I'm talking about things that just didn't exist in reality and only existed in my mind.

He made me think about the process of life and how we walk forward, gather information, and gain context on things that are happening to us. So for years, we're using this information that we're aware of but are totally ignorant of all this other information out there which could help us improve our situation.

It's just like this—in our social service agency, I could worry about something that hasn't happened, like a teacher in school severely punishing

CHAPTER NINETEEN: #529-720

one of the kids we work with and immediately, I get revved up about something that hasn't even happened yet. So, his message was that we shouldn't worry about things that haven't taken place. He just talks about dealing with more fact-based reality.

In terms of my own situation, he helped me realize the truth was that I had put myself in this situation, I was responsible for putting myself in prison, and now, his message was how do I become more conscious and aware of personal growth that's going to translate into some measure of successfully navigating life once I got out. Literally, that was my track.

My mind became acutely aware of why I was there, and I had no choice but to take responsibility and grow from that point forward. There couldn't be any resentment about not being in the NFL—what good would that have done?

The only part that I missed about football was the actual games. All throughout my life, I kept that child-like joy of putting the pads on, putting your jersey on, strapping up your helmet, and taking the field with your teammates. There's a feeling I got when the whistle blew and it was time for the kickoff.

So the only feeling I had about football in prison was related to grieving. When I was in prison, and getting out in my late-20s, I know football at the highest level wasn't coming back. I missed my moment. So there was a grieving process.

But once I started reading, and opening my mind, I could realize that I was done with football as a career path. The more I read, the more things made sense. Football had always been just a vehicle to get out. It was never going to be my whole life—how could it be when even the most successful people are done with it in their 30s. This is the trap of wanting to be a professional football player that so many black kids fall into. Being a professional football player isn't an end in itself. It's not something someone is or can be for their entire life.

At best, football for some people can be a means to an end. It can be a way to get an education, or a way to make a name for yourself which will

227

launch a career selling insurance, or a way to get out of the inner city like it was for me.

But once I had seen outside of my past and my upbringing, and realized that there were other avenues for me to take care of myself and my family, I was like, Oh shit, it never made any sense to think all I could ever do in life was get my body destroyed carrying a football.

The hardest part to reconcile was that I had invested so much time into it, developing my body as an athlete, watching film and studying opponents, and all of it had made so much sense previously but now it made a lot less sense.

Once I systematically thought about it, football and becoming an athlete was presented to me as the best option available to me—and in fact just about the only option other than the streets. That's the track I was on when I had my third juvenile arrest—I was on the track to live in the streets and the adults in my life redirected me towards a track to be an athlete. But sadly, even once I got to Ohio State, it was still only and always about staying on this path as an athlete.

There's very few places, other than sports, for black kids coming from the inner city to develop their identity for the future. Every identity other than athlete seems foreclosed. There's no sense about being a doctor or a lawyer or even a teacher. There's no intense academic environment that develops you in the places that a lot of those bigtime college athletes come from. So, sometimes self-discovery of all our potential can only happen inside of an institution that was forced upon us, like it was for me. This is why my biggest life goal is to create a space where athletes can come and get the psycho-social-emotional development classes I got in prison, but without going to prison, because nobody should have to go to prison to develop as a human.

CHAPTER TWENTY
MACHINE

WHEN I got closer and closer to getting out, after having been in prison for over three years, I got into such a routine that the other guys in my housing unit started calling me the machine.

Literally every day was the same in prison, rise-and-grind. The only difference might be the food—getting an extra piece of chicken on Christmas. That's it. For 4 years straight, I got an extra piece of chicken on Christmas. Other than that, every day was exactly the same.

Think about it, I went into the prison system in September of 2006 and was in Toledo by early-2007. Everything stayed the same for me, day-in and day-out, until I was paroled into a community control halfway house in 2010.

Imagine prison as a dormitory, broken up into 4 housing units—A block, B block, C block, and D block. There were 4 tiers with 4 units, so there were 16 units. My unit was where I lived all day every day for over three years except when I went to the dining hall or recreation. I was in A block and there were 600 people in the A block. The racial breakdown was about 80% black, 10% Hispanic, and 10% white.

When I got to Toledo, they gave us 3 shirts, 3 pairs of pants, a bath towel, a wash rag, and a toothbrush. And some shower shoes. From there, I had a blanket and a sheet, my bedding. This was at intake and then I went to my unit on A block.

I was in Toledo for 38 months. When I walked in, I was immediately recognized possibly because the guards had tipped them off I was coming. Once you get into prison, word travels fast with everything. Someone could have talked to someone in the central office or a correction officer or a unit manager and then word spread.

I think their biggest fear, from the admin point, is that something extreme happens or someone who is well-known is targeted. So, anyone of any notoriety or wealth is separated. There will be more eyeballs on them.

When I first got locked up in the county jail, I was on the 3rd floor, with single-man cells. I could have been upstairs in 9 or 10-person cells, but I wasn't. In Orient, I was just in the general population. And I had a single-man cell in Toledo.

I was in Unit A. There was a big heavy steel door to my room with a very small window, just a few inches wide.

In prison, the lights never go off. There was no lights-off, even after lockdown at 9 pm. The lights are always on. The lights are on all day long. The only light I got in my cell was the light right outside my cell, in the hallway. That was the light I could operate with. I didn't have a light in my room, other than a small one above my sink.

Eventually I had a TV in my room. It was a little 11-inch TV with a remote control that I bought for about $300 from the commissary.

But the first night, I was told to get into my room at 9 o'clock for lockdown and I didn't have a TV or radio or anything at that point.

Prison is like a totally different society. I would go to sleep at 9, like clockwork. They used to call me a machine because I did the same thing every day. I mean I literally did the same thing every day. I don't think everyone else did, but I was focused. I just naturally woke up about 515 or 530 because I was disciplined. I woke up every day at the same time.

One thing I heard every day was the PA system. At 5 o'clock there was a count and, they would announce "Workers to the kitchen." I would hear the CO's keys, and hear people moving around, and I would wake up.

There was a large open space in the housing unit and the speaker was out in that.

As soon as I arrived, there were guys who said if I needed anything, they could hook me up—books, papers, and pencils, or food until I could get to the commissary. There was a microwave in the common area, and

CHAPTER TWENTY: MACHINE

some guys would buy instant noodles and eat those and not even go to the mess hall.

The guys in my housing unit were welcoming to me. Nobody wanted to give me a hard time. There's a lot of tough guys in prison, but I'd like to consider myself somewhat tough as well.

In prison they call this, Picking your shots. People will see how far they can take things. Let me go play basketball and see how rough I can get with you. Let me ask for your shit and see what I can get from you.

This didn't happen to me because I've got a certain demeanor. It's a silent sternness. I'm not an arrogant guy. I respected the environment. There's something I can give off to people though, some confidence, that says, I'm not the one. This is not the guy you want to mess with.

Typically weaker guys would try and befriend everybody. They would try to talk and handshake and get caught up in the antics of prison by sitting at the card table.

I was just humble, I shut the hell up, I minded my business, I wasn't there to do anything other than do my time. I think most guys when they saw that, they were looking to see how am I going to act. So, a few things you have to do when you arrive at prison is you have to go to recreation, you have to go to chow hall, you have to go to your programs. You have to let people see you so you let it be known that you're here, you're around, and you're just like everyone else.

There are guys who come and literally never leave the housing unit. They never leave their pod. They go to the commissary and grab some groceries but they never leave the housing unit for year because they're scared. They sit in their cell all day long.

Prison is a lot of mental jousting. Dudes are constantly jousting with you, asking you to buy them shit for protection, etc. That's what goes on in prison. Bigger guys are pressing smaller guys for sex. When you are coming in, you don't know all this shit exists.

If you just look on the surface level in prison, everybody is just sitting around doing a whole lot of nothing. But once you get there, there is an entire underworld of everything in prison: you got cell phones, you got people smoking weed, you got men having sex with men, you got guys having sex with guards, you got guys gambling, you got dudes getting drunk. It's a whole deal. You got people buying extra food out of the kitchen.

Prison is like the Wild Wild West—anything goes. If you're in prison long enough, you can forget you're in prison, because there is everything that happens on the street that happens in prison. The currency in prison is cigarettes, or items, food items, or favors that you are doing for people. Instead of police on the street you have corrections officers. You've got people trying to get away with schemes, hustling, selling weed and drugs just like they would outside.

People are smoking weed out in the yard. There are 2200 men. Imagine a prison yard is as big as the Oval at OSU and there are 5 guards in the yard, so if people want to smoke weed, and there are 600 men out there, there's no way to watch them all.

I wasn't doing any of that, with drugs or alcohol, because that wasn't my thing. Prison has a great way of showing you what your place is. And after being in prison, I saw that there are a lot of levels of criminals, and I identified that this was a mental hospital. This wasn't for me. There are people who are so far gone.

On the outside, you hear people saying, I'm going crazy. Or someone says, This is driving me crazy. But in prison, through people's eyes or actions, you can literally see people going crazy. I saw people go crazy in prison, the circumstances were so rough. They weren't going home ever again. They had no family support or they had no friends.

Eighty-five percent of the prison was lifers—dudes who had been locked up from the 70s and 80s. The average stay was 15 years. I was in this place with dudes who had murders. You got dudes in there who are serious and there's no way to stay away from them—I was in there amongst them and had to figure out a way to co-exist with them.

But these guys are not as demonic as the media makes them all out to be. These are regular guys but the nature of their crimes was severe. With really crazy guys, you just have to mind your business.

CHAPTER TWENTY: MACHINE

Prison is the master facility where people better mind their own damn business. You might know everything is going on, but you shut the hell up if it ain't none of your business. This is what I did, 100%.

I managed to make some real good friends in prison though, Nathaniel Bibbs, Michael Wagner, Torrence Hearns, Anthony King, and Charles McCoy. I hope these guys can get out on parole but these guys got long sentences. Even now that I'm out, I still talk to these guys on the phone, which costs a dollar. I also communicate with them on email, which costs a quarter. They can get on a tablet in the pod and send me a message to my gmail.

Most of these guys need money to go to the commissary and I've got an app on my phone that lets me put money into their commissary account. I can text a guy in prison the same way I text anybody else and put money in his account. The app is called J-Pay, that's the most common app for this.

These messages take an hour or two to get to them because they get read, I guess. But the messages they send get to me instantly and it only costs them a quarter.

There are so many similarities between prison and the outside. The commissary is basically like a Dollar General. So it's like having a dollar store in a dormitory and you can visit the store once a week. You go there, fill out a shopping list, and give it to the clerk and they do all the shopping and deduct the amount from your account.

The only things that are extremely expensive are the electronics. Other than that, the prices are about the same. So, it took about a month for me to get my TV. My mom and Ashley were putting money into my commissary so I could afford that stuff.

My mom was also trying to help out my brother Michael, who was locked up. While I was in Toledo, Michael was in Ohio State Penitentiary in Youngstown. He got out in 2008 though, while I was still in. He's in Vegas and has been taking care of himself since he got out. No more bullshit, no more hustling.

I got the nickname The Machine after about a year. I got a simple personality. I don't do shit. My life now is literally a lot like it was in prison. I do the same shit every day. I don't gamble, I play chess, and I read. I might play cards to kill time, but otherwise, I worked out, showered, and minded my own damn business.

I knew how to play chess since I was a kid, but there was an older guy in prison named Junior and he was the one who really taught me the strategy. I spent a lot of time playing chess in prison with Junior. It was fun. I got good according to my standards, but you got some dudes in prison who are great. They can play games with their eyes closed, they can play a game backwards.

Chess is all about using your pieces to dictate what you want to do—either setting traps or getting out of traps. I'm trying to move pieces to get to your king and use my pieces to make sure you can't get to my king. But there are guys in there who are great critical thinkers and play for hours on end. Junior is a lifer. I don't know his crimes. You don't say shit about that. It ain't none of your business. You don't talk about anything personal in there. You never ask about crimes.

To a degree, I knew what everybody did. And we knew there weren't any snitches or child molesters either, because those people go to protective custody, which is a different housing unit in the same building.

Typically what every guy did in prison was reading from every source that we could—spirituality, the Nation of Islam was heavy in prison so I heard from those guys. Prison probably has some of the greatest debaters in the world. So you had debates between the guys from the Nation of Islam and Christians—you know, Who is God, What role did Jesus really play, Who was he? These debates happened at the picnic tables and benches in the common area. Guys would just naturally go back and forth periodically about their beliefs during the free time in the middle of the day.

We had 120-130 guys in our housing unit, and we were free to roam around the unit during the day. We were behind plexiglass and the guards were watching us. It was like a neighborhood. There might be altercations if a guy stole something out of someone's cell, or some guy skipping the line to wash your clothes, or if a guy owed you some money from gambling, just

CHAPTER TWENTY: MACHINE

normal prison shit. You had guys getting in altercations but I didn't get into anything other than regular prison shit, playing cards, talking shit, but I didn't get into any fistfights or any big dumbass tussles.

The only stuff I got into was with guys wrestling and messing around the room. You know how guys just talk shit to each other saying, Alright man, let's wrestle. In some ways, even guys who are grown are just big kids so you're messing around saying Dude, I could slam you. Me and a couple other guys we used to wrestle each other and lock up but it's no different than if you're in a locker room. Guys just testing you.

When guys called me The Machine, that was a compliment. I was waking up, working out, showering, reading and writing, reading and writing, reading and writing, and then waiting for mail call about 3:30 each afternoon.

Three times a day we were locked down, 10:00-11:00, 2:30-3:30, and 9 o'clock. Those are standing counts. You had to be standing and off your bed so they can make sure you're alive.

I wasn't around for any escapes or anything but if somebody got their ass beat, they'd see it at lockdown. A lot of guys got their ass kicked. A lot of guys had disagreements, but I'd say 90% of fights happened from gambling and unpaid debts.

If a guy owes another guy money, even a little money, if you're not getting support from home, that's a big deal. If you don't pay, you get your ass kicked. If you fought someone in open space, that was considered cowardly because you were inviting the corrections officers to save you.

Whenever a guy got beat down, the guy who did the beating would get towels so the other guy could clean himself up. This hides the reality from the guards and dudes who got beat up were supposed to just say they got hurt playing basketball.

If you owe money, you could have someone on the outside pay money. Like if a guy owed someone money, his mother could send the other guy's mother a money order. That was a very real thing and if that money didn't get sent, that guy got his ass kicked. I saw this a lot but it wasn't part of my reality. Shit wasn't any of my business so I stayed the hell out of it.

I saw three guys pour boiling hot water on a guy who was in their business. Boiling hot. This is the biggest difference between prison and the real world. There are serious consequences for every action. Every action of semi-disrespect or wrongdoing, there is physical retribution taken, immediately. There was a higher level of accountability and respect in prison than in society.

If you knew before you did anything wrong that someone would hold you accountable for every single thing, you would walk through society a lot more consciously. Put it like this, this is the common denominator throughout the entire prison, there is accountability: knuckles in your face, getting your ass stomped, or getting a knife in you. So, guys respect each other. Guys don't lie. If I know I don't want to be part of this lifestyle, I stay away from it.

If I'm a drug dealer and I give a guy drugs in prison, I'm not going to get paid until I can demand that money and actually collect it. I saw a guy give another guy drugs, and when the dude dealing tried to get his money the next day, the guy who got the drugs walked up on the dealer with his guys, spit in his face, and said, Motherfucker try and take it from me.

So, you're waking up and it is intense every single minute of every day. It is repetitive and almost mundane, sure, but there is an intensity to how mundane it is because the repetitiveness of every single day could lull you to sleep but you can't ever let that happen. Every action has consequences.

You had to be alert every minute of every day. So we're on edge every minute of every day. It could be something as simple as if you're hanging with an idiot. If you're hanging with an idiot and he does something, that's on you too.

I had a young guy who I was hanging out with, and that young guy goes and whoops another guy and takes his shoes. For no reason. He didn't realize that the other guy was a Muslim. So pretty soon there were 50 Muslims coming after him.

But they came to me saying, Yo, your young dude took our dude's shit and he needs his shit back. So, now I had to go have a conversation with this guy, Yo, you have to give that guy his shoes back and fight him again. This shit happened. You got Muslims deep in the joint, hundreds of these dudes.

And you got gangs in the prison. I'm just Maurice Clarett, who the hell am I on my own? I'm tough on the football field or tough in real life, but one person isn't going to defeat the Bloods, Crips, Heartless Felons, or Folks. Gangs were never my thing. I was just going to mind my own business, make myself better, and stay the hell away from what wasn't my business.

That's the biggest thing in prison, minding your own damn business. You just have to stay the hell away from everybody else's business. I didn't have any drugs or alcohol issues in prison because that's how you get wrapped up in more shit. I didn't need that in my life anymore.

There's a significant population of guys in prison who are trying to get themselves together and getting ready to leave. There was a space for that, so trying to get myself together didn't make me a target. Everybody else recognized hustling wasn't my life anymore and gave me that space.

So prison worked for me, and it works for a lot of guys. You just have to be determined to stay the hell out of gossip, stay out of prison politics like who is hustling or who's got weed—that was none of my business.

I was in Kellah Konteh's office within a couple days of arriving in Toledo and I was ready to do it. At that point, I knew I needed to do something with myself. There were book clubs and classes on alcohol abuse, substance abuse, and parenting. These were led by social workers or some of the inmates.

There was even Toastmasters in there, and AA, and after going through these groups, they asked me if I wanted to host some of those classes.

I did a lot of Toastmasters in the evenings. That was fun. It was all run by inmates, 100%. We went through the whole official program. Toastmasters must have been one of the most fun things I did, teaching me how to speak. I didn't realize how many deficiencies I had in my language. My biggest gain was being confident and speaking in front of people.

I just gained the confidence of getting up in front of people. Those dudes in prison are critical dudes. They were brutally honest, having no reservations about telling me I was horrible if I was horrible.

There was a bulletin board in my housing unit and there were lots of clubs and classes. All I had to do was sign up for them. I signed up for AA and NA together. We didn't really work the 12 steps but we worked out of the big book. We had one big book for the whole class. They called it AA but it was really just a platform for guys to express what drinking and drugging had done to their lives and how it put them into bad situations.

I didn't do the lead by myself but I shared it. It had to do with being honest with the statistics. Almost 85% of guys who did crimes, did them under the influence. We were literally just talking about how being under the influence caused you to do things that weren't responsible. I would just speak my part, talk about what I did, and that was pretty much it. I did AA and NA for 2 years and I bet I did Toastmasters for about a year and a half.

Kellah Konteh ran the book club about A Long Way Gone, about a child soldier, Ishmael Beah. He was snorting dope and shooting heroin as a child soldier, but then he made his way to Oberlin College and started raising awareness of this international tragedy. I did group activities with Kellah, though he got promoted while I was there. He created an environment for a lot of guys to improve themselves. The next guy was Mr. Smith, who was appointed by Kellah Konteh.

Everybody asks me what I remember from when I was in prison. In particular, they want to know what it was like when Barack Obama got elected president of the United States. When Obama was running for president, we didn't even feel it. The night he got elected, I was in my room watching it on TV, but I didn't even feel it. It was cool to see but I wasn't connected to it and we weren't like the guys celebrating in the streets in black neighborhoods around the country. It didn't affect my world one bit.

The next day, there weren't even guys hooting and hollering, no high-fives. I remember being somewhat proud in the moment. If you're in prison for life, it doesn't really matter. You don't even feel the holidays, no gift exchanges, maybe guys smoke a little weed on New Year's Eve, but when I say it's like that movie Groundhog Day where you wake up and every day is the same, that's the only way to explain it.

CHAPTER TWENTY: MACHINE

After a while, I started counting the months I had been in. I got done counting the days pretty quickly, so I started counting the months. It was easy to count the months and then years with the sports seasons. I watched basketball, baseball, and football and this way I just passed the different seasons.

I didn't know exactly when I was getting out so it's not like I had a date circled on the calendar. I didn't know the date I would go back to Franklin County Common Pleas Court for my hearing, etc. I roughly knew I was going to file my papers in February of 2010, but I had no clue when they were going to get back to me. That happened in April or May; I got transported to Columbus, appeared in front of the judge, went to the halfway house, and got out.

CHAPTER TWENTY-ONE

OUT

THE LONGER I was in prison, the closer I got to being done with my sentence, the longer it felt and the more things bothered me. It felt more like I was actually incarcerated towards the end than the beginning when I was changing and growing more as a responsible adult. When I was ready to get out, I mean I was ready.

In the beginning of my sentence, when there was so much time in front of me and I wasn't getting out anytime soon, I just worked on myself and developing my mind. To be honest, the first few years were the greatest period of development in my life so far.

And this development lasted all the way until I had the realization that my date was within 90 days and then 60 days, and then it just felt like I was eager to get out. At that point, I was ready to go and join society again and make my contributions. I was ready to get out and be a responsible adult in the world and be a good husband and a good father.

The last 7 days felt like 7 months because the only thing on my mind now wasn't how can I develop myself, it was get me the hell out of here.

I was just counting the days. The last few days in Toledo, I was feeling ready to go. I wasn't scared or nervous. I felt like I was a more functional person. I knew the growth that had taken place inside of prison because I had the same discipline that motivated me in football to be better. This was a transferable skill that I developed in prison. So I just knew that I was a much better person coming out of prison than this dude running around selling drugs and robbing people before I went in.

But I knew when I got out, I had to go to a halfway house for a minimum of 4.5 months. I knew that was going to be in Columbus. That was predetermined from before I went to prison. So one day I finally left Toledo in handcuffs, getting transported from the prison to the county jail, and I was in the county jail for 3-4 days waiting to see the judge. I had to see him and he could visibly see I was a changed man ready to live on the outside.

I weighed 212 when I got out of prison, losing 50-60 lbs easy. I was on a vegan diet at one point, just eating the bare minimum. I didn't realize it was vegan at the time. I was just trying to tighten up my discipline and challenge myself and see how much of a minimalist I could become. Looking back on it, I think it was sort of pride. Comfort inside of discomfort. Prison is supposed to be uncomfortable but my own discipline allowed me to take control of my circumstances. I was working out every day doing push-ups, sit-ups, jogging—I was in great shape. Prison took everything else away. I would naturally wake up in the morning just charged up, trying to win the day. It's the same thing I'm doing now.

Really, the mentality people see now, I've been doing this shit since 2007. Literally getting up at 5 or 6 in the morning, working my ass off, taking a shower, being diligent, eating my food, making the most out of each day, going to sleep, waking up, and doing the same thing the next day. I have the same discipline every day.

There had been so much encouragement from the outside while I was in prison that I knew I had a lot of people supporting me when I got out and rooting for me to succeed.

While I was incarcerated, Tressel and I wrote each other a few times. I think he initiated the conversation, encouraging me. Tressel's message is the same now as when I was incarcerated: Hey, continue to do the right thing moving forward. He reached out to me because he was writing The Winner's Manual and he said I got a chapter that I want to include you in and I want your permission to use your name. He said, I hope that despite everything that happened that you get your life together.

CHAPTER TWENTY-ONE: OUT

I remember Mike Tomlin, the coach of the Steelers, wrote to me. And Jerry Angelo, the GM of the Bears, who was from Youngstown. These were just guys who reached out and wanted to encourage me. I never worked out for them or played for them.

I never knew what I would get in the mail and one day a letter from the Pittsburgh Steelers came in, and pretty soon after that an envelope that said Chicago Bears. Stuff like this meant the world to me because they had a lot better shit to do than write me. It was just cool to think that someone of that stature in the football world would write me. Someone who was extremely busy and has lots of shit to do. I'm not saying everybody else didn't have shit to do but these guys were running multi-million dollar organizations.

In order to be released to community control, I had to go in front of the same judge and my lawyer was with me. The judge asked me what did I learn from prison. He asked if given the opportunity can I get out and do the right thing. By then, I was ready to get the halfway house process started. I pretty much knew once they came and got me from prison that I would be released even though I could have been turned down. But I knew I had built up enough credibility.

In prison, it went from like everybody wondering is this guy going to come in and think that this is a joke or is he going to take this as a chance to improve himself. If I had to sum prison up in one phrase, I would say that on a daily basis I was just minding my own business and making myself a better person. How I basically interacted with other people, getting my stuff done on a daily basis to improve myself—that's how I gained the respect of people around me.

Another reason I knew I could succeed when I got out is that toward the end of my incarceration, I became a mentor to younger guys, encouraging them to read more, exercise more, and get themselves together. By the time I left, it was a graduation process like graduating from college—Commencement, a beginning.

I had started mentoring guys both formally and informally for a while. I had been hosting some of those pyscho-social-emotional support classes.

There were a few guys who facilitated groups like Toastmasters and other little classes that you have in prison.

After I had been through them and guys looked at me as somebody who was disciplined, I knew I had basically done what I needed to do in prison. So I became one of the leaders of the classes, a facilitator. I enjoyed this because it felt like this is what helped me and allowed me to learn to think and understand how to think and to understand why I'm thinking how I'm thinking and how I could change that. That was interesting to me.

There's definitely guys in prison who come at it from the position of wanting to grow. George Jackson of the Black Panthers said prison either breaks a person or makes them stronger and lots of people enter it as an opportunity thinking I'm ready to grow the hell up.

A lot of guys had been in multiple prisons, but not every prison had the same programs. People now talk about judicial reform—in the 80s and 90s when these prisons were built, nobody was saying Hey, let's make time and carve out rehabilitation spaces for them. It was more like let's house these guys and give a space for recreation and a place to eat but nobody was building physical spaces for people to develop. So if a guy wanted to leave his wing in prison, you literally only have hallways, showers, and cafeterias. There were no ancillary rooms. This prison in Toledo had a library and a couple classrooms, so I was lucky.

I was a mentor both inside my housing unit and inside the class. I was also able to take some classes from Ohio University while I was in prison. I was completing the work but I couldn't afford to pay the tuition for the credit. It wasn't free. Actually a gentleman who graduated from Ohio State and was a professor, he and his wife had basically paid for me to take those classes. He had reached out to me and said he graduated from Ohio State and was a professor there and said if you want to take some classes, I will pay for you to go back to school.

So, OU had correspondence courses that I could take but what happened was after paying for the initial course to get me started, this kind gentleman passed away. The big expense for those courses was getting someone to proctor the exams. I couldn't afford to pay the proctor to take the exams, so

CHAPTER TWENTY-ONE: OUT

I would do all the work but then I couldn't do the tests and get the credit. That was okay though, because I was getting the knowledge. Mainly I was taking courses in Philosophy and Psychology.

It crossed my mind to get my degree when I got out, but I wasn't ever motivated to actually get the degree even though I am always educating myself. The one thing that dominated my thinking however about getting out was that I was just flat broke. I was starting from scratch with no money whatsoever.

When I left the county jail, all I had was sneakers and undergarments but the halfway house gave me a list of things I needed and my mother had to buy them and leave them for me at the halfway house.

The county delivered me there after I appeared in front of the judge and was granted my release. It was called a community-based correctional facility but we just referred to it as a halfway house and I needed to live there another 4.5 months.

While I was living there, I went back to Ohio State. I started taking classes in summer 2010 from the halfway house. They would let me out to go to class. The tuition was paid for by my lawyer, Mike Hoague.

I signed up for an African American Studies class. The motivation to finish was just a pride thing—to say I didn't stop on this college process that I started. I was getting to campus with some of the former players I knew. They would come grab me at the halfway house and take me there, which was really kind of them.

These were guys who were out of Ohio State, out of the NFL, just living in Columbus. I was just like any other serious student who was actually trying to learn. In fact I got an A- in that class.

But in the fall, I went to Omaha to play in the United Football League. I don't know how they found me, but I got a letter through the halfway house and it said, Hey, we have an opportunity for you to play football. When I got out, I had no intention of ever playing football again in my life but I was dead broke and had a family to support.

So basically, I went out to Omaha. It was the GM who had been at the Broncos who found me, Ted Sundquist. He tracked me down and asked if

I would like to play for them. I said Yes but only because I was broke and they were going to pay me $50,000. I was like cool so he said can you come and try out. I was in shape from being in prison. My body had recovered but I knew the whole move to recruit me was just making headlines for the league.

Even when I went through the drills and worked out and was catching footballs and all that bullshit, I knew I wasn't the same person. I was in shape but I wasn't in a football-player's mind. There was no way I was going to run through walls anymore and embrace the sheer violence of the game—not once I had turned my mind on and developed into a responsible adult. I just couldn't rationalize destroying my body and my brain.

Football is a violent game, any way you slice it. It's violent by design—it's intended to be violent and when it's played at the highest level, like it was during our championship season of 2002, it was super violent. Look at the National Championship game—Willis McGahee got his knee popped by Will Allen and even during the broadcast, Keith Jackson said Will came in like a truck and that's about right.

Even though McGahee had a nice career in the NFL, his knee was never the same and I can't imagine what it's going to be like for him as an old man. This is what bigtime college and NFL football players sign up for and after a few years of turning my brain on in prison, I just couldn't get into this headspace again. I knew I could make it on the outside with my brain and not my body.

When I got out of prison, I was vigilant about everything. There was an intensity that I picked up in prison that I didn't have before. In prison nobody talks to each other, in prison everybody wakes up on edge just because of the environment. In prison there's just an intensity that you have to have every day just to exist in that environment. So, coming out of prison, I still had that intense attitude of self-monitoring every action of how I presented myself to people and how I did everything.

I had to get an interstate compact to get permission to leave Ohio and go to Omaha. Playing football was considered a job and this is how I was able to go to Nebraska. So, I told Ashley and Jayden that I could go and

CHAPTER TWENTY-ONE: OUT

make some money. They were still living in Youngstown at the time. I went out there and played football for the first season. We played 8 games and I made $50,000. Instead of getting money after each game like everybody else, I asked Ted Sundquist just to keep it and give it to me in a lump sum at the end.

That was in the fall. I thought this was a way to get some money. Even when I was out there on the field physically, I was still institutionalized in my mind. I would go to practice and when I would come home, guys would leave practice and come back to the hotel where we were staying—these guys would go out and socialize but I would come back to the room and I didn't realize it but I was just totally cool with just sleeping in the bed and being in the room the whole day. I was just going back to my cell. We would literally be done and I was conditioned to sit inside my room all day.

There were guys I had played with and against on the team, but these guys were just recently either released from the NFL or weren't too far removed, so their mentalities were totally different. They were trying to get back in the league, they were social, some guys had money and all this other shit. I was a dude who didn't have a thousand dollars to my name. So I would just go out and practice, come back and rest, practice, and come back and rest, every day.

It was easy for me to see some destructive behaviors in other people. Being in prison where life is highly regimented and highly disciplined, I could see that some of these guys were self-destructive. I wasn't intervening though or working with them even though they knew I had been in prison. I was just minding my own business. I was so dead set on making the team just to get the money that shit I was seeing didn't bother me.

I worked incredibly hard to make the team so I could get that money, but I didn't have any joy running guys over. The first few times I got hit when we had equipment on, I thought, This shit ain't for me anymore. It didn't make any sense to go sit in the cold tub for what, go to practice for what, watch film for what. None of it made sense to me as my future.

Every once in a while, I would feel some joy putting on my jersey and going out there and running the ball in the open field. There's just nothing like that feeling in the world—but I couldn't think about doing it as a career professionally. I didn't want to watch film anymore, I didn't want to blow up linebackers on a lead block, and I certainly didn't want to be in any more head-on collisions.

As a child, being a football player was the only roadmap I had to escape my situation—it was all I thought I had to offer the world. But I became a man in prison and opened up my mind to many other paths. I realized after I got out that there were so many other things I was capable of. There was so much more opportunity and more that I had to offer the world.

When I was a child, I spoke like a child, I thought like a child, and I acted like a child. But now that I was out of prison, it was time to put aside my childish things and speak like a man, think like a man, and act like a man.

ACT III

EPILOGUE

I CAME BACK to Ohio after playing in Nebraska in 2010, and actually went back there the following year to play, just to make some more money. At that point, running a football was my most marketable skill.

After two seasons banking some money by playing for the Omaha Nighthawks, I came back to Ohio and started doing some business in transportation and logistics, and also started my public speaking.

My first opportunity came at Quinnipiac University, where I was invited by Professor of Law Marilyn Ford. I owe her a lot since she started me on this path where I've now spoken at over 400 universities and organizations.

I've been public speaking since 2012 and have spoken at Notre Dame, Florida State, Alabama, Kentucky, Mississippi State, Austin Peay, Arizona State, Florida, Virginia, U Conn, U of Cincinnati, Ohio University, Indiana, Georgia Southern, U of South Florida, Texas A&M, and many others.

This has earned me the nickname the "athlete whisperer" because I can communicate with these guys because I sat where they were sitting and they listen to me. I also give talks to men who are incarcerated, and to religious groups. My main message is simple: encouragement. I just like encouraging people. If people ask me what I like to do most, it's give encouragement.

In 2016, I started a social service agency in Youngstown and we called it The Red Zone. We started with 7 people and now we've got about 130 between Youngstown and Columbus.

The Red Zone provides social support services to people in need—young people, old people, people who are using, people who have quit using, etc. Our motto is simple: we are dedicated to helping our clients discover their strengths and abilities to assist them in reaching their full potential.

This is the work I was put on this planet to do and I have found my purpose.

The question that everybody asks me is whether I regret not getting to play in the NFL. I can say 100% that the fact that I didn't play in the NFL doesn't eat at me at all. The only thing that gets to me is that I wasn't prepared for my opportunity when it came up. It bothers me that I had so much other shit going on that I didn't have a clear mind and make the most of my opportunity with the Broncos. There was so much stuff that bogged me down at Ohio State and that followed me to California and I was just avoiding my daily realities, usually hiding behind drugs and alcohol.

I didn't even know how to sort through it or figure a starting point to get through it. Everything with the drinking, drugging, partying—it was just taking me to another space mentally to not deal with the stuff I should have been. It was escapism. But the fact that I didn't score a touchdown in someone's uniform in the NFL, I don't even give a damn, you know?

It only hurts me because I took so much pride in practicing. It hurt me that I didn't seize my chance after years of conditioning my body and lifting weights and watching film and being able to intelligently break film down and prepare myself the way I had prepared myself in high school and Ohio State. But the game of football, I just don't care about it. It's not a big part of my identity.

I've been asked to coach a few times but I don't have that much interest in that either. I have more interest in talking to kids in a computer lab, asking them what they're looking at and why—talking to them about taking books out of the library and exploring big ideas.

I explained this to someone recently: the greatest funnel in the world is ESPN. It is the dangling carrot and most kids want to get on that stage in some capacity. You have a huge population of undereducated black and other poor kids who come from inner cities or very rural areas and all they can think about is sports. I want to be part of opening their eyes to all of life's possibilities, outside of sports.

EPILOGUE

I have a different perspective on rural America now. I met a lot of guys in prison from rural America. I used to think that if you were from rural America you just didn't understand life but now I know that rural America and inner-city America can be like the exact same thing. These people in inner cities and rural communities have a lot in common: their education is under-funded, there's good teachers but lots of bad ones, and many of them have a bad family environment as well. So, they think the only way out of this reality is to play sports or become an entertainer or do some shit they've seen on TV. That's the only place for most kids growing up to find a roadmap out.

But the percentages of succeeding on those paths are gravely low and they are getting lower. Even guys who get drafted into professional sports leagues, which is a small percentage, have a gravely low probability of making enough money to be set for life. For instance, this is what everybody thinks happens when you make the NFL—that you're set for life but that is emphatically not the case and somebody needs to be out there telling even the All-Americans in Power Five conferences that. Football ain't their future. The NFL is getting younger and cheaper every year—careers are getting shorter and guys are making less money. They all need to have a plan for their future other than football. Like me, their real life starts when they get done with football.

It's not realistic to think you're going to have an NFL career and be set for life but you've got kids pouring everything into something that's nothing but a dream and foreclosing all of their other potential. Even if they make it to the pros for a few years, they're still going to need to know how to live life in their 30s, 40s, and 50s.

Identity foreclosure is as bad as the opiate and heroin epidemic now because of the lives it is destroying. People aren't achieving up to their potential. For some reason the whole goal of so many young males is to get a scholarship and just becoming one of these college athletes like that's the ultimate goal of life. And then when they do get there, that is if they do get there, so many of them are not academically prepared—they don't have a real understanding of what they want to do with themselves other than play football or basketball once they get there.

So then they're shuffled into all these classes that were created to help them stay eligible to stay on the field and are shuffled through 4 years of that bullshit and the likelihood of getting to the NFL is almost nil. I asked Les Miles once, Would you put your own children in the courses that your football players take? He had no answer for that.

But let's say a college football player hits the lottery and gets drafted, chances are still unbelievably low that they can make a team and hang on until they qualify for a pension. But they don't even get to collect that until they're much older, like 30 years later at the earliest

Most likely, even guys who have great college careers bounce around from roster to practice squad to roster to practice squad until they have to hang up their cleats. The NFL is called Not for Long for a reason.

And when they finally face reality and give up football, then they're just done. They're not relevant anymore. They've created a whole bunch of money for their college and maybe some notoriety and this big brand for everyone else but they've got nothing to show for it. If they graduated, maybe they can go back and sell insurance or real estate but if not, they've got nothing.

It's not the system's fault—the system is what it is. If I created a money-making system I might create it so that it benefits me but I would try to do it in a way that doesn't consume so many lives in the process and particularly doesn't consume the lives of so many young African American males.

Colleges and universities and conferences and TV networks and bowl games have all created a system that at the most fundamental level benefits them, at the expense of the players. The players are nothing but fungible goods. They're just disposable.

Look at the way now that people are saying it doesn't even make any sense to pay big money to a running back in the NFL—because other than an elite few backs, they are all just interchangeable and every year there's more of them coming out of college whose bodies aren't yet completely destroyed so it makes better financial sense to have a back who is new to the league and then toss him on the scrap heap and get another fresher one.

But you'd hope that somebody would be conscious enough to help the people whose labor builds the multibillion dollar bigtime football industry in this country and that's the players. Nobody turns on the TV to watch the coaches. It's not Nick Saban, Urban Meyer, or Dabo Swinney who generate billions of dollars—it's the players. It's players whose names you might not know whose bodies or brains have been destroyed, and some players who even gave their lives for football.

Probably we can't change the system at a macro level. NFL teams and universities need the revenue streams at this point, conferences and television networks need the product, and hotels and restaurants and stores have all been created by this engine.

But the closer you look at it, you start to understand what needs to change—the system needs to treat the players with humanity and dignity. I mean college players can look around their campus and see their jerseys getting sold everywhere and even if their name isn't on the back, their number is, and the university is pocketing all that money.

I think the solution is that college football players should just play football and be enrolled in a few classes—maybe physiology, anatomy, even financial management—and then when they're done they should really take classes in pursuit of a degree or career for four years or however long it takes. But the colleges and universities shouldn't be allowed to wipe their hands clean of the players until they are prepared to succeed in the world. It's called alma mater for a reason—the college becomes your mother and a mother doesn't turn her back on her kids just because they failed out or left early to take their shot and tried to make some money.

A football scholarship should be sort of like going into the military you serve your time and then the military pays for your education. There should be a G.I. Bill for college football players. In this system, at first you just play football and mainly concentrate on it, taking actual academic courses that will help you be a better athlete. And when you're done, if you don't go to the NFL, or even if you do go for a short period of time, then you go back to your college or university and get your degree.

Let's just tell the truth, if it weren't for the athletic department, most of these guys wouldn't be there. They wouldn't have even qualified for admission. There isn't anything on most campuses to deal with guys reading on the 9th-grade level. Why would there be? The reality is that the football players are primarily if not exclusively there to play football and make money for the university. So being a football player should be just like the military. You go be a hero, maybe win a national championship instead of saving the country, then they pay for your college and you start your future life when your football career is over.

This is the only realistic way to do it. The absolutely unrealistic and impossible part for most of the players is that they're supposed to be getting an education while they are playing football. Many of them couldn't even get their degree if they were spending 40-50 hours/week going to classes, meeting with tutors, and visiting professors in office hours for extra help. They're just not qualified or prepared. They know they wouldn't be there if it weren't for football and it's the football coach who renews their scholarship every year, not their professors. On top of that, so many of them aren't even taking the academics seriously at this point because they think they're going to the NFL.

These bigtime college players were identified in high school as standout football players, they were recruited by high school coaches with promises their college would send them to the NFL, and their classes are secondary or even lower than that despite the sound bites about going to this school or that because of the academics.

Playing football at OSU for me was a full-time gig. It was way more than 40 hours a week of practice, lifting, and film that enabled me to help my team win a national championship. We were all putting in those hours—even guys whose names you don't remember.

Especially during the season which is the entire fall semester, we were easily putting in 50-60 hours/week on football. Now you've got teams playing every day of the week, missing classes and the college football playoffs bleeding into spring semester.

And you have to look at the course schedules players take to facilitate their primary commitment to succeeding on the football Field. For lots of players, they just go into General Studies, African American Studies, or Communications. What the hell is that? Guys have to have skills to get employed. You have to be employable. You can't just learn some general things or understand communications. I didn't have a major that I remember and even if I did, I doubt it was anything practical or anything that would have helped me get a job outside of football. Now, I want to learn more about the mechanics of entrepreneurship. I want to compile courses that I'm interested in, enhancing what I'm doing now.

For a lot of other guys playing football or basketball in bigtime programs, especially guys who come from the streets, I think they would do great as social work majors. In this major, they can learn about themselves. They can also get a real practical training so that someday they can get a job, maybe even working inside bigtime football and basketball programs with athletes like themselves. Or they could work with kids in the inner cities—kids who believe all they can ever be is a football or basketball player.

Think about it, an army of black male social workers who had formerly been athletes would be pretty credible in terms of teaching young black kids about a future outside of sports. Little black kids don't need no more athletes coming back to the 'hood hosting football or basketball camps. Little black kids don't need no encouragement to play sports. What they need is to start learning to cage their rage, and learning about responsible adult culture when they're teenagers so they don't have to learn it in prison like I did.

If I really think about it, just about everybody I ran with as a kid—all those people I talked about in the beginning of this book—they're either in prison or dead. Even the older guy I broke into the house with in 8th grade just got murdered a few years ago.

I was like the ringleader of most my friends because I got into selling drugs in 6th grade and I was getting in trouble before them, but I was lucky and got caught at 13 and 14 and went to juvenile detention before things got too serious. Then I started playing football, which definitely saved my life, 100%.

When I look at all my guys from the south side, they're either in prison or dead. We just experienced so much trauma watching other people get killed and other craziness and it screwed us up. Everyone is either screwed up or in prison or dead except for me and that's because of football so I'm incredibly grateful I got to play the game and get saved.

I guess the last thing I want to say is that I'd like to graduate from Youngstown State as a point of pride for kids in Youngstown. A lot of people think if you are from Youngstown and go there you're a failure. I'm trying to promote to these kids in Youngstown that I want to go there and remove that stigma because it's a great university which offers people a lot of potential to become successful in life.

But on the other hand, it's kind of like an ego thing for me to graduate from Ohio State, to finish what I started. I get people coming up to me all the time, white ladies in Bexley, near the Columbus School for Girls, where Jayden goes—they say, I've been paying attention to you since you got out of prison and I appreciate you turning yourself around. There are absolutely a lot of people rooting for me.

I'm helping to coach my daughter's basketball team so I'm traveling in a lot of circles—suburban affluent circles—and people are rooting for me. I've said it before, nobody has fans that show love like Ohio State and I'm still feeling that love. It's a positive force in my life and people are expecting great things from me. I'm just absolutely invested now in lifelong learning—mine, and everyone else's. All I want to do is learn everything I can and I hope the next time I'm on ESPN is when I graduate from college.

ACKNOWLEDGMENTS

I WOULD LIKE to show my appreciation to everyone who has participated in the process of writing this book. Very few people I've mentioned this project to have been anything other than unequivocally supportive. For sure there are still detractors in and around Columbus but they are becoming more and more scarce as Maurice performs incredibly valuable service to distressed communities in Ohio, and tours the country as an advocate for mental health and substance abuse awareness. Maurice faced a lot of criticism for raising the issue of homelessness in Columbus during media coverage before the 2002 National Championship game, but now everyone can see his commitment to social justice is heartfelt. People deserve a second chance and Maurice is making the most of his.

Thanks to everyone who read and commented on the manuscript: Gwendolyn Cartledge, Professor in the College of Education at Ohio State, who gave valuable feedback on the first section of the book; Steve Guinan (MFA), who is writing an excellent book himself about the Toledo Troopers (Ohio's outstanding women's professional football team from the 1970s); Kelli Monedero who gave it the first full reading and let me know it had great potential; Jill Smith, who showed me ways it could be used in a language arts curriculum; Julia Nusken, an OSU grad from the '50s and family friend since I was a kid; Robert W. Turner II, whose own outstanding book—Not For Long—was a great inspiration to us; Jason Manganaro (MFA), my buddy from Ohio State who met with me weekly to go over detailed aspects of the manuscript; Pierre Lucien, whose close reading and encouragement over the last two weeks helped convince me this book was ready to go; and finally, to my gracious and studious wife, Brieanne Beaujolais, who was so focused on her candidacy exams the last 3 months that I didn't want her to give up the time necessary to read the book, but who finally whipped through it last weekend (after she passed!) and caught about 20 mistakes that nobody else did.

– Bob Eckhart, September, 2019